# School–Community Relations

Douglas J. Fiore

EYE ON EDUCATION
6 DEPOT WAY WEST, SUITE 106
LARCHMONT, NY 10538
(914) 833–0551
(914) 833–0761 fax
www.eyeoneducation.com

**Library of Congress Cataloging-in-Publication Data**

Fiore, Douglas J., 1966–
    School community relations / by Douglas J. Fiore.
       p. cm.
    Includes bibliographical references and index.
    ISBN 1-930556-27-6
    1. Community and school—United States. I. Title.

    LC221 .F56 2002
    371.19′0973—dc21

                                       2001055604

10 9 8 7 6 5 4 3 2 1

Editorial and production services provided by
Richard H. Adin Freelance Editorial Services
52 Oakwood Blvd., Poughkeepsie, NY 12603-4112
(845-471-3566)

## Also Available from EYE ON EDUCATION

**The Emerging Principalship**
Linda Skrla, David Erlandson, etc.

**Money and Schools, 2nd ed.**
David C. Thompson and R. Craig Wood

**Human Resources Administration:**
**A School-based Perspective, 2nd ed.**
Richard E. Smith

**Introduction to Educational Leadership**
**and Organizational Behavior**
Patti L. Chance and Edward W. Chance

**Thinking Through the Principalship**
Dianne E. Ashby and Samuel E. Krug

**Dealing with Difficult Teachers**
Todd Whitaker

**Dealing with Difficult Parents**
Todd Whitaker and Douglas J. Fiore

**Staff Development: Practices That Promote**
**Leadership in Learning Communities**
Sally J. Zepeda

**Creating Connections for Better Schools:**
**How Leaders Enhance School Culture**
Douglas J. Fiore

**The Principal's Edge**
Jack McCall

**Urban School Leadership**
Eugene T. W. Sanders

**Research on Educational Innovations, 3rd ed.**
Arthur K. Ellis

# *The School Leadership Library*

## David Erlandson and Alfred Wilson, General Editors

This series identifies the knowledge and skills you need to master the ISLIC standards and/or the proficiencies assessed in your particular state. Each book offers practical aids such as sample letters, memos and checklists.

**The Emerging Principalship** Linda Skrla, David Erlandson, et al.

**Leadership** Gary M. Crow, L. Joseph Matthews, and Lloyd E. Mccleary

**Information Collection** Paula M. Short, Rick J. Short, and Kenneth H. Brinson, Jnr.

**Problem Analysis** Charles Achilles, John Reynolds, and Susan Achilles

**Judgment** James Sweeney and Diana Bourisaw

**Organizational Oversight** David A. Erlandson, Peggy L. Stark, and Sharon M. Ward

**Delegation** Michael Ward & Bettye MacPhail-Wilcox

**Implementation** Anita M. Pankake

**Instruction and the Learning Environment** John M. Jenkins & James W. Keefe

**Measurement & Evaluation** James McNamara, D. Erlandson, & Maryanne McNamara

**Student Guidance and Development** Mary Ann Ward and Dode Worsham

**Resource Allocation** Scott Norton & Larry Kelly

**Staff Development** Sally J. Zepeda

**Motivating Others** David P. Thompson

**Interpersonal Sensitivity** John R. Hoyle and Harrison M. Crenshaw

**Oral and Nonverbal Expression** Ivan Muse

**Written Expression** India J. Podsen, Charles Allen, Glenn Pethel, and John Waide

**Working in a Legal & Regulatory Environment** David J. Sperry

**Philosophical and Cultural Values** George Crawford and Janice Nicklaus

# About the Author

Dr. Douglas J. Fiore, a former teacher and principal, is currently a faculty member in the Division of Educational Studies at Virginia Commonwealth University where he works with graduate students in Educational Administration and Supervision. He is the author of *Creating Connections for Better Schools: How Leaders Enhance School Culture* and is co-author with Dr. Todd Whitaker of the best selling *Dealing with Difficult Parents and with Parents in Difficult Situations*. He has also written numerous articles and is a presenter at many national conferences for both teachers and administrators.

Doug and his wife Lisa live in Midlothian, Virginia, with their three daughters, Meagan, Amy, and Katherine.

# Acknowledgments

I wish to acknowledge the contributions of many individuals who have assisted in the creation of this work. Without the assistance and support of many, this book would not have been possible.

Drs. Jeanne R. Fiene, Western Kentucky University, Clarence Fitch, Chicago State University, Gene Gallegos, California State University in Bakersfield, Christine M. Imbra, St. Cloud State University, Ramona Lomeli, Illinois State University, Anna Hicks McFadden, Western Carolina University, Kelly McKerrow, Southern Illinois University, Eleanor A. Perry, Arizona State University West, William Rosier, West Virginia University, Mark Schmidt, North Dakota State University, Edward Seifert, Texas A&M-Commerce, and Linda C. Tillman, Wayne State University all served an important role as reviewers for initial drafts of this manuscript. Without question, their insights and expert suggestions improved this textbook. As I have taught much of this material to graduate students at both the State University of West Georgia and at Virginia Commonwealth University, I also wish to thank those students for listening, learning, and providing meaningful feedback.

Thanks also go to the following people for providing their real-life examples of great school-community relations which became the "showcase" features sprinkled throughout the pages of this book: Dr. William C. Bosher, director of the Commonwealth Educational Policy Institute in Richmond, Virginia, Mr. David Conrad, music director in the Manteno School District, Manteno, Illinois, Dr. Douglas DeWitt, assistant professor at Minnesota State University, Ms. Doreen Duncan, former fifth grade teacher at Northwest Elementary School in Tampa, Florida, Dr. Sondra G. Estep, professor at Governor's State University, Ms. Nancy Fahnestock, math teacher at Godby High School in Tallahassee, Florida, Dr. David Haney, assistant professor at North Dakota State University, Mr. Gregory Karas, fourth grade teacher at Parkview Elementary School in Valparaiso, Indiana, Dr. Dale Lumpa, principal at Charles Hay Elementary School in Englewood, Colorado, Dr. India Podsen, associate professor at North Georgia College and State University, Ms. Johnna Riley, resource teacher at R.C. Longan Elementary School in Richmond, Virginia, Mr. Seth Weitzman, principal of Hommocks Middle School in Larchmont, New York. The examples provided by these individuals serve to verify the benefits of strong school-community relations.

Special thanks to Bob Sickles, Publisher and President of Eye on Education. In addition to great guidance and support, Bob has given me freedom and respect, two helpful luxuries. He also has a keen understanding of many of the concepts contained in the pages that follow, and my ideas have gained clarity as a result of many conversations with him.

Finally, heartfelt thanks go to my wife Lisa and my daughters Meagan, Amy, and Katherine. The love, support, and encouragement from these four gifts ultimately explain why and how this work was made possible.

# Table of Contents

About the Author . . . . . . . . . . . . . . . . . . . . . . . . . . . . v
Acknowledgments . . . . . . . . . . . . . . . . . . . . . . . . . . . vii
Preface . . . . . . . . . . . . . . . . . . . . . . . . . . . . . . . . . . xv

1   **Paying Attention to Public Opinion** . . . . . . . . . . . . . . 1
      Trends in the Public's Perception . . . . . . . . . . . . . . . . . . . 4
      Misconceptions Regarding Public Opinion . . . . . . . . . . . . . 9
      The Purpose of A Plan . . . . . . . . . . . . . . . . . . . . . . . . 11
      Three Kinds of Plans . . . . . . . . . . . . . . . . . . . . . . . . . 15
         The Coordinated Plan . . . . . . . . . . . . . . . . . . . . . . 15
         The Centralized Plan . . . . . . . . . . . . . . . . . . . . . . . 16
         The Decentralized Plan . . . . . . . . . . . . . . . . . . . . . 16
      Chapter Summary . . . . . . . . . . . . . . . . . . . . . . . . . . 18
      Case Study Analysis . . . . . . . . . . . . . . . . . . . . . . . . . 19
         A Tale of Two Cities . . . . . . . . . . . . . . . . . . . . . . . 19
         Questions for Analysis . . . . . . . . . . . . . . . . . . . . . . 20

2   **Reading the Pulse of the Community** . . . . . . . . . . . . . 21
      Get to Know Community Leaders . . . . . . . . . . . . . . . . . . 21
         Look to Formal and Informal Leaders . . . . . . . . . . . . . 21
         Look to Local Civic Organizations . . . . . . . . . . . . . . . 22
      Neighborhood Schools . . . . . . . . . . . . . . . . . . . . . . . 25
      Important First Steps . . . . . . . . . . . . . . . . . . . . . . . . 25
         Neighborhood Visits . . . . . . . . . . . . . . . . . . . . . . . 25
         A Neighborhood Tea . . . . . . . . . . . . . . . . . . . . . . . 29
      Don't Forget the Parents . . . . . . . . . . . . . . . . . . . . . . 30
         Information Shared by the Teaching Staff . . . . . . . . . . . 30
         Information Shared by the Students . . . . . . . . . . . . . . . 31
         Information Shared by Business and Community Leaders . . . . . . 32
         Information Shared by Other School Administrators . . . . . . . . 33
      Multiculturalism and School–Community Relations . . . . . . . . . 34
      Chapter Summary . . . . . . . . . . . . . . . . . . . . . . . . . . 36
      Case Study Analysis . . . . . . . . . . . . . . . . . . . . . . . . . 37
         Changing Landscapes . . . . . . . . . . . . . . . . . . . . . . 37
         Questions for Analysis . . . . . . . . . . . . . . . . . . . . . . 37

3   **Establishing Everybody's Role** . . . . . . . . . . . . . . . . . 39
      School–Community Relations at the District Level . . . . . . . . . 39
         The Superintendent . . . . . . . . . . . . . . . . . . . . . . . 40
         Mistakes Made by Superintendents . . . . . . . . . . . . . . . 42
         The Director of School–Community Relations . . . . . . . . . 43
      School–Community Relations at the Building Level . . . . . . . . . 45

The Principal . . . . . . . . . . . . . . . . . . . . . . . . . . . . . . . . . 45
The Teacher . . . . . . . . . . . . . . . . . . . . . . . . . . . . . . . . . . 48
The Office Staff . . . . . . . . . . . . . . . . . . . . . . . . . . . . . . . . 49
Organizational Standards . . . . . . . . . . . . . . . . . . . . . . . . . 51
Goals 2000 . . . . . . . . . . . . . . . . . . . . . . . . . . . . . . . . . . 52
Interstate School Leaders Licensure Consortium (ISLLC) Standards . . 60
The National PTA. . . . . . . . . . . . . . . . . . . . . . . . . . . . . . 63
Community Schools . . . . . . . . . . . . . . . . . . . . . . . . . . . . . 64
Chapter Summary. . . . . . . . . . . . . . . . . . . . . . . . . . . . . . . . 65
Case Study Analysis. . . . . . . . . . . . . . . . . . . . . . . . . . . . . . 66
The Balancing Act . . . . . . . . . . . . . . . . . . . . . . . . . . . . . . 66
Questions for Analysis. . . . . . . . . . . . . . . . . . . . . . . . . . . . 66

**4 Communicating Effectively: Everybody's Job** . . . . . . . . . . . . **67**
The Communication Process. . . . . . . . . . . . . . . . . . . . . . . . . 68
Idea Formation . . . . . . . . . . . . . . . . . . . . . . . . . . . . . . . . 68
Idea Encoding. . . . . . . . . . . . . . . . . . . . . . . . . . . . . . . . . 69
Communication Channel . . . . . . . . . . . . . . . . . . . . . . . . . . 69
Receiver Decoding . . . . . . . . . . . . . . . . . . . . . . . . . . . . . . 71
Nonverbal Communication: It's Not What You Said,
But How You Said It . . . . . . . . . . . . . . . . . . . . . . . . . . . . 72
Communication Barriers . . . . . . . . . . . . . . . . . . . . . . . . . . . 75
Language Barriers . . . . . . . . . . . . . . . . . . . . . . . . . . . . . . 75
Cultural Barriers . . . . . . . . . . . . . . . . . . . . . . . . . . . . . . . 75
Barriers Inherent in Specific Physical Disabilities. . . . . . . . . . . . 76
Barriers Related to Time . . . . . . . . . . . . . . . . . . . . . . . . . . 77
Overcoming Communication Barriers . . . . . . . . . . . . . . . . . . 77
Perception Checking . . . . . . . . . . . . . . . . . . . . . . . . . . . . 77
Communicating Regularly. . . . . . . . . . . . . . . . . . . . . . . . . . 78
Communicating Purposefully. . . . . . . . . . . . . . . . . . . . . . . . 79
Chapter Summary. . . . . . . . . . . . . . . . . . . . . . . . . . . . . . . . 80
Case Study Analysis. . . . . . . . . . . . . . . . . . . . . . . . . . . . . . 81
All the News That's Fit to Print—And Then Some . . . . . . . . . . 81
Questions for Analysis. . . . . . . . . . . . . . . . . . . . . . . . . . . . 81

**5 Opening Up to Your Internal Publics** . . . . . . . . . . . . . . . . . **83**
The Principal as Role Model . . . . . . . . . . . . . . . . . . . . . . . . . 84
Visibility Is the Key . . . . . . . . . . . . . . . . . . . . . . . . . . . . . . 85
The Need for Effective Human Relations Skills . . . . . . . . . . . . . 86
The Student as an Internal Public . . . . . . . . . . . . . . . . . . . . . 87
The Use of Discipline. . . . . . . . . . . . . . . . . . . . . . . . . . . . . 90
Teachers—The Most Important Adults in the Building. . . . . . . . . 91
The Friday Focus—A Tool for Positive Internal Communication . . . . 92
Positive Relationships with Noninstructional Staff . . . . . . . . . . . 93
Other Members of the Internal Public. . . . . . . . . . . . . . . . . . . 95
Substitute Teachers. . . . . . . . . . . . . . . . . . . . . . . . . . . . . . 95
Student Teachers . . . . . . . . . . . . . . . . . . . . . . . . . . . . . . . 97
The Importance of the School Secretary . . . . . . . . . . . . . . . . . 97

The Entire School Staff: The Key to Strong School–
    Community Relations . . . . . . . . . . . . . . . . . . . . . . . 98
Chapter Summary . . . . . . . . . . . . . . . . . . . . . . . . . . . 99
Case Study Analysis . . . . . . . . . . . . . . . . . . . . . . . . . 100
    "Class" Parties . . . . . . . . . . . . . . . . . . . . . . . . . . 100
    Questions for Analysis . . . . . . . . . . . . . . . . . . . . . . 100

**6   Embracing Your External Publics . . . . . . . . . . . . . . 101**
Appropriate Parental Involvement . . . . . . . . . . . . . . . . 101
    Involving Parents While They Are at School . . . . . . . . . 102
    Welcome to Our School? . . . . . . . . . . . . . . . . . . . . 104
    Involving Parents While They Are at Home . . . . . . . . . 105
Other Members of the External Public . . . . . . . . . . . . . . 107
    Establishing Key Communicators . . . . . . . . . . . . . . . 109
    Where to Start with Key Communicators . . . . . . . . . . . 110
    The Importance of Community Members with Grown Children . . . 111
    Intergenerational Programs in Schools . . . . . . . . . . . . 112
Presenting Students to the Community . . . . . . . . . . . . . 113
    Athletics . . . . . . . . . . . . . . . . . . . . . . . . . . . . . 113
    Plays . . . . . . . . . . . . . . . . . . . . . . . . . . . . . . . 114
    Other Artistic Endeavors . . . . . . . . . . . . . . . . . . . . 114
    Academic Competitions . . . . . . . . . . . . . . . . . . . . 114
    Be Forewarned . . . . . . . . . . . . . . . . . . . . . . . . . 115
Chapter Summary . . . . . . . . . . . . . . . . . . . . . . . . . . 115
Case Study Analysis . . . . . . . . . . . . . . . . . . . . . . . . . 116
    That's Not What I Meant to Say . . . . . . . . . . . . . . . . 116
    Questions for Analysis . . . . . . . . . . . . . . . . . . . . . 117

**7   Improving Media Relations . . . . . . . . . . . . . . . . . 119**
All the News That's Fit to Print . . . . . . . . . . . . . . . . . . 120
    When the Reporter Initiates the Contact . . . . . . . . . . . 120
    When the School Leader Initiates the Contact . . . . . . . . 122
    Involving Staff Members in the Process . . . . . . . . . . . . 123
    The News Release . . . . . . . . . . . . . . . . . . . . . . . . 126
Communicating Through Local Radio . . . . . . . . . . . . . . 127
    Spreading the Good News . . . . . . . . . . . . . . . . . . . 130
    Public Service Announcements . . . . . . . . . . . . . . . . 130
Lights, Camera, Action! . . . . . . . . . . . . . . . . . . . . . . 132
    You Look Marvelous . . . . . . . . . . . . . . . . . . . . . . 134
Do Not Feed the Monsters . . . . . . . . . . . . . . . . . . . . . 135
    Be Proactive . . . . . . . . . . . . . . . . . . . . . . . . . . . 135
    We All Make Mistakes . . . . . . . . . . . . . . . . . . . . . 136
Parting Shots . . . . . . . . . . . . . . . . . . . . . . . . . . . . . 137
Chapter Summary . . . . . . . . . . . . . . . . . . . . . . . . . . 139
Case Study Analysis . . . . . . . . . . . . . . . . . . . . . . . . . 139
    I Think It's True What They Say About the Squeaky Wheel . . . . . . 139
    Questions for Analysis . . . . . . . . . . . . . . . . . . . . . 140

**8  Putting It All on Paper** . . . . . . . . . . . . . . . . . . . . . . **141**
   Three Kinds of Readers . . . . . . . . . . . . . . . . . . . . . . . . . 141
      The 20-Second Reader . . . . . . . . . . . . . . . . . . . . . . . 141
      The Newspaper Reader. . . . . . . . . . . . . . . . . . . . . . . 142
      The Novel Reader . . . . . . . . . . . . . . . . . . . . . . . . . . 142
   Does Impressive Language Make the Impression You Desire? . . . . . . . 143
   The School Newsletter. . . . . . . . . . . . . . . . . . . . . . . . . . 144
      Columns of Type . . . . . . . . . . . . . . . . . . . . . . . . . . 146
      Font Size and Style . . . . . . . . . . . . . . . . . . . . . . . . . 146
      Pictures and Graphics. . . . . . . . . . . . . . . . . . . . . . . . 146
      Headline Wording. . . . . . . . . . . . . . . . . . . . . . . . . . 146
      Paper Size . . . . . . . . . . . . . . . . . . . . . . . . . . . . . . 147
   Newsletter Topics . . . . . . . . . . . . . . . . . . . . . . . . . . . 147
      The Use of Technology . . . . . . . . . . . . . . . . . . . . . . . 148
   The Student Report Card . . . . . . . . . . . . . . . . . . . . . . . . 150
   A Personal Letter from the Principal. . . . . . . . . . . . . . . . . . . 151
      Words or Phrases to Avoid. . . . . . . . . . . . . . . . . . . . . . 154
   Written Communication from the Classroom. . . . . . . . . . . . . . . 156
   Communicating Via the World Wide Web . . . . . . . . . . . . . . . . 159
      Points to Consider. . . . . . . . . . . . . . . . . . . . . . . . . . 161
   Chapter Summary . . . . . . . . . . . . . . . . . . . . . . . . . . . 162
   Case Study Analysis. . . . . . . . . . . . . . . . . . . . . . . . . . . 163
      The Write Stuff. . . . . . . . . . . . . . . . . . . . . . . . . . . . 163
      Questions for Analysis . . . . . . . . . . . . . . . . . . . . . . . 163

**9  Saying What You Mean—Meaning What You Say** . . . . . . . . **165**
   Telephone Etiquette . . . . . . . . . . . . . . . . . . . . . . . . . . 165
      Telephone Calls From the Principal. . . . . . . . . . . . . . . . . . 167
   Face-to-Face Conversations . . . . . . . . . . . . . . . . . . . . . . . 168
   Speaking to a Large Group . . . . . . . . . . . . . . . . . . . . . . . 170
   Communicating During a Campaign . . . . . . . . . . . . . . . . . . 172
      Communicating with a Citizen's Advisory Committee. . . . . . . . 175
   The Campaign's Conclusion . . . . . . . . . . . . . . . . . . . . . . 177
   Chapter Summary . . . . . . . . . . . . . . . . . . . . . . . . . . . 178
   Case Study Analysis. . . . . . . . . . . . . . . . . . . . . . . . . . . 180
      Pass the Antiperspirant. . . . . . . . . . . . . . . . . . . . . . . . 180
      Questions for Analysis . . . . . . . . . . . . . . . . . . . . . . . 180

**10  In Crisis Situations, You Must Have a Plan** . . . . . . . . . . . **183**
   The Importance of Planning . . . . . . . . . . . . . . . . . . . . . . 183
      Select Individuals to Serve on Crisis Response
        and Aftercare Teams. . . . . . . . . . . . . . . . . . . . . . . 185
      Establish a Headquarters for the Crisis Response
        and Aftercare Teams. . . . . . . . . . . . . . . . . . . . . . . 185
      Select an Individual to be the Official Spokesperson
        During a Crisis . . . . . . . . . . . . . . . . . . . . . . . . . . 186
      Establish a Procedure for Activating Community
        Support Services . . . . . . . . . . . . . . . . . . . . . . . . . 186

Establish a Procedure for Developing Channels
of Communication . . . . . . . . . . . . . . . . . . . . 187
Establish a Procedure for Controlling Rumors. . . . . . . . . . . . . 187
Establish a Procedure for Assessing the Crisis Management Plan. . . 188
Establish a Procedure for Bringing Closure to the Crisis . . . . . . . 189
Communicating in a Time of Crisis . . . . . . . . . . . . . . . . . . 192
Media Relations in Crisis Situations . . . . . . . . . . . . . . . . . . 194
Provide Facts About the School and the Crisis. . . . . . . . . . . . 194
Log All Information Released to the Public . . . . . . . . . . . . . 194
Release Names of Victims Only After the Next of Kin
Have Been Notified. . . . . . . . . . . . . . . . . . . . . . 195
Be Aware of Photographers on Campus—You Have Every
Right to Control Photographers on Your Property . . . . . . . . 196
Repeat Key Messages as Often as Possible and Stay Focused
on Those Messages . . . . . . . . . . . . . . . . . . . . . 196
Dealing with the Aftermath of a Crisis . . . . . . . . . . . . . . . . 196
Crisis Aftermath . . . . . . . . . . . . . . . . . . . . . . . . . . . . 197
Chapter Summary . . . . . . . . . . . . . . . . . . . . . . . . . . . 199
Case Study Analysis . . . . . . . . . . . . . . . . . . . . . . . . . . 200
3...2...1...Action! . . . . . . . . . . . . . . . . . . . . . . . . . 200
Questions for Analysis . . . . . . . . . . . . . . . . . . . . . . . . 200

**11 Three Opportunities to Shine** . . . . . . . . . . . . . . . **201**
Open House. . . . . . . . . . . . . . . . . . . . . . . . . . . . . . 202
Open House Tours . . . . . . . . . . . . . . . . . . . . . . . . . 202
Open House Programs . . . . . . . . . . . . . . . . . . . . . . . 203
Classroom Visits. . . . . . . . . . . . . . . . . . . . . . . . . . . 205
Timing Is Everything . . . . . . . . . . . . . . . . . . . . . . . . 206
Advertising the Open House—Calling All Parents . . . . . . . . . 207
The Cleanliness of the School . . . . . . . . . . . . . . . . . . . 208
Parent–Teacher Conferences . . . . . . . . . . . . . . . . . . . . . 209
Helping Teachers Prepare for Conferences. . . . . . . . . . . . . 213
Conducting the Conference . . . . . . . . . . . . . . . . . . . . 215
Convocations and Celebrations. . . . . . . . . . . . . . . . . . . . 217
Graduation. . . . . . . . . . . . . . . . . . . . . . . . . . . . . . 219
Awards Programs. . . . . . . . . . . . . . . . . . . . . . . . . . 220
Chapter Summary . . . . . . . . . . . . . . . . . . . . . . . . . . . 221
Case Study Analysis . . . . . . . . . . . . . . . . . . . . . . . . . . 222
But They Scare Me. . . . . . . . . . . . . . . . . . . . . . . . . . 222
Questions for Analysis . . . . . . . . . . . . . . . . . . . . . . . . 223

**12 Evaluating Effectiveness and Building Confidence—
The Future** . . . . . . . . . . . . . . . . . . . . . . . . . . **225**
Determing the Effectivess of Your School–Community
Relations Efforts. . . . . . . . . . . . . . . . . . . . . . . . 226
Verifying Results in School– Community Relations. . . . . . . . . 226
Making Intangibles More Tangible . . . . . . . . . . . . . . . . . 230
School Choice in the Twenty-First Century . . . . . . . . . . . . . . 232

Chapter Summary . . . . . . . . . . . . . . . . . . . . . . . . . . . 235
Case Study Analysis . . . . . . . . . . . . . . . . . . . . . . . . . 236
    The Proof is in the Pudding . . . . . . . . . . . . . . . . . . 236
    Questions for Analysis . . . . . . . . . . . . . . . . . . . . . 237

**References** . . . . . . . . . . . . . . . . . . . . . . . . . . . . **239**

**Index** . . . . . . . . . . . . . . . . . . . . . . . . . . . . . . . **243**

# Preface

This book presents and discusses the essential elements of a successful school–community relations plan for all schools. It presents evidence of the importance of keeping the public connected to the schools we share. Furthermore, it explains the benefits of having an effective school–community relations plan, as well as the pitfalls of failing to do so. Finally, it brings to light for all who are studying school administration the necessity for administrators to make sound school–community relations a top priority of theirs.

The study of school–community relations, though an integral part of the graduate curriculum of most programs in educational administration, is sadly viewed by some as nonessential. Some institutions of higher education, along with some of our public school systems, fail to see the importance of this vital subject and place it in a secondary position to courses dealing with stricter managerial content. However, the vast majority of people associated with improving the training of school administrators do, thankfully, realize that school–community relations are essential to effective school leadership. Though this was always true, the times in which we currently work to improve the quality of our educational institutions demand even more that leaders build strong, lasting relationships with stakeholders. The changing role of the effective school administrator requires a stronger understanding of school–community relations than was ever the case before. If one examines the behaviors of the best school administrators, either in preschool settings, K–12 schools, or institutions of higher education, these behaviors will certainly show a tremendous priority placed on effectively communicating with, and involving, the publics that support our schools.

School administrators must understand and deal with the public's deep concerns regarding education on a daily basis. Sometimes this concern, voiced by a single parent, involves a method of behavior correction or a curricular choice made by a teacher. At other times, the concern, voiced by a community association such as a church or civic group, is centered on a ceremony or other schoolwide celebration. Still, at other times the concern involves something that the school leader has little or no control over, such as a school's testing program or state regulations for the inclusion of students with special needs.

In each of these instances, the school administrator must have the skills to communicate effectively. He or she must possess an aptitude for listening and must have a plan for responding to and effectively dealing with the concern. Proactively understanding the community's perceptions; local, state, and federal trends in education; and the resources and power lying at their disposal, allows administrators to demonstrate that they really are leaders.

The skills and knowledge base required for effective school–community relations are vast and always changing. The study of school–community relations is, therefore, vitally important if school leaders are to truly *lead* our schools. In fact, in many recent polls conducted by various school administrator associations, principals and superintendents rated school–community relations as the first or second most important aspect of their job. Furthermore, administrators consistently state that they wish they had received more training in this arena. As this book goes to press, both the National Association of Secondary School Principals (NASSP) and the National Association of Elementary School Principals (NAESP) have strands in their upcoming annual conferences that deal exclusively with the principal's ability to work with a school's many publics. Similarly, the American Association for Higher Education (AAHE) includes a strand in its national conference regarding the need to understand students' family responsibilities and community experiences. All levels of education are in need of leaders who understand and appreciate the contributions made by their various publics.

This book gives you the information necessary to become a skilled school administrator in the area of school–community relations. It provides you with the necessary background information, and it equips you with many tried-and-true techniques for improving your ability to understand and communicate with your publics. Each chapter concludes with a bulleted summary designed to ascertain the extent to which you have internalized the concepts presented. Finally, each chapter contains a case study. These case studies assist you in applying the information learned to a real-life situation faced by a school leader.

With issues of school choice, vouchers, site-based management, and school safety continuing to grab headlines all across the country, school leaders and those in training need to understand how to deal with the publics served by our schools. In the pages that follow, I fulfill that need. I wish you well as you work toward making your schools all that they can be and as you strive to communicate your efforts and accomplishments to all who will listen.

*Douglas J. Fiore*

# 1

# Paying Attention to Public Opinion

Literature in virtually all disciplines regularly proclaims one inescapable fact: schools have changed just as the world has changed. Educational literature, in particular, is prone to comparisons of what life used to be like, how students used to behave, and how schools used to function. Whether or not the "good old days" were quite as good as people remember them to be, though fodder for debate, is really irrelevant. The inescapable fact once again is that schools have changed.

One way that our schools have changed is in their relationships with the many publics that they serve. Ask parents, community leaders, teachers, or administrators questions about the role they perform in our schools in comparison to what they perceive it to have been in previous generations. Most of them will tell you that it is quite different. From an administrative point of view, strong communication skills are far more significant than they once were. The involvement of stakeholders in school-related decisions is now an expectation. The public owns the public schools, and, perhaps for the first time, it realizes it does.

The trend in recent years has been for school leaders in all capacities to focus increased attention on their relationships with the many publics served by their schools. This focus has come from all levels of school administration, from the school board to the superintendent to building level administrators. As anybody involved in our schools can attest to, the focus has not really stopped at this level either. Teachers and staff are finding themselves paying increasingly more attention to their communication skills and strategies, their relationships with parents and guardians, and their overall image, as perceived by the general public. They, like their colleagues on the administrative team, are concerned with truly understanding the public's opinion of our schools.

The question this trend begs is, "Why? Why are educators, particularly those in leadership positions, so concerned with public relations and public opinion?" Answers to this question, though linked to the concept of change, are as numerous as the publics themselves. For one thing, we are finding ourselves spiraling more deeply into the Information Age. This Age is characterized by almost instantaneous access to information.

The skills required to receive this information are minimal, and as the days progress a greater number of people discover that this is so. Gone are the days when the general pubic acquired all of its information about our schools from within the local community. Now, wherever people happen to be, they have information about most of our schools at their fingertips. The technological explosion of the Information Age has armed people with the tools and the technologies to get virtually any and all information that they desire.

Along with the disappearance of a bygone era void of much technology, we have also bid farewell to the days when much information, such as one school's standardized test performance in comparison with a neighboring school's performance, was concealed from or unknown to the general public. We have bid farewell to an era in which people concerned themselves more with what was happening in their own communities than in the rest of the world. Today, the public demands information about school performance. John and Jane Q. Public insist that it is their right to know how students in their neighborhood school are performing in comparison with other students anywhere in the world. They insist that budgetary information, salaries, and curricular choices be known to them, and they want a voice in arriving at all school-related decisions. School administrators who missed out on training in the area of school–community relations find John and Jane difficult to deal with. They do not know how to respond to these demands for involvement. The response, however, is really quite simple and rudimentary.

School leaders need to welcome this involvement. Not only must they welcome it, but school leaders now have the responsibility to ensure that the public is correctly informed. It is not enough to simply welcome involvement passively. The active role of school administration requires leaders to listen and to inform. Although access to information is virtually limitless, so is access to misinformation. School leaders, skilled in all aspects of school–community relations, have the ability to keep misinformation in check. These leaders demand that those they work with have the skills to work with our publics and to stop working against them or behind their backs. To do otherwise is to create a negative image that will be damaging to our nation's schools.

The smart school leader of the twenty-first century knows how important public involvement is to the future of public education. He or she understands what the community thinks of the school he or she is leading. This leader has two fingers squarely on the pulse of public opinion and utilizes this information to inform the public when information is needed or desired and to confirm or alter the public's perceptions when they appear to be inaccurate. The leadership skills, the human relations skills, and the communication skills needed to be such a leader are changing rapidly in response to the transformation in the way in which the public perceives their role in education. The smart school leader understands this and works very hard at improving these skills. Finally, this leader realizes that our schools are just that—*our* schools. Therefore, this leader gives voice to the many publics, understands their concerns, and keeps them well informed.

Giving these publics a voice that will be heard is an essential component of effective school–community relations. If we really believe that the key to making all schools great is to link them with the real world for which they intend to prepare students, then we will make every effort to involve the real world in our planning, implementation, and assessment efforts. These three words—planning, implementation, and assessment—are key words in developing our school–community relations plans.

It is no longer acceptable for school administrators to focus their communication efforts solely on public relations. This is because the idea of public relations implies that school leaders ought to be doing little more than informing, persuading, or selling school success to their constituents. Whereas this may have been enough years ago, such one-way communication is now passé at best. The days of *public relations* plans in schools were characterized by such one-way communications. That is to say that the school communicated information to the community (usually parents) that school leaders felt the community ought to know. There was little, if any, opportunity for the community members to give meaningful input to the school leaders. Communication in this regard flowed in one direction only, from the school leaders to the community.

The result of efforts like these is an informed public, but not an empowered one. Community members know something about what goes on in a school, but they have no voice. The public schools in America wind up doing a very poor job of either representing the public or preparing young people to impact the public in a system characterized by one-way communication.

What is needed is a school–community relations plan that is built on two-way communication. Information flows from the public to the school and from the school to the public. When plans like this are in place, then schools really do become essential parts of the community. In subsequent chapters, specific techniques and ideas for accomplishing two-way communication and designing the essential components of a school–community relations plan will be explored. The emphasis first must be on understanding the public's perception. School leaders absolutely must understand how the public views our schools if they are to begin responding to, enhancing, or altering these views.

# Trends in the Public's Perception

An important first step for school administrators to take involves their understanding of the public's perceptions. The Gallup Organization in tandem with Phi Delta Kappa (PDK) has been conducting public opinion surveys about the perceptions people have of American educational institutions for more than 30 years. The purpose of these polls is to provide information about the public's feelings and attitudes to those making decisions about American public education. The results, shown annually in *Phi Delta Kappan*, tell us that the public's opinion of our schools and their effectiveness has changed somewhat over the last quarter century. However, the changes are not as significant or as negative as one might imagine, given the growing skepticism about our schools' effectiveness portrayed in certain social and political settings.

The *Phi Delta Kappa/Gallup Poll of the Public's Attitudes Toward the Public Schools* (Rose & Gallup, 2001), though widely recognized in the educational community, is by no means the only educational poll that the public has access to. Numerous organizations conduct public opinion surveys at the state, regional, and national levels. Shell Oil Company is one example of a corporation that also produces an educational attitude survey. The results shown, as is the case with many of these surveys, are somewhat similar to those shown by PDK/Gallup. In a recent Shell education poll, for example, just 25 percent of respondents rated the nation's public schools as excellent or good, whereas a whopping 66 percent rated them as fair or poor (Shell Oil Company, 1998). These ratings have declined steadily since the first Shell poll was conducted in the 1970s.

Also conducted are polls and surveys that pay particular attention to national spending priorities. Every two years, for example, the University of Chicago's National Opinion Research Center conducts such a survey. One finding that has been consistently shown in this survey is that the public feels that education is one area where the country should be spending more money. A 1996 study released prior to that year's presidential elections indicated that voters were more concerned about education than they were about crime or taxes. Similar results have been shown in studies published during many election years over the past two decades. These studies all indicate, at a minimum, that the public thinks education is extremely important.

With the wide recognition and easy access of the *PDK/Gallup Poll of the Public's Attitudes Toward the Public Schools*, all school leaders are prudent to pay attention to its results and to look for trends over time. It is important to note, however, that school leaders also need to have their own methods for ascertaining their community's perceptions of the school they are leading. Specific ways in which this can be done are presented throughout this book.

The data in the most recent PDK/Gallup report suggests the following conclusions:

♦ public schools benefit when a large number of people have close contact with them;

♦ a significant part of the public seems to be persuaded that children today receive a better education than in the past;

♦ people tend to prefer smaller schools at a time when the trend is toward larger schools;

♦ public school parents want more say in decisions related to the public schools.

Although these conclusions need not drive all of the decisions that school administrators must make, they do provide administrators at all levels with information that ought to be considered.

Exhibit 1.1. shows results from 1976 and 2001 as a means by which to compare/contrast public attitudes over a 25-year period. Although the data does not show public responses to many key questions, it does address the public's perception of the quality of public schools during the particular two years depicted. Note that these results represent the public's perception of the local schools in their community.

As mentioned earlier, although there are some apparent discrepancies between the public's perceptions of our schools in 1976 and their perceptions in 2001, there are also some noticeable similarities. Further, the perception of our schools' effectiveness is not declining, as some skeptics would like us to believe. As the above exhibit illustrates, in 1976, 42 percent of respondents gave their local schools a grade of A or B. Also in 1976, 16 percent of respondents gave their local schools a grade of D or F. The figures represented by these ratings are more negative than are their 2001 counterparts. In 2001, the percentage of respondents rating the schools with an A or a B is 51 percent, while those giving local schools grades of D or F equal 13 percent. It is worth noting that this is the highest percentage of respondents grading schools with an A or B in the poll's history. Although that fact does represent good news that educators should celebrate, it still represents a relatively small change from the percentage replying similarly in 1976.

Further improvements are noted when we look at the responses of public school parents in isolation. With this group, we see that 50 percent rated the schools as deserving an A or a B in 1976, whereas 62 percent felt the same way in 2001. In 1976, 30 percent of this group rated the schools with a C, the grade assigned by 25 percent in 2001. Finally, in 1976, 15 percent of public school parents felt their local schools deserved a grade of D or F whereas 12 percent felt that way in 2001. These figures seem to represent a slight, positive shift in the percentage of public school parents who

# Exhibit 1.1. Attitudes Toward Public Schools in Community—1976 and 2001

*Students are often given the grades A, B, C, D, and FAIL to denote the quality of their work. Suppose the public schools themselves, in this community, were graded in the same way. What grade would you give the public schools here— A, B, C, D, or FAIL?*

| Grade | National Totals | | No Children in School | | Public School Parents | |
|---|---|---|---|---|---|---|
| | *2001 %* | *1976 %* | *2001 %* | *1976 %* | *2001 %* | *1976 %* |
| A & B | 51 | 42 | 47 | 38 | 62 | 50 |
| A | 11 | 13 | 8 | 12 | 19 | 16 |
| B | 40 | 29 | 39 | 26 | 43 | 34 |
| C | 30 | 28 | 39 | 26 | 25 | 30 |
| D | 8 | 10 | 8 | 9 | 8 | 10 |
| FAIL | 5 | 6 | 4 | 7 | 4 | 5 |

have confidence in the public educational institutions in their communities, particularly in terms of the A and B grades. At the very least, they represent a small decrease in the percentage of public school parents who express serious dissatisfaction (as implied by grades of D or F) in our schools. Whether or not there is a significant difference between those parents who considered our schools to be failing in 1976 and those feeling similarly in 2001 is not nearly as important as recognizing that public school parents are continuing to express some degree of dissatisfaction. We should celebrate our successes, as indicated by these polls. We must also, however, pay attention to the 37 percent of parents who feel that the schools in their communities only deserve grades of C, D, or F. This recognition can only come about by first acknowledging that the polls exist.

Although all of this information might be confusing or even disconcerting to many school administrators, a deeper understanding of these poll results offers some further hopeful news. As the PDK/Gallup polls have consistently shown, the general public always looks more favorably on the schools in their local community than they do on the nation's schools as a whole. In fact, whereas Exhibit 1.1. indicated that only 13 percent of respondents felt that their local school deserved a grade of D or F in 2001, Exhibit 1.2. shows that number climbing to 19 percent when respondents were asked to rate the nation's schools as a whole. These differences become even more pronounced when one examines the attitudes of *public* school parents. This group, in particular, is ambivalent about the quality of our nation's public school. Though principals would love to see all of our nation's schools being rated more favorably by the general public, they do find great relief in knowing that at least *their* public thinks that *their* school is better than most others.

---

### Exhibit 1.2. Attitudes Toward Public Schools in Nation—2001

---

*How about the public schools in the nation as a whole? What grade would you give the public schools nationally—A, B, C, D, or FAIL?*

| Grade | National Totals | No Children in School | Public School Parents |
|-------|-----------------|-----------------------|-----------------------|
|       | 2001 %          | 2001 %                | 2001 %                |
| A&B   | 23              | 22                    | 25                    |
| A     | 2               | 1                     | 2                     |
| B     | 21              | 21                    | 23                    |
| C     | 51              | 53                    | 47                    |
| D     | 14              | 13                    | 15                    |
| FAIL  | 5               | 5                     | 4                     |

---

Furthermore, and equally important for school administrators to understand, in virtually all polls, the public indicates that education ought to be a national priority worthy of increased attention and spending. A June 1999, NBC/Wall Street Journal poll, for example, found improving public education outranking such issues as guaranteeing the financial integrity of Social Security, promoting strong moral and family values, and increasing tax cuts. This, too, is very important for school leaders to take note of. Although the criticisms leveled against the nation's schools may be troubling, the support indicated by the public's ranking of education's importance as a national priority should be encouraging. Remember, in addition to the NBC/Wall Street Journal poll, similar results are consistently shown in the National Opinion Research Center surveys.

As PDK/Gallup polls further illustrate, these feelings of education's importance extend to the state level as well. Whereas 50 percent of PDK/Gallup respondents favored spending state budget surpluses on public schools, only 31 percent thought the surplus would be better spent on tax cuts (Rose, Gallup, & Elam, 1998). This specific question was not addressed in the 2001 survey, because the nature of the 2000 election year indicated more questions should focus on particular political agendas.

School leaders need to be aware that the public, as expressed in these polls, does want the nation's schools to get better. Many members of the public appear willing to spend money in this regard, indicating a stronger level of support than many administrators realize. Though the public does question the educational achievements made by our schools nationally, by and large members of the public appear to be more satisfied with the local schools attended by their own children. These findings are important to take note of because their existence may make it difficult for school administrators to take a reactive stance based on the assumption that the public does not support their schools. This assumption, as poll results indicate, is patently false. Therefore, it will not work for school administrators to throw their hands up in the air and exclaim that the public does not support education. Understanding what these polls have to say about the public's attitudes allows school leaders to take a proactive stance on school–community relations. They inform administrators of what the public feels they are doing well, which in turn gives institutions' school–community relations plans a direction and a focus. It is important to note that school administrators should not base all of their decisions on public opinion. Doing so is hardly proactive. Rather, school leaders must understand that they are very well served to be *aware* of public opinion. This awareness leads to more informed decisions, which in turn creates fewer surprises.

It also must be noted that school principals do not need to wait for the results of these national polls to begin their understanding of public opinion. Instead, successful school leaders ought to conduct some of their own research regarding their public's attitudes and beliefs about their school's effectiveness. This research can come in many forms, as will be illustrated in subsequent chapters. All research forms are useful because they accomplish two very significant goals. First, they give the principal important information about public opinion. Second, surveying the local school community to ascertain its perceptions causes many people to feel as though they are important to the school. This examination, in and of itself, often produces desirable results in terms of school–community relations. Many people—be they parents, business leaders, or community neighbors—want nothing more than to feel listened to.

Though there are numerous sources for assisting administrators in surveying public opinion, school administrators unfamiliar with conducting their own public opinion research could consider Phi Delta Kappa International to be a valuable resource. The organization offers customized opinion polling services to individual schools or districts. Also, Phi Delta Kappa International makes PACE (Polling Attitudes of the Community on Education) materials available. These materials, geared toward the nonspecialist in research methodology, include detailed information on constructing questionnaires, sampling, interviewing, and analyzing data.

Thus far, this chapter has focused primarily on the role of polls that inform school leaders of their *external public's* opinions, that is the opinions of those individuals who spend most of their time outside of the school's walls. As explained, knowledge of these poll results helps to inform administrators' decisions in terms of their external communication. External communication, the focus of Chapter 6, includes all communication between the administrator and the school stakeholders outside of the school facility. Equally important to strong school–community relations is the school administrators' ability to understand and involve their *internal publics*. These people, often taken for granted because of an assumption that their regular role within their schools automatically keeps them informed, cannot be ignored. This concept is the focus of Chapter 5. The best school–community relations plans involve strong, regular, and purposeful communication with both the internal and external communities of our schools. Subsequent chapters are devoted to methods school leaders can use to strengthen communications with both of these groups.

## Misconceptions Regarding Public Opinion

By paying close attention to the public's perception of schools and their effectiveness, leaders are able to deal more effectively with misconceptions when they arise. Though there may be reasons for some to criticize the schools in their community, by and large the criticisms endured by public education have involved serious misconceptions. David Berliner (1993) stated that American schools have been damaged over the years by many unsubstantiated claims. Among these claims are the notions that education spending is wasteful and that American students are lazy and unproductive. These claims, according to Berliner, lead to the greater misconception that America's productivity has fallen as a result of an inadequate system of public education. Consider the words of Phillip Schlechty: "Some would return to a past golden era when all parents were supportive and most children learned what it was intended that they learn. These people do not seem to know that there never was a golden era" (1997, p. 1).

The following examples are just a few that help to counter some of the misconceptions about our nation's schools. They provide some startling information that illustrates the problems existing in "the good old days." Essentially, these statements illustrate what Phillip Schlechty so eloquently stated. Throughout American educational history, there have been problems perceived by the public. This is not a new phenomenon. These are facts that school administrators must understand if they are to provide proper leadership for contemporary school communities.

- Only 40 percent of Americans who entered school in 1945 completed four years of high school. Fifty years later, that number had risen to 80 percent.

- In 1889, 335 out of 400 colleges found it necessary to set up special preparatory departments to compensate for the deficiencies in entering freshman.

- In 1941, the Naval Training Corps reported that 62 percent of college freshman tested failed a test of basic mathematical reasoning.

- When the U.S. Army was testing recruits prior to World War I, they found so many illiterate inductees that two intelligence tests were developed—one for those who were literate and another for those who were illiterate. (Schlechty, 1997)

None of this information should be cause for celebration among the devoted members of the educational community. There still is much work to be done in our nation's schools. It must be noted, though, that problems have existed for a long time. The evidence simply does not support the cry that American public education is declining. In fact, in many ways, the nation's public schools have exceeded some of the goals they may have been founded for. They may not have been founded, many argue, for the purpose of creating a society in which virtually all citizens were literate. Yet, the *Human Development Report, 1995* from the United Nations indicates that 99 percent of Americans are literate. The percentage of functionally literate Americans (those who can read well) is less than most school leaders would like. However, the United States is clearly among the world's leaders in terms of the number of adults who can read. This represents a significant educational goal that has been met. Apparently, the good old days were not quite as good as some people remember them to be, and today is not quite as bad either.

## Showcase

In order to promote our school through linkages with the business community, the staff and I designed a Readers Are Leaders Week. Every day for one week, every classroom had a community leader come and read to them. The outcomes of the project went far beyond my original vision. Most Reader–Leaders entered the school somewhat nervous but all left relaxed, smiling and asking what they could do for our school. The most common comments revealed a confidence in our school and a positive feeling about the next generation. In one week, our school made 75 business–community connections. The readers included a realtor, banker, photographer, lawyer, stockbroker, engineer, land developer, and hospital personnel. We understood that we could maximize media coverage of this event if we included government leaders. State and U.S. representatives and senators, local politicians, and the State Superintendent of Schools all participated or sent a representative. Later, when I attended a community function with the superintendent, it was wonderful to have so many business people approach us with positive comments about our school.

*Sondra G. Estep, Ph.D., former Principal, James B. Eads Elementary, Munster, IN, now Professor, Governors State University, IL*

## The Purpose of A Plan

Being cognizant of public opinion helps school administrators build a foundation upon which they can develop a plan. The knowledge of public opinion, therefore, is not an end. Instead, it is a means by which the administrator begins to formulate the school–community relations plan for his/her particular school. The term *school–community relations plan* has been mentioned rather casually thus far. What is actually meant by this term? How can school–community relations be planned since they involve so many different people? First of all, not only can they be planned, but also they must be planned. Sadly, there are school leaders who consider school–community relations to be something that just happen. These people, believing that such relations cannot really be planned, lead their schools with a "fly by the seat of your pants" attitude. The best leaders among this group do experience some success, due to an innate or well-developed ability to make decisions. For the most part, they make good decisions and often find support for their ideas.

However, there is a real danger in leading in this way. Planning, so widely talked about in education, is considered by most to be essential to success. With the public having greater access to our schools, there are many more opportunities for interaction between the school leader and the public than there ever were before. One bad decision or ill-timed comment can be far more devastating for the school leader of today than it would have been say a decade or so ago. It stands to reason that as a greater number of people have quick and easy access to information about our schools, skills of judgment and decision making become more critical for school leaders to master.

The application of planning to school–community relations is, therefore, obvious. Failure to plan for school–community relations is an invitation for disaster. Beach and Trent (2000) suggest that the following characteristics of a planning system ought to be present as educational leaders seek to develop their school–community relations plan:

- *Simplicity:* Most school systems do not have the resources to establish a full-time planning position. Therefore, time constraints will require a planning system that is straightforward, simple, and easily managed.

- *Visibility:* Visibility should be a prime consideration in communicating key elements of the school–community relations program. While educational leaders can communicate a great deal of information without ever being seen by constituents, being visible demonstrates to many a higher level of commitment (Fiore, 1999).

- *Accountability:* Outcomes of the school–community relations plan must be tangible and measurable. Planners should be sensitive to the need to visibly demonstrate these outcomes.

- *Brevity:* An effective school–community relations plan should be succinct and to the point, using language appropriate to a wide audience. (p. 252)

Paying attention to these elements allows the school leader to create a plan that can be implemented and continuously revised. When such elements are part of a school–community relations plan, then leaders do not need always to "think on their toes." Instead, as issues arise, the school leader will be equipped with a structure in which to relate to the larger community.

We must pause to pay particular attention to one of the characteristics mentioned above because of its unquestionable importance, not only to school–community relations planning, but to effective school leadership in its broadest sense—visibility. As numerous studies have confirmed (Fiore, 2001; Whitaker, Whitaker, & Lumpa, 2000), school leaders who are visible improve staff morale, communicate better with parents, know more students, and generally improve the climate and culture of their schools. In research conducted in 261 schools, it was found that staff perceptions of a positive school culture were significantly higher in schools in which the principal was considered to be visible often (Fiore, 1999). Just as a lack of visibility will hurt an administrator's ability to relate to members of a school community, so too will it hurt the leader's ability to be seen as an effective leader.

Because the demands of good school–community relations can be somewhat time consuming, school principals need to realize that there is much to be gained by performing some of their management responsibilities while wandering around. Principals who are visible and practice Management by Wandering Around (MBWA) (Frase & Melton, 1992) demonstrate a real commitment to being with people. As the authors state, "MBWA leaders are seldom found in their offices during school hours. MBWA principals are on their feet, wandering with a purpose. They spend their time in classrooms and hallways, with teachers and students." The importance of this visibility cannot be overstated. Critical to any school–community relations plan is the notion that the leader must be both visible and accessible to constituents to the maximum extent possible. It must be noted, however, that this visibility is not a task in and of itself. Rather, there are many tasks that principals can accomplish while wandering around their facilities. However, some strong planning skills are required to make such task accomplishment more possible.

Planning in school–community relations is really no different from planning in other educational contexts, such as curriculum. It does not, as some would imply, limit possibilities, but it instead creates them. Consider the well-planned teacher. He or she enters the classroom each day with a plan that contains learning objectives, instructional methodology, and evaluation of some form. Because of this plan and the teacher's understanding of the plan's long and short-term goals, the teacher is able to deviate from the plan somewhat if the needs of the learners require it. The unplanned teacher, on the other hand, often finds it difficult to let students' needs lead him/her down an unintended path because of a lack of understanding of long and short-term goals. There is a fear that perhaps the teacher and students will find themselves in an area with which they are unfamiliar—that they will never be able to find their way back. The same logic applies to school–community relations. Having a plan, whether it be for crisis management, the publication of a school newspaper, or ideas for conducting parent–teacher conferences, provides the educator with a framework from which to begin. As long as the objectives of the plan are understood and met, then there is some room for deviation from it. The "fly by the seat of your pants" method of planning virtually guarantees that different people on different days will do drastically different things.

It must also be noted that an effective school–community relations plan bases itself on solid action, not just thoughts, words, or intentions. School–community relations are about things that must be done. As most experienced school leaders can attest to, upwards of 90 percent of school–community relations can be traced to what is actually done in a school. This only leaves 10 percent to be dependent on listening and verbal and written forms of communication. With this in mind, the best school–community relations plan is most strongly influenced by what is done in school on a regular basis. In other words, it can no longer be assumed that an attractive monthly newsletter alone constitutes strong school–community relations. It may be an important component, but school–community relations, as is the case in all relationships, represent things that are done to build a greater sense of commitment among people.

Here is one final note about school–community relations planning. As is the case with all strategic planning, a yardstick is needed to assist in measuring a plan's effectiveness. As long as the planner understands the goals of the plan, this yardstick can be used to measure the design before it is finalized and put into action. Exhibit 1.3. provides a checklist to be used as such a yardstick.

---

### Exhibit 1.3. Checklist for School–Community Relations Plan

---

- ◆ Does the plan make use of appropriate and varied communication channels for the various audiences involved?
- ◆ Do all individuals with responsibility in the school–community relations plan know what the goals and objectives are?
- ◆ Does the plan contain strategies for involving all stakeholder groups whenever possible?
- ◆ Are the goals, objectives, and desired outcomes of the school community relations plan consistent with the school philosophy and the state's laws?
- ◆ Are the goals, objectives, and desired outcomes stated in measurable terms to the extent possible?
- ◆ Has the design of the plan's strategies and activities considered available human resources, funds, and facilities?
- ◆ Does the plan distinguish between long and short-term goals and objectives?
- ◆ Are there provisions in the plan for future audits of its effectiveness and results?
- ◆ Is the school community relations plan tailored to the specific needs of the school and its community?
- ◆ Does the school community relations plan take into account the need for in-service education of the staff?

---

School administrators who fail to understand the need for a sound school–community relations plan are inviting trouble. Those who build a plan, but fail to ever check up on its effectiveness, are in an equal amount of trouble. Instead, school administrators must have a plan, carry it out as effectively as possible, and periodically audit or check on its effectiveness. Again, these steps are not only true in school–community relations. They are simply the essence of good planning.

## Three Kinds of Plans

Though the actual design of a school's community relations plan contains characteristics unique to the needs of the particular community served by the school, a point that will be further elaborated upon in subsequent chapters, the organizational framework under which it was created will fall into one of three categories. These three categories form the basis for understanding who in the organization is responsible for the design, coordination, and implementation of the school–community relations plan. Described below, they are coordinated, centralized, and decentralized plans.

### The Coordinated Plan

A school–community relations plan that is coordinated involves a strong degree of cooperation between central office administrators and administrators at the school building level. The roles and responsibilities of these administrative positions complement one another and are neatly fit into a clearly articulated plan. At the central office level, there is often somebody employed as the director or coordinator of school–community relations. This person serves as a valuable resource person to the principal, reinforcing the work being accomplished at the building level. Additionally, the director of school–community relations at the central office level may assume responsibility for establishing media contacts on behalf of the school, resolving complaints from parents or other community members in cooperation with the principal, and assisting the principal in assessing the effectiveness of the individual school's school–community efforts.

A coordinated school–community relations plan that is organized and carried out effectively offers an excellent opportunity for cooperation and consistency within a school system. The building principals in such plans have great discretionary power, which they usually appreciate. However, they operate within a structural framework that is established cooperatively between the central office and the school. This collaboration leads to an increased likelihood that goals will be the same and that viewpoints in regard to school–community relations will be common. Such a framework also, in many cases, increases the likelihood of support from the central office administration. Confluence of goals and viewpoints causes the increased likelihood of such support.

## The Centralized Plan

When a school–community relations plan is centralized, the responsibility for the program belongs solely to the superintendent and his/her designee. At the school building level the principal has little, if anything, to do with the overall plan. Though the principal obviously must interact with members of the community on a regular basis, this interaction takes place independently of the school system's goals and intents. As such, the formal school–community relations plan is far less personal than it is in the coordinated model. The emphasis in a centralized school–community relations plan is on relations with groups of people, not with individuals.

Supporters of a centralized plan base their support primarily on the fact that the superintendent is almost always the best-known public figure in a school system. It is typically the superintendent who belongs to key civic organizations and is seen by the public as the chief representative of the schools. Because the superintendent does not have a school building to lead throughout the school day, the nature of the job, it is argued, allows for greater opportunities for community involvement to take place. In many ways, the superintendent has the most accurate finger on the pulse of the community.

Those who disagree with the effectiveness of a centralized school–community relations plan do so because it ignores individual needs. The centralized plan assumes that people's needs throughout a community are similar. In many school systems, particularly larger ones, the demographics vary greatly from one school to the next, making the similarity of needs among school communities rare. Also of concern is the possibly flawed notion that the superintendent knows the community best. Many argue that although the superintendent may know the larger community well, the building level administrators best understand the populations served by each individual school.

## The Decentralized Plan

A school–community relations plan that is considered to be decentralized places most of the responsibility on the shoulders of the building principal. There is little, if any, formal involvement in the school–community relations plan on the part of central office administration. The result is a more personal relationship between the school and the community it serves. Principals, understanding much more about their local community than those at the central office do, base decisions on the understandings they have of their population's needs and interests.

The decentralized plan is very common in schools today. Most people believe that it is logical to assume that the building principal, of all those on the administrative team, has the best understanding of their community. The common belief is that the principal is in the best position to develop a school–community relations plan that will be of the most benefit to his or her own particular school.

However, this type of plan also has some critics. Some argue that a plan that is too decentralized usually involves a neglect of school–community relations on the part of central office administrators. If plans are all developed locally, then the superintendent and his or her administrative team do not really have a significant role to play. This exclusion often leads to a lack of support from the top, which is harmful to the school in a time of dissension. Furthermore, in school systems already replete with dissension or conflict between teachers and administrators, the plan may be further weakened by the lack of central office involvement. Finally, some principals simply falter in their school–community relations without some guidance, direction, or support coming from the central office.

There are pros and cons to all three of these types of plans (see Exhibit 1.4.). The effectiveness of one type over another is probably less a function of the plan's framework and more a function of the principal's ability to be a leader. It is important for building level administrators to understand that regardless of the label they can affix to their school district's school–community relations efforts, it is the principal's responsibility to develop and maintain positive relationships with the school community–both internally and externally.

## Exhibit 1.4. Pros and Cons of School–Community Plans

|  | *Pro* | *Con* |
|---|---|---|
| *Coordinated Plan* | Increased likelihood of consistency and confluence of values. Little room for misinformation between central office and school building leadership. | Difficult to accomplish in larger school systems. |
| *Centralized Plan* | Superintendent is in the best position to coordinate school–community relations efforts. Schools usually receive similar treatment because one person is responsible for communication. | Deals only with groups of people. Individual needs of each school are ignored. |
| *Decentralized Plan* | The principal understands their school's individual needs best and is in the best position to readily communicate with their community. | Leads to inconsistency within a school system and lack of involvement from central office. |

# Chapter Summary

- It is of paramount importance that school leaders understand what the public really thinks of our schools.
- The public has a tendency to rate their local schools much higher than they rate our nation's schools as a whole.
- Many people want an increased say in decisions made at the local school level.
- When asked to rank order our nation's priorities, a high percentage of Americans do believe that education ought to be considered priority number one or two.
- Misconceptions about public school effectiveness abound. Increased awareness of these misconceptions helps school leaders to correct them.

- It is very important for school leaders to have a clearly articulated plan for school–community relations.
- The school leaders visibility ought to be an important component of this plan.
- School leaders need a yardstick of some kind to measure their school–community relations plan's effectiveness.
- There are essentially three types of school–community relations plans: (1) coordinated, (2) centralized, and (3) decentralized.

# Case Study Analysis

## A Tale of Two Cities

Joe Thompson had been a teacher in the Sunnyvale Community Schools for 12 years. During that time, he became highly respected in the affluent community served by the school and was a favorite teacher among parents and students. When he accepted a job as principal of Westview Elementary School, located in a blue-collar community some 30 miles down the river, the entire Sunnyvale Community mourned the loss of their favorite teacher. However, all were convinced that Joe's no-nonsense approach would make him as successful in the principalship as he was as a teacher.

At the Westview Open House meeting the following September, Joe addressed the parents in attendance for the first time. "First of all, I want to inform you of how excited I am to be the new principal here at Westview," he began. "However, I'd be lying if I didn't say that I am disappointed by the lack of attendance at tonight's meeting. Now I realize you are not the parents who need to hear this, as you obviously care about your children's education. I am concerned, however, that so many Westview parents appear not to care. As research shows, children will not be successful in school without parental involvement."

Though the rest of Joe's address went very well, as he highlighted some ambitious goals for his new school, there were some parents in attendance who had been offended by Joe's opening comments. These parents knew how badly their neighbors wanted to be in attendance. Many of them, it was commonly understood, simply couldn't be because the community's chief employer, Northwire Industrial, required employees to do shift work. Within a few days, word of Joe's open house speech had gotten around the community and his office telephone began a constant ringing.

"How dare you imply that I don't care about my children," one mother exclaimed.

"Who are you to come into this town and judge our lifestyle," screamed a father.

"Maybe if you held open house at a convenient time for parents, we would have been there," yelled another parent.

Joe closed his office door, sat back in his chair, and wondered where he had gone wrong.

## Questions for Analysis

1. How has Joe Thompson's lack of understanding of his community hurt his early tenure at Sunnyvale?

2. What are some steps Joe could have taken to prevent the current situation he's faced with from developing?

3. Does Joe suffer from any misconceptions about his new community? If so, what are they?

4. If you were Joe, what would you do next?

# 2

# Reading the Pulse of the Community

In Chapter 1, the importance of understanding what the public really thinks of our schools was discussed in great detail. Paying close attention to the public's perception of schools and then using this knowledge to design a school–community relations plan that fits and creates lasting connections was referred to. In this chapter, these concepts are expanded upon. Particular attention is paid to the significance of understanding exactly what your community expects from your school and what your school needs from your community. With this knowledge, school administrators are best able to design and implement the most effective school–community relations plan for the community they serve.

## Get to Know Community Leaders

### Look to Formal and Informal Leaders

Every community, regardless of size or location, has individuals who are considered to be the community leaders. Often these people are seen in this light because of the status of the jobs that they hold. For instance, in many communities, bank presidents, leading attorneys, and medical doctors have traditionally emerged as community leaders. Some communities see school administrators, higher education faculty, contractors, builders, and religious leaders in this leadership capacity. Although the specific occupations of community leaders vary from one community to the next, all communities seem to have individuals who emerge in these leadership roles.

In addition to these more easily identified community leaders, there are many communities that have what is referred to as "pockets" of leadership. These "pockets" refer to smaller subgroups within the community that may have an individual or group of individuals they view as their leaders. Examples are some churches, private schools, ethnic groups, and/or minority groups. This is not to imply that everywhere these groups are found they are existing as a subgroup or "pocket." It is certain, however, that in some communities groups that do not fit the description of the community norm find themselves forming an unofficial subgroup. These subgroups or "pockets" have their leaders as well. They may not be leaders in the broader community, but these "pockets" of leadership exert great influence over the people who may be a part of their "pocket".

School leaders must be aware of who holds leadership positions, either formally or informally, within these groups and within the community in its broadest sense. They must form professional relationships with these leaders in order to understand the needs and desires of the community members they represent. In most communities it is virtually impossible for a school leader to get to know, even on a shallow level, all of the members of the community. For this reason, the school leader must make every effort to begin forming relationships with the community leaders. By understanding who these individuals are and what interests they may be representing, the school leader can begin developing plans for including them in the school–community relations plan for their school. How to specifically accomplish this will be discussed later in this chapter.

For now, the focus is on how the school leader can go about getting to know these community leaders. Since the size and demographics of communities have such variation in them, what are some steps school leaders can take to begin the process of getting to know their community's leaders? Then, what specifically should be done with the information collected from these community leaders? The answers to these questions begin with the leader's willingness and ability to reach out to the different groups within the community. A great place to start is with local civic and cultural organizations.

## Look to Local Civic Organizations

People who assume leadership roles in many communities frequently do so, at least in part, through their association with local civic organizations. Although membership in many civic organizations is open to any members of the community desiring to serve, we are all aware of some organizations that limit their membership to individuals holding identifiable leadership positions within the community. Though our own feelings of social and community justice may or may not support all of these organizations, it is difficult to deny the fact that many community leaders are found to have some association with these civic groups. It is also true that many of these organizations perform valuable services for the communities in which they are located. This provides school leaders with one more rather compelling reason why they should get to know leaders of civic organizations.

If school leaders desire to understand who the community leaders are, then they must look to these organizations. There is no implication here that the school leader must necessarily join any of the organizations. It is important, however, that the school leader is aware of who the members are and how leaders in the organization can be contacted. This information is of great value whenever the school leader is seeking a community outlet for garnering support for any type of school initiative. Not only can these organizations be great sources of funding, but the support they can lend in other ways may be equally important to the school leader. Exhibit 2.1 lists some of the more common organizations found within American communities. Absent from this list are organizations that profess or practice a particular religion or faith. These organizations can also be very important to the school leader, because they represent either majorities of the community or a community pocket, as referred to earlier. Although some of these organizations may be unfamiliar in your particular community, and other prominent local ones may be absent from the list, Exhibit 2.1 lists some of the more common organizations to look for.

## Exhibit 2.1. Major Civic and Cultural Organizations

- ◆ AARP
- ◆ AMVETS
- ◆ American Red Cross
- ◆ American Cancer Association
- ◆ Kiwanis International
- ◆ Boy Scouts of America
- ◆ Girl Scouts
- ◆ Rotary International
- ◆ Lion's Club
- ◆ Fraternal Order of Police
- ◆ Jaycees
- ◆ Delta Kappa Gamma
- ◆ Chamber of Commerce
- ◆ Arts Council
- ◆ Historical Society
- ◆ Tourism Development Authority
- ◆ VFW
- ◆ YMCA
- ◆ Salvation Army

By getting to know leaders of these organizations, school leaders will have at their disposal a tremendous connection to public opinion. Though a large segment of any given community will not be represented by these organizations and must be reached through alternative means, these organizations will provide access to the opinions of a large percentage of community leaders.

It is wise, therefore, for school administrators to arrange to speak to these groups whenever they implement or propose a program that would benefit from community support. Many of these organizations hold regularly scheduled meetings and enjoy having school personnel present innovative and necessary information about their school's goals and/or programs. Again, it is important to note that the responsibility for actually presenting to these groups is not solely the school administrator's. Many programs are presented better by the teachers and students involved in them. For example, when starting a conflict resolution program in elementary schools, many school leaders have found that the faculty sponsor and some select students are far better at presenting the information than they themselves would be. Additionally, the members of the civic or cultural organization receiving the presentation often enjoy the opportunity to hear from youngsters at their meetings. In addition to meeting the organizations' goals of staying connected to the community, the school administrator, by scheduling such opportunities to inform, will meet the school's goals of creating an informed and supportive public.

## Showcase

The Burnsville Chamber of Commerce and the Burnsville/Eagan/Savage Schools in Burnsville, Minnesota have an outstanding formal partnership. The Burnsville Chamber is an active organization that is involved in all aspects of community life, including local education. Unlike many Chambers of Commerce, the Burnsville Chamber is not a social club. The Chamber has an active Education committee that annually sponsors a series of highly successful events designed to contribute to the growth and well being of the community's students. These events include: an annual Career Carnival in which over 100 local professional and business owners visit with and counsel over 1,000 students and parents; an Ethics in the Workplace workshop given to over 100 students annually; and a series of shadow days that provide students a firsthand look at different career opportunities. These events are imbedded in different class curriculums and have become an integral part of many students' educational experience.

*Douglas DeWitt, former Principal, Burnsville*
*High School, Burnsville, MN, now Assistant Professor,*
*Minnesota State University*

# Neighborhood Schools

It was once true that schools were considered integral parts of the neighborhoods in which they were located. Many readers can attest to this reality through their own personal memories and through testimony of walking through their neighborhood to their schools each morning. However, as some of our nation's neighborhoods have eroded, so, too, have the perceptions of the school as a good neighbor. In several of our nation's biggest cities, steps are being taken to reverse this process and return schools to the status of valued neighbor. This is being done in places like Boston, Los Angeles, and New York City because of an understanding that real school reform cannot occur if it ignores the circumstances of students' lives outside of school. The school itself must be returned to the status of "community beacon" so that students who lead impoverished lives can have something safe to rely on. Improving educational outcomes for students requires much more than attending to academic content and standards. The conditions in the neighborhood also have to be considered (Maeroff, 1998).

The return of schools as valued centers of the neighborhood is happening in some places. However, many communities cannot relate to this experience. Today, with many communities building schools on huge parcels of land set apart from the rest of the community, a neighborhood feeling between the school and the community just does not exist. Though I do not intend to be to harsh in my judgment of the particular location of schools in our communities, many people feel nostalgic over the loss of the neighborhood school. However, these feelings are not only induced because many schools are physically isolated from the community, they are often induced because of an emotional isolation. There are many people who literally live next door to a school, yet they feel very disconnected from the building and all of its inhabitants. For these people, school leaders need to demonstrate that they recognize that a relationship with community leaders will only take a school so far. The taxpayer living next door must also believe that he/she is important to the school and that the school family desires a relationship with him/her. Such a bond or relationship is accomplished through being a good neighbor. Good neighbors, I think we would all agree, communicate with and care about one another.

# Important First Steps

## Neighborhood Visits

Sound advice for any new school administrator is to take some time to personally visit the houses surrounding your school. Though you may temporarily feel like a door-to-door salesperson, you will be amazed and pleased at the reaction many neighbors have to this idea. These visits need not be long, but they should be focused on the fact that you are a new neighbor and you just want to say "hello." You may even bring a set of specific questions that you want answered to assist you in ascertaining the extent to which the neighbor likes living near the school. Although this discussion will tell you a great deal about discipline as students walk to and from school and behavior on the playground if you have one, it should not be the main focus of your visit. The purpose of this initial visit needs to be simply saying "hello."

Exhibit 2.2 illustrates a sample script of how to approach these neighborhood visits. For obvious reasons, the script cannot be carried too far, because one can never precisely anticipate what the neighbor will say in reply.

---

## Exhibit 2.2. The Initial Visit

"Good afternoon (morning). My name is Melissa Simone and I'm the new principal next door at Crestwood Elementary. Since we're going to be neighbors, I thought I'd like to just stop by and introduce myself. It's important to me that my family enjoys positive relationships with our neighbors. As I get to know my new school family even better, I'm going to be sure that I impress upon them the value of good neighbors. How long have you lived here? What have been some of the best things about living next to our school? What are some of the most difficult aspects? I don't want this to be the last time we ever speak. Please fell free to drop by the school and visit me whenever you'd like to. It was a pleasure meeting you."

---

Although the mock introduction illustrated by the above example leaves no obvious room for response, your judgment must be trusted in determining how to deliver this mini speech. For example, it would certainly be unwise to read this monologue, leaving no opportunity for a reply from the neighbor. However, delivered in a conversational and genuine tone, this little speech accomplishes a few important goals:

- It demonstrates a proactive approach. By making the visit in the first place, the school leader establishes that he/she wants to take the first step in relationship building.
- It introduces the concept of the school functioning as a family within a neighborhood. This allows the neighbor to see the school in a friendlier, more personal way.

- It invites the neighbor to share and be open without forcing the neighbor to do so.
- It demonstrates that, as leader, you are interested in hearing about both the positive and negative aspects of your school.
- It leaves the neighbor with an open invitation to contact you if problems ever do arise.

Again, visiting neighbors and introducing yourself will not be feasible in all situations. Some schools have no neighbors who are close in proximity. Other schools are situated amidst high-rise apartment buildings containing hundreds of residences. There are still other, yet unmentioned reasons why such visits are not possible for all administrators in all settings. However, for the administrators housed in schools where such visits are at least feasible, an opportunity for understanding the community is being missed if you do not take advantage of these situations. For those in communities where such visits are difficult, there probably are creative ways that you, too, can get out into the community more. Such steps must begin with a conscious choice on the part of the administrator, though. What is needed is the belief that taking these steps is indeed important.

Though Exhibit 2.2 illustrates a visit by a new principal, slight modifications can make this technique just as valuable for veteran leaders who have worked at the neighborhood school for many years. Rather than introducing yourself as the new principal, open with a statement such as, "We've been neighbors for some time, but until now we just haven't had ample opportunity to meet and to talk."

It may be more comfortable and more appropriate in a particular community for the administration to send a notice in the mail informing neighbors that the principal intends to be walking the neighborhood and visiting in the near future. Again, each individual school leader must use his/her judgment in determining whether this is a good step or not. In situations where it is wise to notify neighbors via mail before surprising them with a visit, a letter such as that illustrated in Exhibit 2.3 may be beneficial.

## Exhibit 2.3. A Welcoming Letter

Dear Neighbor,

As principal of Crestwood Elementary School for the last (*insert appropriate time*), I have tried to recognize the value of forming and maintaining valuable relationships with our school's neighbors. Since we all coexist within the same small geographical area, I feel it is important to understand how we can best be neighbors to one another. As we all become so busy during the courses of our days, we have not had ample opportunities to get to know each other to the extent that I feel it is important to do so. Because some of you have children in our school, some of us have had occasions to meet and speak before. However, those of you without children in our school are equally important to all of us at Crestwood.

During the week of October 5–9, I will be walking through the neighborhood with the sole purpose of getting to know our neighbors better. If you are available when I'm in the neighborhood, I'd love to visit with you briefly. If you are unavailable or would prefer not to be bothered, I understand completely. Simply feel free to drop by the school and visit with me at your convenience.

Looking forward to being great neighbors, I remain,

Sincerely,

Melissa Simone, Principal

As was the case in Exhibit 2.2, the sample letter depicted in Exhibit 2.3 accomplishes some very important goals. Specifically, it:

- Proactively introduces or reintroduces the administrator to the neighbors. This demonstrates the importance that the administrator gives to seeking out partnerships with the school's neighbors.
- Establishes the reasons why the administrator thinks communication with neighbors is important.
- Informs the neighbors when the administrator intends to be walking through the neighborhood to meet with people.
- Gives the neighbor a safe and easy way to choose not to interact with the administrator during that time frame.

◆ Sincerely invites and welcomes the neighbors to visit the school whenever they would like to.

Also worth noting is that the wording here is merely offered as a generic suggestion. Only you know the phrasing that would be appropriate in your particular community. Modify accordingly, so that you feel more comfortable with the process.

Once again, it may feel awkward to begin communicating with neighbors of the school, as this section of the text has suggested you should. If so, the feelings of discomfort are probably caused by the fact that such communication is not typically done in our schools. This brings up a crucial point to consider when planning any aspect of a school–community relations plan, namely that just because things have been done a certain way for a long period of time does not indicate that they should continue to be done that way. The statement has been made that if you always do what you've always done, you'll always get what you've always gotten. Perhaps, instead, things need to be done differently for an even longer period of time. Making friendly contact with the neighbors of your school makes for smart school–community relations. There are important perceptions of your school that only close neighbors of the school can have. For example, these individuals know, from an outsider's perspective, how much noise emanates from your school throughout the day. They know the degree to which loitering or vandalism is taking place on school grounds. They understand, better than anybody, about traffic patterns and problems that may be created at different points in the school day. These neighbors often have strong perceptions of your school; perceptions that are based on direct, objective observations. Because, in many ways, perception is reality, failure to acknowledge, appreciate, and, where appropriate, alter these perceptions is simply that—failure.

Remember, too, that a leader is somebody whom people will follow to a place they otherwise might not go. It is imperative that school administrators act as leaders in regards to communicating with the public. Doing so may at times feel awkward, but good communication simply will not happen without strong, committed leaders.

## A Neighborhood Tea

Some school leaders prefer to have regularly scheduled meetings of their neighbors inside the school building. Often there are refreshments served at these gatherings, but that is not an essential component. Each individual leader must use his/her own judgment to determine the particulars of these events.

What is essential is that the event be communicated to the neighbors in a timely and accurate fashion. It is almost always easier to attract parents to the school than it is to attract those adults with no familial ties. With this in mind, a school leader desirous of hosting a neighborhood tea or similar gathering must take extra steps to ensure that the neighbors receive the invitation. Often, this involves mailing the invitation, followed up by a telephone call urging the neighbors to attend.

To prevent these events from simply being informal gatherings of neighbors, which is something the school does not necessarily need to be involved with, the school leader should have a focused agenda for each meeting. Topics that may be included for discussion are: how to improve traffic patterns, monitoring students prior to the school's official arrival time and after the school's official departure time, and the formation of a neighborhood watch committee charged with overseeing the students' and the building's protection during nonschool hours. The session should also always include some type of question and answer period, which puts the neighbors in a position to feel as though the entire meeting was not planned in advance. Plans are good, but a certain amount of free expression gives everybody the feeling that his or her issues are important.

Regardless of whether "tea" and/or other refreshments are served, the school neighbors must come away from these meetings with the realization that they are important. The meetings must be handled in such a way to communicate that the school is an important part of the neighborhood. They must illustrate the importance of community.

## Don't Forget the Parents

The most common way in which school leaders typically learn about the community in which their school is located is through the parents of the students they serve. Although a good deal of this information is perceived directly by the leader, there is still more information that the leader gets through indirect means. Examples of indirect means include:

◆ Information shared by the teaching staff

◆ Information shared by the students

◆ Information shared by business and community leaders

◆ Information shared by other administrators

Paying attention to what these groups have to say about parents in the community will assist the school administrator in forming the best possible notion of the parents' needs, feelings, and desires. Let us examine some specific ways that teachers, students, business and community leaders, and fellow administrators inform the school leader about the attitudes of parents.

### Information Shared by the Teaching Staff

Teachers have many formal and informal interactions with a variety of parents during a typical school year. Open house activities and parent–

teacher conferences are two of the most often used formal interactions that yield tremendous information to teachers about the parents' feelings toward the school and its staff. Through these opportunities, teachers have the chance to engage in meaningful two-way communication with parents. Though the structure of the occasions may limit the extent to which communication can truly be two-way, open houses and parent– teacher conferences are characterized by their objective that teachers will communicate with parents and parents will communicate with teachers.

Because attendance at these events may vary considerably from one community to the next, the amount of information about parent attitudes that they yield will also vary. There are, however, many informal ways in which teachers gather information about parent attitudes. It is through these informal interactions that a great deal of understanding regarding parents' attitudes and feelings can be realized. Informal interactions that can be quite informative include:

- Notes from parents
- Conversations in the hallway
- Parents chaperoning field trips or other school activities
- Classroom parent volunteers

## Information Shared by the Students

Teachers who get to know their students on a personal level engage in many meaningful conversations with them intended to be of assistance in the teaching–learning process. In addition to the benefits that relationships can have on teaching–learning, they are also opportunities to learn about feelings, beliefs, and attitudes. Students often reflect the attitudes of their parents. Although it is not always the case, many times through conversations with the students, teachers are able to learn quite a bit of significant information about the parents' feelings regarding schooling. Though not the primary reason why such relationships are important, this adds even more credence to the notion that teachers benefit greatly by taking the time to listen to the hearts and minds of their students.

The same logic applies to the role of the school administrator. Because this leader does not have a regular class of students to meet with on a daily basis, relationships of the same quality as those formed by teachers are difficult to attain. However, this is one important reason why the best school administrators are visible to all stakeholders throughout the school day (Fiore, 1999; Whitaker, 1997). In the case of the students, this visibility breeds familiarity and comfort, which will ultimately foster more positive, honest relationships.

## Information Shared by Business and Community Leaders

In most communities, some business and community leaders are also parents. Though not always true, a large percentage of these leaders send their children to the public schools in the community. Therefore, there is an additional reason for formulating partnerships and relationships with these business and community leaders. Namely, these people give you very important information about the attitudes and beliefs of some of your students' parents.

This points to one additional reason why it is important for school leaders to form partnerships with business and community leaders. Such partnerships, in addition to creating tremendous support for the school and its goals, become trusted channels of communication for the school leader. Business and community leaders, particularly those who are parents, know a great deal about what parents in the community think of the school. Their positions as leaders give them access to a good deal of public opinion. Relationships with these people really can become wonderful, efficient channels of communication with a percentage of your school's parent population.

---

## Showcase

Due to declining enrollment in our high school, I recently planned a Realtor's Breakfast to be held at our school. I contacted the Tallahassee Board of Realtors and asked them to have one of their weekly meetings here. My goal was to encourage them to sell property on our side of town, as we continue to struggle with enrollment. I convinced the two local grocery store chains and one bank that if we can persuade more people to move to this side of town, they too would prosper. They agreed and they made donations to help us out. Students in our graphic arts computer classes created banners, posters, and programs for the event. Rather than using honor roll students to serve breakfast, I instead chose students who were not on track to graduate. I wanted to show confidence in them that few had shown. The students handled themselves beautifully and I had an opportunity to show our school in a whole new way that not only helped our image, but most importantly helped our students.

*Nancy Fahnestock, Math Teacher,*
*Godby High School, Tallahassee, FL*

---

# Information Shared by Other School Administrators

One of the skills that school administrators continually hone throughout their careers is how to work with parents. Even before becoming administrators, teachers develop better skills for dealing with parents with each passing year. Books like *Dealing With Difficult Parents and With Parents in Difficult Situations* (Whitaker & Fiore, 2001) provide assistance for dealing with challenging parents and challenging situations. The result is an informed and experienced cadre of educators who can provide great assistance to administrators in understanding parents and how to work well with them. For this reason, administrators can turn to their administrative colleagues, particularly if new to the community, for a great deal of useful information about parents. If the administrative colleagues know very little about the particular parents they're being asked about, their experiences can certainly help in generalizing information that will still be helpful.

Professional literature in school administration can also yield a great deal of help in learning about what parents want from their child's school. In the May, 1998, issue of Educational Leadership, for example, Dorothy Rich summarizes efforts in Anchorage, Alaska, and in Rochester, New York, to discover what parents think about their children's teachers. The goal of these districts' leaders is to utilize this information to enhance home–school connections. Rich suggests that the following questions be used by school leaders to discover parent attitudes:

- Does the teacher appear to enjoy teaching and believe in what he or she does in the school?
- Does the teacher set high expectations and help children reach them?
- Does the teacher know the subject matter of the class and how to teach it?
- Does the teacher create a safe classroom where children are encouraged to pay attention, participate in class, and learn?
- Does the teacher deal with behavior problems fairly and consistently?
- Does the teacher make clear what my child is expected to learn?
- Does the teacher treat my child fairly and with respect?
- Does the teacher contact me promptly with any concerns about my child's academic and behavioral performance?
- Does the teacher provide helpful information during conferences?

◆ Does the teacher use a variety of communication tools to report progress and student needs?

◆ Is my child's teacher accessible and responsive to me when I call or want to meet?

◆ Does the teacher work with me to develop a cooperative strategy to help my child?

A list of questions such as these is a great starting point for discovering parent attitudes in your school community. Additionally, these questions illustrate the school's commitment to working with parents in order to meet the needs of their children. Just as the case was made in Chapter 1 that it would not be prudent for school leaders to base all of their decisions on public opinion, parental responses to these questions ought not be taken without a grain of salt. Parental attitudes may be skewed somewhat from reality. However, utilizing responses to questions such as these will provide school leaders a better understanding of where to begin in their dealings with parents and their accompanying feelings and attitudes.

## Multiculturalism and School–Community Relations

Here at the dawn of the twenty-first century, it is clear that people from other countries and from other cultures find the United States to be a source of freedom and opportunity. In fact, with the exception of the first decade of the last century (1901–1910), we have seen a marked increase in the number of people who are immigrants to the United States (Immigration and Naturalization Service Statistics Division, 2001). What used to be an urban phenomenon is quickly becoming an experience that administrators from varying communities have in common. Our neighborhoods and, consequently, our schools, are becoming increasingly multicultural. The benefits that this multiculturalism can bring to our educational system will be realized only if school leaders first understand the needs of these cultural communities.

Chapter 4 pays attention to the differing nonverbal behaviors that various cultures exhibit and use in communication. It is important that school administrators are aware of these differences, but they are only one small part of the cultural understanding required to make people from all cultures feel welcomed and valued at school. This is alarming news to administrators who are watching the population in their school community change before their very eyes. Without training to help understand the new cultures arriving at their schools, these administrators either feel lost and insecure, or they become defiant and refuse to adjust to the needs of the changing community. Both of these reactions are mistakes. Reactive behavior seldom enhances communication. For this reason, school leaders must proactively familiarize themselves and their staff members with all cultures that are part of their school communities.

This familiarization does not occur accidentally. Becoming familiar with and showing appreciation for various cultures take a concerted effort, particularly if the culture in question is new to the community. The school administrator must, therefore, reach out to members of the community who can assist him/her in designing staff development or workshop sessions to make staff members aware of customs, traditions, and rituals that may be a part of the new culture. This is the only way that the staff will have to begin showing sensitivity and appreciation for the individuals whose pasts are rooted in the new culture. Once there is an awareness of the community's multiculturalism, then the leaders of the school can incorporate ideas from all cultures into the culture of their school. In doing so, they will create a new school culture that over time will strengthen the sense of community within the school. Examples of some ways that different cultures can be woven into a school's existing culture include:

- Celebrating diversity through pictures and posters adorning the school.
- Preparing written materials in all languages that are used as primary languages in students' homes.
- Bringing cultural sensitivity into the school cafeteria through menu choices reflective of the community's diet.
- Acknowledging and educating students about holidays and customs that are integral parts of the community's many cultures.
- Reexamining existing school dress codes to see if there are rules and regulations that are insensitive to the dress of different cultures.
- Ensuring that respect for, and appreciation of, diversity are essential components of the school's mission and vision statements.

It is important that all school leaders recognize the power and significance of their school's culture. They must realize that all that happens inside of a school is inexplicably tied to the culture of that school. School culture, representing the shared attitudes, values, beliefs, and behaviors of members of the school family, forms the foundation for student achievement, staff morale, parent satisfaction, and school climate (Fiore, 1999).

Failure to develop a school culture respectful and representative of the community's culture can doom a school to failure. If all school–community relations were merely public relations, then communicating with the public would be all that is required. However, the best school–community relations plans involve more than just communication. They involve a desire to welcome people and to alter some of our own conceptions to include those of our community. This creates the strong tie between school culture and school–community relations.

School culture consists of the commonly held beliefs of teachers, students, and principals that guide such characteristic behaviors as learning activities, grouping practices, and the ways that teachers talk with each other and evaluate student achievement (Heckman, 1993). If these beliefs and resulting characteristic behaviors work for the school but are in conflict with the community, then it will be very difficult for the school to relate successfully to community members and make them feel important. School–community relations can only be strengthened when the community and the school share a common culture. Multicultural communities, therefore, need to develop a common culture that includes everybody. The lead for such an activity must be the school.

Reading the pulse of the community is an important first step. Responding to the pulse, and continuing to read and modify it, are absolutely necessary if school administrators wish to be leaders in school–community relations.

## Chapter Summary

- ♦ School administrators must get to know the leaders in their school's community.
- ♦ In many communities, leaders can be found holding membership in civic and/or cultural organizations.
- ♦ School administrators must also pay attention to subgroups in their community. They must form relationships with leaders of these groups as well.
- ♦ It is up to the school leader to introduce and reintroduce the school to its neighbors. These neighbors must be shown the important position they hold in the school community.
- ♦ School leaders must continuously reach out to parents for support.
- ♦ The many cultures represented in a community should all find a place in the school.
- ♦ By fostering and developing a common school culture focused on the needs and aspirations of students and their families, school leaders perform their most important school–community relations task.

# Case Study Analysis

## Changing Landscapes

The demographics of the Leland High School community had changed quite a bit during the last four or five years. Carolyn Jackson, Leland's principal, felt that in many ways the school community she was hired to lead six years earlier had somehow disappeared. Fewer than two percent of the student body spoke a language other than English in their homes when Carolyn was hired. Today that figure was at about 25 percent. There were houses of worship popping up in the community that Carolyn didn't recognize, and at least a half dozen ethnic food markets, complete with marquees that Carolyn could not read, had opened within the past year.

What troubled Carolyn Jackson the most was that parent participation had dropped off dramatically in recent years as well. Carolyn was hired largely because of her people skills; Leland was not starving for instructional leadership six years ago when she started. Now, as test scores in the school were showing a rapid decline, the very parent involvement she was so proud of seemed to be disappearing as well. The school lost two of its most valued business partnerships within the past three years, as a few local businesses left the neighborhood, yielding way for the new ethnic markets that now characterized Leland High School's neighborhoods.

The students and the few parents Carolyn knew were great people, in her judgment. Leland still had much to be proud of, as there were fewer student disruptions and better attendance than at any other high school in the district. Still, something was missing. Carolyn Jackson stared out her office window and wondered how she could rekindle the spirit of Leland High School and her own spirit that used to be tied directly to it.

## Questions for Analysis

1. What advice would you give Carolyn Jackson as she struggles to rekindle what she perceives as the missing spirit?
2. How can Carolyn compensate for the loss of business partnerships in this school community?
3. Are there ways in which Carolyn can utilize her strong people skills to increase parental involvement at Leland?
4. What has been Carolyn's biggest failure at Leland in recent years?
5. If you were principal of Leland High School, what would your plan be for improved school–community relations? What would you do first?

# 3

# Establishing Everybody's Role

Successful school–community relations do not occur accidentally. Rather, they are achieved by calculated efforts. As the best school leaders already realize, the efforts required are necessary. Though time-consuming, working hard at establishing, maintaining, and nurturing healthy school–community relations is the right thing to do if our ultimate goal is the realization of an educational system that all constituents are a part of.

It is very important to note that the efforts required to develop these positive school–community relations ought not come from a single source. In fact, in today's climate, it would be impossible for this to happen. Years ago it may have been appropriate for school districts to hire an individual to single-handedly oversee public relations. To foster the kinds of school–community relations that are necessary today, however, it is totally unreasonable to expect one person to be responsible for these public relations tasks. Parents are busier and, in some cases, more critical of schools. Politicians, though always interested in education, are feeling an increased sense of urgency to be involved in the business of schooling. Taxpayers are demanding more accountability for the money they feel is being drained from their homes and given to the schools. These actions are true regardless of the size of the school or school system you are working in. School–community relations are everybody's responsibility. To be successful, everybody who has a stake in the union between schools and their communities must recognize the significance their role has in the process of developing healthy school–community relations.

## School–Community Relations at the District Level

In some parts of the country, a school district consists of a single school. In other areas, school districts are defined by county boundaries, creating some metropolitan districts with upwards of 200 schools. Obviously, there will be differences between these two extremes in both the number of employees who work directly on fostering positive school–community relations and the specific responsibilities that these individuals are charged with carrying out. This being said, there are similarities in what school districts of varying sizes do to keep school–community relations positive and nurtured. Outlined below are the responsibilities of key personnel working in district offices in "typical" school districts. Though the specific job titles of some of these individuals may differ from the titles held by their counterparts in districts you are familiar with, the required job tasks are similar. This section ends with a broader summary of district-level responsibilities so that these responsibilities may be compared/contrasted with the "typical" building-level responsibilities that many principals and/or their designees are charged with carrying out.

## The Superintendent

It would defy logic if this text failed to discuss the critical role of the superintendent in a school district's school–community relations plan. As the chief officer of a district, the superintendent can be, and usually is, the most influential member of the certificated staff. This is not only true because of the importance of a superintendent's particular tasks relative to school–community relations. Rather, what is referred to here is the importance of the superintendent's leadership in making school–community relations a priority. A leader, it is argued, is an individual whom people will follow to a place that they would not otherwise go by themselves. In this regard, the superintendent who is a true leader exerts tremendous influence over the success or failure of his or her district's school–community relations plan. This influence is not necessarily exerted because of any tasks that the superintendent carries out. Instead, leadership is exerted through the moral authority, or the authority vested in the superintendent based on subordinates' perceptions of his/her values and beliefs, rather than by tasks or edicts. As Schlechty (1990) maintains, superintendents can delegate almost every type of authority they have with the exception of moral authority. Moral authority rests in the office of the superintendent and is, therefore, much more difficult to delegate or empower others to possess. If the superintendent does not use his/her moral authority to get people enthused about strong school–community relations, but attempts to delegate such tasks instead, then there is little hope that any majority of stakeholders will be excited about the process. Therefore, the specific tasks of the superintendent, which vary considerably from one school district to the next, are not nearly as important as the belief system of the superintendent and his/her willingness to use the moral authority accompanying the office to make positive school–community relations a priority for everybody.

Having made this point, there are tasks relative to many school–community relations plans that are best assigned to the superintendent. They are simply not carried out as effectively in the absence of moral authority.

Among the school–community tasks often carried out by the superintendent are the following:

- Bringing members of their administrative team together in a way that each individual benefits from the knowledge, skills, and experiences of the others relative to school–community relations.
- Establishing and maintaining open communication channels within the school system (internal communication).
- Developing and nurturing open communication channels between the school system and the public (external communication).
- Developing and championing the basic school system policy for creating relationships between the school and the community.
- Taking the initiative to keep the school board, the staff, and the general public informed of school matters.
- Ensuring that the school system's plans for school–community relations are assessed and evaluated, and then seeing to it that the findings of these assessments are made available to the school board.
- Making sure that influential groups and community leaders are provided with factual information that will cause them to act on behalf of the community's children and their education.

In addition to performing the above tasks, the superintendent must act as a model for what the school system believes in and hopes to accomplish in terms of school–community relations. In this regard, he/she must always remember that the only way to get other administrators and staff members to be visible in the community is to model this behavior first and foremost. This requires the superintendent to do many of the things discussed in Chapter 2. The superintendent must be aware of who the community leaders are and must actively seek their support and counsel on school matters.

In many districts, superintendents serve on the boards of local civic and community organizations. In this way, the superintendent models the importance of community involvement to all members of the school community. An additional benefit from such involvement is that it affords the superintendent an opportunity to engage regularly in meaningful two-way communication with community leaders. As expanded upon in Chapter 4, two-way communication involves both listening and informing. It is the purest way to ensure that the interests and concerns of all parties communicating are addressed. Superintendents who spend all of their work time in the office find little opportunity to engage in two-way communication. As such, these individuals find themselves expert at one-way communication, that is, giving information through memoranda and news releases with little opportunity for public response. By being involved with community leaders through service to community and civic groups, the superintendent has much greater opportunity for meaningful two-way communication with constituents.

## Mistakes Made by Superintendents

The job responsibilities of the modern day superintendent can be overwhelming. As the public demands greater accountability for student achievement, lower taxes, and safer schools, overworked superintendents can often forget the importance of school–community relations and experience pitfalls that can cause real damage. Below are six of the more common mistakes superintendents make that hurt their school system's overall school–community relations. Although the list does not report every mistake made by every superintendent, it illustrates some of the more common pitfalls that many readers will recognize.

1. **Listening to and responding to parental complaints without referring them to the proper channels.** Superintendents understand the importance of responding to parental concerns. The mistake occurs when they listen to and respond to these concerns without first ensuring that the problems are dealt with at the appropriate level. A superintendent who fails to refer building-level concerns to the appropriate place justifiably upsets principals and teachers. This behavior also creates a climate of micro managing, which is very unnerving to those at the school level.

2. **Failing to listen to principals, other administrators, and teachers.** Although the superintendent is ultimately responsible for the school system's school–community relations plan, the wise superintendent recognizes that employees are great sources of public information and further recognizes that these employees often have a keen understanding that leads to very good suggestions regarding school–community relations. The superintendent needs to make employees feel as though their suggestions are listened to.

3. **Making political appointments.** Whether we like it or not, there is a political element to some of the decisions made in our schools. People are hired or dismissed, bids are accepted, and contracts are awarded for reasons that sometimes have political foundations. The superintendent concerned with school–community relations should avoid politics and base

decisions on what is best for students and the school system, not for political gain.

4. **Making decisions on matters about which they are ignorant.** In an overzealous attempt to show people that they are knowledgeable and qualified, some superintendents make decisions about issues on which they are ill informed or ignorant. Rather than seeking out the counsel of those who best understand the issues (other administrators, teachers, staff, parents, students), some superintendents make the mistake of thinking that they must have all the answers. This arrogance causes some damaging decisions to be made.

5. **Showing more concern for finances than for employee welfare.** The financial solvency of some school systems is one of the more stressful aspects of the job for superintendents. However, schools are about people first. The superintendent who fails to demonstrate an understanding of this priority can cause great harm to the school system's efforts at positive school–community relations.

6. **Failing to have both an internal and an external publication that shows the activity of their office.** Chapters 5 and 6 go into great detail about the importance of internal (within the school system) and external (outside of the school system) communication. Because there is a certain degree of mystery surrounding people's ideas of what the superintendent does all day, it is prudent for the superintendent to regularly publish information for all stakeholder groups. This is the superintendent's way of both keeping people informed and of demonstrating accountability to all who are associated with the school.

Anybody who has had any experience with the superintendency can surely recognize how easy it can be to experience the above pitfalls while still caring about the school system and working very hard at being its leader. For this reason, the list is not intended as a condemnation. It does illustrate two important realities, though. First, the superintendent is a significant player in a school system's school–community relations plan. Second, successfully modeling appropriate school–community relations behaviors requires a deliberate attempt on the part of the superintendent.

## The Director of School–Community Relations

Because the importance of school–community relations is finally being realized, many school systems employ a full-time administrator to oversee this significant function. This individual, designated by the superintendent, formulates, carries out, and assists others in adhering to the school system's school–community relations plans.

Because each school system designs its administrative cabinet differently, the actual title given to the administrator directing school–community relations varies considerably from one place to the next. Exhibit 3.1 shows the most commonly used position titles.

---

### Exhibit 3.1. Position Titles

---

The director of school–community relations is sometimes called:

♦ Assistant Superintendent
♦ Assistant to the Superintendent
♦ Director of Information and Community Relations
♦ Director of School–Community Relations
♦ Director of Information Services
♦ Director of Publications
♦ Coordinator of School Information
♦ Public Information Officer

---

Note that these titles represent a change in the way we now think of school–community relations. Previously these relations were known simply as public relations. The responsibilities individuals in these leadership positions typically assumed indicated that they should be referred to with such titles as public relations officer, director of public relations, or director of information and public relations. Words such as "communication" and "community" have now become much more commonplace in these titles, representing a shift in how we view the essential duties that are required.

As the occupation titles vary, so do the specific responsibilities assumed by the director of school–community relations. This variance has a great deal to do with the size of the school system. In some larger school systems, for example, the director of school–community relations assumes a major research responsibility. That is, the director and the director's office staff design all surveys, sample the appropriate populations, gather and analyze the data, interpret the results, and make recommendations based on their interpretations. The directors in these larger districts have immense responsibility in recommending policies to the school board based on public opinion and research. They are often skilled in both qualitative and quantitative analyses, and they can assist the school staff in interpreting survey results.

Many smaller school systems do not have the resources to perform these functions. Because their populations are much smaller and often less diverse, they do not have as much need for a director with research capabilities. In the smallest of districts, public opinion can be understood through steps as simple as town meetings and open houses. In many of these school systems, if there is a director of school–community relations, that person's primary function is to write news releases and newsletters.

Exhibit 3.2 lists some of the most common, generalized responsibilities that this district-level official often assumes:

---

### Exhibit 3.2. Duties of the Director of School–Community Relations

---

- Interpret school board policies to the public
- Serve as a source of information to the community regarding school matters
- Assess public attitudes and opinions and keep appropriate school personnel informed
- Compose and/or edit all written communications (internal and external) from the school system
- Interface regularly with members of the media
- Assist school officials with crisis management plans
- Provide and/or arrange for staff development or in-service training in the area of school–community relations for all school personnel

---

## School–Community Relations at the Building Level

### The Principal

Just as the superintendent exerts tremendous influence over the school system and significantly molds and alters the system's approach to school–community relations, the principal influences the school. As the chief administrator, it is the principal whose leadership determines the degree to which the school enjoys positive and productive relationships with the communities it serves. The principal, through deliberate behaviors and innate values and beliefs, sets the tone for communication patterns, partnership formations, and/or alienation.

## Showcase

Principals need to understand that a positive and productive relationship with the central office is good for kids. A few ideas that may help school buildings with this issue are:

♦ Always send minutes of building meetings to central office personnel.

♦ Always introduce central office personnel and board members at public events.

♦ When communicating with other principals via e-mail, copy to appropriate central office staff.

♦ Praise teachers in front of, and to, central office staff.

♦ Understand that to make change in any situation you need to deal with the appropriate people.

♦ Communicate with all people as peers.

♦ Everyone is important.

♦ Never take credit.

♦ Always give credit.

♦ Approach issues from a "we," not an "I," point of view.

♦ Know you may not have all the information.

♦ Know that you can always get better

♦ A final comment is if principals remember that everyone is trying to do their best it helps with positive and productive communication.

*Dr. Dale Lumpa, Principal, Charles Hay*
*Elementary, Englewood, CO*

Many studies have been done regarding the influence that more positive and more negative principals have on the climate, culture, and overall environment of a school (Fiore, 1999; Whitaker, 1997; and Stolp, 1996). These studies conclude that the principal, more than any other individual in the school, determines the degree to which people feel welcome, accepted, and comfortable within the school's walls. Without these feelings, any attempt at involving the community in schools will be severely challenged.

As was true when speaking of the superintendent's role, the principal's role in school–community relations is largely a leadership issue. There are certainly tasks that the principal must attend to relative to school–community relations, but the values and beliefs that guide the principal's behavior are even more important. In other words, a principal who really believes that our schools belong to the publics they serve will be more in tune with the importance of school–community relations. A principal who believes, as former first lady and now Senator Hillary Clinton said, that it "takes a village" to raise a child, will emphasize relationships with all school stakeholders. A principal who believes in, and thus engages in, continuous and deliberate two-way communication with internal and external groups will find school–community relations tasks to be a natural outgrowth of all that they do on a regular basis.

This being true, the following tasks of the school principal relative to school–community relations are important parts of the principal's job. They, like the superintendent's responsibilities, differ somewhat from one school to the next. Like the superintendent's tasks, however, these tasks ought to be recognizable and applicable to most principalships:

- Being a good listener whenever others speak with him/her
- Being tactful and diplomatic in all relationships
- Creating meaningful professional development activities that assist the staff in developing strong communication skills
- Promoting an open-door policy and being accessible to students, parents, staff, and others
- Keeping the superintendent informed of successes and failures relative to the school's overall school–community relations efforts
- Recognizing and celebrating the accomplishments of all members of the school family
- Maintaining school publications that keep internal and external groups informed about what's going on in the school

There are other responsibilities that principals assume, depending largely on the size of their school and staff and the demographics of their community. However, the list above highlights many of the significant responsibilities as confirmed by several studies (Fiore, 1999; West, 1993; and Schueckler & West, 1991).

While there are implications throughout this book for all school employees desirous of improving their school's overall relationship with the community, the major focus is on the role of the principal. Even if the principal is not directly responsible for a particular school–community relations task, he/she still plays a significant role in seeing to it that the task is carried out by the person who is responsiblee. In larger schools, for example, there are assistant principals or vice principals who play a role in the school's school–community relations plan. Though tasks vary considerably from one environment to the next, what follows are seven critical roles for assistant principals or vice principals at virtually any school level:

- Act as liaison between the principal and staff members
- Maintain positive rapport with staff members
- Communicate effectively with parents and students
- Strive to motivate students and faculty
- Work on maintaining high morale among staff
- Illustrate professional demeanor with all stakeholders
- Establish a disciplined student body

Without discussing each administrative position within a school system and without allowing much devotion to the different environmental factors among and between our schools, it is clear that the administration plays a large role in a school or school system's ability to develop and maintain positive school–community relations. For this reason, books like this are written, and graduate courses are developed, to illustrate to prospective and practicing administrators how keenly important their role is. However, another group that is vitally important to any school or school system's success in this regard is the teachers. These individuals, on the front line of education, can make or break a school's efforts at maintaining positive school–community relations.

## The Teacher

You might say that every decision made by a teacher and every action taken by a teacher affects school–community relations to some degree. Though most of a teacher's time is spent working with students, the attitudes and feelings that students have about their teachers spill out into the rest of the community through home dialogue, schoolyard games, and to some degree the students' achievement. Think of these words by noted child psychologist, Haim Ginott:

> I've come to the frightening conclusion that I am the decisive element in the classroom. It's my personal approach that creates the climate. It's my daily mood that makes the weather. As a teacher, I possess a tremendous power to make a child's life miserable or joyous. I can be a tool of torture or an instrument of inspiration. I can humiliate or humor, hurt or heal. In all situations, it is my response that decides whether a crisis will be escalated or de-escalated and a child humanized or dehumanized.

Through these behaviors, which humanize or dehumanize and escalate or de-escalate, teachers impact the attitudes that their students have about school. Not only do these attitudes have a profound effect on the students' feelings, but they necessarily wind up affecting what parents think of the school. By and large, if children are miserable in school, then their parents will be miserable, too. Miserable parents are logically less willing to be involved positively in schooling. Miserable parents also tend to say miserable things at work and in the community about their child's school. The effect that these derogatory remarks have on school–community relations can be devastating for a school.

Because of these devastating effects, school administrators have a responsibility to create a culture in their school that prohibits students from being made to feel dehumanized. By doing so, the administrator exerts great influence over the behaviors of teachers. The administrator makes it known that students, even those in need of correction, are treated with dignity in their school. In this way, school administrators provide great assistance to teachers in promoting positive school–community relations.

This being said, there are specific tasks that teachers perform in advancing a school's school–community relations plan. These tasks include:

- Being visible and accessible to students and parents
- Communicating regularly and purposefully
- Demonstrating a positive attitude about school
- Taking pride in the physical, child-centered appearance of their classroom
- Forming and maintaining business partnerships between the school and the community
- Teaching students the value of communities and the importance of being community members

There are certainly times in a teacher's professional life when the teacher is annoyed by a decision that an administrator or the school board has made. One of the most damaging things a teacher can do in those instances is to speak negatively about the administrator or board member in public. The professionalism required of teachers mandates that they understand the influence their words have within the community. Though it is perfectly justifiable for a teacher to be unhappy with decisions made or actions taken, the professional teacher keeps these professional problems at work and does not vent his/her negative feelings out in the community. It is up to the school leader to set the tone and verbalize this expectation. Again, in this way, the school leader can exert tremendous influence over the teacher's ability to advance or inhibit the school's school–community relations goals.

## The Office Staff

The office staff, whether consisting of a single secretary or a group of staff members with secretarial, administrative, and or bookkeeping duties, plays a significant role as well in advancing or inhibiting a school's school–community relations plan. In Chapter 5, attention is paid to the communication patterns of the secretary. As the voice of the school, it is the secretary who has the most direct contact with school stakeholders. The administrator must, therefore, be sure that the secretary understands the significance of his/her role in school–community relations. Much of the information supplied in Chapter 5 is applicable not only to the school secretary but also to any individuals in the main office who have contact with the public.

Because communication patterns of the office staff get treatment in Chapter 5, the focus here is on the physical appearance of the main office. Just as nonverbal body language influences a person's perceptions, so does the physical appearance of the school office. If I use kind words to speak with you, but I do so with a scowl on my face, you may begin questioning how genuine my comments are. In the same way, a school secretary may speak in a friendly tone, but if the office appearance conjures up opposite feelings, then you may begin questioning how genuine the school secretary is being with you.

Consider Exhibits 3.3 and 3.4 as examples. Both of these are signs that were hung in schools with which I am familiar. Both of these signs say something about the atmosphere in the office. They may say that the atmosphere is fun and that people who work there have senses of humor. Or, these signs may say something else. Exhibit 3.3, for example, can imply that this school is not a place where people enjoy coming to work.

Because signs such as these are open to different interpretations, the office staff must be mindful about their display. Failure to do so could lead visitors to the office to draw incorrect conclusions that could, in some cases, damage a school's image. Though successful school–community relations are about much more than mere image building, the image that the public has of a school is an important factor in that school's ability to foster and maintain the kinds of relationships that are desired.

It is up to the school administrator to ensure that the tone set in the main office is one that is consistent with the image the school wishes to portray to the community. In this way, the administrator exhibits the leadership necessary to assist the office staff in doing their part to foster positive school–community relations.

## Exhibit 3.3. Sick Day Sign

I've used up all of my sick days, so I'm calling in DEAD!

## Exhibit 3.4. Procrastination Sign

PROCRASTINATION on your part does NOT

Constitute an EMERGENCY on my part!

Not to be ignored in this section is the role of the food service staff. Without question, what is served at school and how it is served certainly affects public perceptions. Because food is served to students, staff, some parents, and visitors, the food service staff members are in great positions to affect dramatically the morale of the entire school community. The same can be said of bus drivers, the custodial staff, and virtually every single employee of the school. Each individual, without regard to the specific role he or she plays, has both responsibility for, and effect on, school–community relations. He or she may not always realize this, though. That is why it is ultimately up to the building-level administrator to make school–community relations a conscious and important part of everybody's job.

## Organizational Standards

As more and more educational institutions turn their attention to the importance of sound school–community relations, educational organizations such as the National PTA and the National Education Association also adopt standards or principles that schools ought to embrace in order to be in full concert with the organization's mission and purpose. This section focuses on standards from important organizations and agencies, beginning with the federal government.

## Goals 2000

Goals 2000, the educational legislation initiative introduced by former Secretary of Education Richard Riley, is replete with directives speaking to the importance of bridging existing gaps between our public schools and the communities in which they are located. Complying with the goals outlined in this legislation virtually requires schools to value collaborative relationships with community members. Exhibit 3.5 outlines the goals as the 103rd Congress of the United States declared them. Note elements of school–community relations, which have been woven through much of this legislation's fabric.

---

### Exhibit 3.5. National Education Goals (GOALS 2000)

---

(1) SCHOOL READINESS.—

(A) By the year 2000, all children in America will start school ready to learn.

(B) The objectives for this goal are that—

(i) all children will have access to high-quality and developmentally appropriate preschool programs that help prepare children for school;

(ii) every parent in the United States will be a child's first teacher and devote time each day to helping such parent's preschool child learn, and parents will have access to the training and support parents need; and

(iii) children will receive the nutrition, physical activity experiences, and health care needed to arrive at school with healthy minds and bodies, and to maintain the mental alertness necessary to be prepared to learn, and the number of low-birthweight babies will be significantly reduced through enhanced prenatal health systems.

(2) SCHOOL COMPLETION.—

(A) By the year 2000, the high school graduation rate will increase to at least 90 percent.

(B) The objectives for this goal are that—

(i) the Nation must dramatically reduce its school dropout rate, and 75 percent of the students who do drop out will successfully complete a high school degree or its equivalent; and

(ii) the gap in high school graduation rates between American students from minority backgrounds and their non-minority counterparts will be eliminated.

(3) STUDENT ACHIEVEMENT AND CITIZENSHIP.—

(A) By the year 2000, all students will leave grades 4, 8, and 12 having demonstrated competency over challenging subject matter including English, mathematics, science, foreign languages, civics and government, economics, arts, history, and geography, and every school in America will ensure that all students learn to use their minds well, so they may be prepared for responsible citizenship, further learning, and productive employment in our Nation's modern economy.

(B) The objectives for this goal are that—

(i) the academic performance of all students at the elementary and secondary level will increase significantly in every quartile, and the distribution of minority students in each quartile will more closely reflect the student population as a whole;

(ii) the percentage of all students who demonstrate the ability to reason, solve problems, apply knowledge, and write and communicate effectively will increase substantially;

(iii) all students will be involved in activities that promote and demonstrate good citizenship, good health, community service, and personal responsibility;

(iv) all students will have access to physical education and health education to ensure they are healthy and fit;

(v) the percentage of all students who are competent in more than one language will substantially increase; and

(vi) all students will be knowledgeable about the diverse cultural heritage of this Nation and about the world community.

(4) TEACHER EDUCATION AND PROFESSIONAL DEVELOPMENT.—

(A) By the year 2000, the Nation's teaching force will have access to programs for the continued improvement of their professional skills and the opportunity to acquire the knowledge and skills needed to instruct and prepare all American students for the next century.

(B) The objectives for this goal are that—

(i) all teachers will have access to preservice teacher education and continuing professional development activities that will provide such teachers with the knowledge and skills needed to teach to an increasingly diverse student population with a variety of educational, social, and health needs;

(ii) all teachers will have continuing opportunities to acquire additional knowledge and skills needed to teach challenging subject matter and to use emerging new methods, forms of assessment, and technologies;

(iii) States and school districts will create integrated strategies to attract, recruit, prepare, retrain, and support the continued professional development of teachers, administrators, and other educators, so that there is a highly talented work force of professional educators to teach challenging subject matter; and

(iv) partnerships will be established, whenever possible, among local educational agencies, institutions of higher education, parents, and local labor, business, and professional associations to provide and support programs for the professional development of educators.

(5) MATHEMATICS AND SCIENCE.—

(A) By the year 2000, United States students will be first in the world in mathematics and science achievement.

(B) The objectives for this goal are that—

(i) mathematics and science education, including the metric system of measurement, will be strengthened throughout the system, especially in the early grades;

(ii) the number of teachers with a substantive background in mathematics and science, including the metric system of measurement, will increase by 50 percent; and

(iii) the number of United States undergraduate and graduate students, especially women and minorities, who complete degrees in mathematics, science, and engineering will increase significantly.

(6) ADULT LITERACY AND LIFELONG LEARNING.—

(A) By the year 2000, every adult American will be literate and will possess the knowledge and skills necessary to compete in a global economy and exercise the rights and responsibilities of citizenship.

(B) The objectives for this goal are that—

(i) every major American business will be involved in strengthening the connection between education and work;

(ii) all workers will have the opportunity to acquire the knowledge and skills, from basic to highly technical, needed to adapt to emerging new technologies, work methods, and markets through public and private educational, vocational, technical, workplace, or other programs;

(iii) the number of quality programs, including those at libraries, that are designed to serve more effectively the needs of the growing number of part-time and midcareer students will increase substantially;

(iv) the proportion of the qualified students, especially minorities, who enter college, who complete at least two years, and who complete their degree programs will increase substantially;

(v) the proportion of college graduates who demonstrate an advanced ability to think critically, communicate effectively, and solve problems will increase substantially; and

(vi) schools, in implementing comprehensive parent involvement programs, will offer more adult literacy, parent training and life-long learning opportunities to improve the ties between home and school, and enhance parents' work and home lives.

(7) SAFE, DISCIPLINED, AND ALCOHOL- AND DRUG-FREE SCHOOLS.—

(A) By the year 2000, every school in the United States will be free of drugs, violence, and the unauthorized presence of firearms and alcohol and will offer a disciplined environment conducive to learning.

(B) The objectives for this goal are that—

(i) every school will implement a firm and fair policy on use, possession, and distribution of drugs and alcohol;

(ii) parents, businesses, governmental and community organizations will work together to ensure the rights of students to study in a safe and secure environment that is free of drugs and crime, and that schools provide a healthy environment and are a safe haven for all children;

(iii) every local educational agency will develop and implement a policy to ensure that all schools are free of violence and the unauthorized presence of weapons;

(iv) every local educational agency will develop a sequential, comprehensive kindergarten through twelfth grade drug and alcohol prevention education program;

(v) drug and alcohol curriculum should be taught as an integral part of sequential, comprehensive health education;

(vi) community-based teams should be organized to provide students and teachers with needed support; and

(vii) every school should work to eliminate sexual harassment.

(8) PARENTAL PARTICIPATION —

(A) By the year 2000, every school will promote partnerships that will increase parental involvement and participation in promoting the social, emotional, and academic growth of children.

(B) The objectives for this Goal are that—

(i) every State will develop policies to assist local schools and local educational agencies to establish programs for increasing partnerships that respond to the varying needs of parents and the home, including parents of children who are disadvantaged or bilingual, or parents of children with disabilities;

(ii) every school will actively engage parents and families in a partnership which supports the academic work of children at home and shared educational decision making at school; and

(iii) parents and families will help to ensure that schools are adequately supported and will hold schools and teachers to high standards of accountability.

---

In examining the contents of the eight goals listed in Exhibit 3.5, the importance of school–community relations is crystal clear. Not only is Goal 8 clearly directed at improved parent involvement, but also Goal 4 refers to business and community partnerships, and the need for relationships with other community groups is implied throughout the legislation.

Although each presidential administration will promote its own school improvement agenda, it is certain that some form of improved school–community relations will be advocated in any national plan. This is because of the increased recognition that schools cannot educate children alone. The school leader who recognizes this will find great support in federal legislation.

As evidence, consider the educational initiatives enacted during the first 100 days of President George W. Bush's term in office. His program, "No Child Left Behind" (Exhibit 3.6), which subsequently became the reauthorized version of the Elementary and Secondary Education Act, contains elements that are obviously different from those of Goals 2000. Most notable of these elements are the proposals regarding school choice and charter schools funding. However, there are themes relative to school–community relations and parental involvement that are quite consistent with the themes in Goals 2000. This illustrates again that the federal government, regardless of the majority party or the individual in the President's office, is well aware of the role parents play in education and the importance of this role to positive school–community relations.

---

### Exhibit 3.6. Title IV
### (No Child Left Behind)

---

### Promoting Parental Options and Innovative Programs

### (Title IV)

### Overview

The purpose of Title IV is to promote parental choice and to increase the amount of flexible funds available to states and school districts for innovative education programs.

Systems are often resistant to change—no matter how good the intentions of those who lead them. Competition can be the stimulus a bureaucracy needs in order to change. For that reason, the Administration seeks to increase parental options and influence. Parents, armed with data, are the best forces of accountability in education. And parents, armed with options and choice, can assure that their children get the best, most effective education possible.

### Summary of Proposals

**Promotes Charter Schools.** Funding will be provided to assist charter schools with start-up costs, facilities, and other needs associated with creating high-quality schools.

**Broadens Education Savings Accounts.** The amount of funding that can be contributed annually to these accounts will be increased to $5,000 and allowable uses of funds will be expanded to include education-related expenses in Kindergarten through 12 th grade.*

**Expands School Choice.** A school choice fund will be created and administered by the Secretary of Education to demonstrate, develop, implement, evaluate, and disseminate information on innovative approaches that promote school choice.

**Consolidates Categorical Grant Programs to Send More Dollars to Classrooms.** Overlapping and duplicative grant programs will be consolidated into one flexible grant for innovative programs and sent to states and school districts. Funds may be used for local innovative programs, as well as to provide choice to students in persistently failing or dangerous schools so they can attend adequate, safe schools of choice.

**Expands Public–Private Partnership in School Construction.** States are currently allowed to issue a certain number of tax-exempt bonds for private contractors to build public facilities, such as airports and low-income housing. Public school construction is currently not an allowable use of such bonds. By allowing private activity bonds to be used for public school construction, local districts across America will be able to leverage additional funds to be used for school construction and repair. The amount of bonds in each state able to be used for public-private partnerships in school construction would be based on the state population.

---

Although there may be modifications to some of this plan's components, particularly those involving the controversial decisions of using state money to fund nonpublic schools, it is clear from the summary of Title IV that the Bush administration intends for parents to have more choice in the schools their children attend.

Furthermore, the Bush plan, as sent to the 107th Congress, clearly seeks to strengthen the relationships between school personnel and students' families. Again, though modifications may occur, look at the wording in Exhibit 3.7 from Senate Bill S.7.

# Exhibit 3.7. Subtitle C— Parental Involvement

SEC. 221. STATE PLANS.

Section 1111 (20 U.S.C. 6311) is amended—

(1) by redesignating subsections (d) through (g) as subsections (e) through (h), respectively; and

(2) by inserting after subsection (c) the following:

"(d) Parental Involvement.—Each State plan shall demonstrate that the State will support, in collaboration with the regional educational laboratories, the collection and dissemination to local educational agencies and schools of effective parental involvement practices. Such practices shall—

"(1) be based on the most current research on effective parental involvement that fosters achievement to high standards for all children; and

"(2) be geared toward lowering barriers to greater participation in school planning, review, and improvement experienced by parents."

SEC. 222. PARENTAL ASSISTANCE.

Part D of title I (20 U.S.C. 6421 et seq.) is amended to read as follows:

"PART D—PARENTAL ASSISTANCE AND CHILD OPPORTUNITY

"Subpart I—Parental Assistance.

"SEC. 1401. PARENTAL INFORMATION AND RESOURCE CENTERS.

"(a) Purpose.—The purpose of this part is—

"(1) to provide leadership, technical assistance, and financial support to nonprofit organizations and local educational agencies to help the organizations and agencies implement successful and effective parental involvement policies, programs, and activities that lead to improvements in student performance;

"(2) to strengthen partnerships among parents (including parents of preschool age children), teachers, principals, administrators, and other school personnel in meeting the educational needs of children;

"(3) to develop and strengthen the relationship between parents and the school;

"(4) to further the developmental progress primarily of children assisted under this part; and

"(5) to coordinate activities funded under this part with parental involvement initiatives funded under section 1118 and other provisions of this Act.

"(b) Grants Authorized.—

"(1) In general.—The Secretary is authorized to award grants in each fiscal year to nonprofit organizations, and nonprofit organizations in consortia with local educational agencies, to establish school-linked or school-based parental information and resource centers that provide training, information, and support to—

"(A) parents of children enrolled in elementary schools and secondary schools;

"(B) individuals who work with the parents described in subparagraph (A); and

"(C) State educational agencies, local educational agencies, schools, organizations that support family-school partnerships (such as parent-teacher associations), and other organizations that carry out parent education and family involvement programs.

"(2) Award rule.—In awarding grants under this part, the Secretary shall ensure that such grants are distributed in all geographic regions of the United States."

---

## Interstate School Leaders Licensure Consortium (ISLLC) Standards

Developed in 1996 as the *Standards for School Leaders*, what are now commonly referred to as the ISLLC standards have become the framework on which many higher education programs in school administration and many state licensure requirements are built. These six standards, arrived at by the School Leaders Licensure Consortium under the direction of the Council of Chief State School Officers, attempt to develop a common core of knowledge regarding the elements of effective school administration. It is universally accepted that the six ISLLC standards do, in fact, identify important qualities, characteristics, and behaviors of effective school leaders.

The ISLLC standards appear in Exhibit 3.8 (p. 62). Pertinent to the study of school–community relations is the undercurrent of communication and stakeholder engagement practices woven throughout these six standards.

Standard 1, for example, illustrates the necessity for school leaders to share their school's vision with the larger community. Further, this standard requires the leader's vision to be supported by the school community. Such support can only be gathered through effective two-way communication techniques.

In Standard 2, the importance of a school culture conducive to student learning and staff professional growth is emphasized. The development and sustenance of such a culture requires leadership centered on communicating with, and engaging, all stakeholders. As discussed in one of my previous books, Creating Connections for Better Schools: How Leaders Enhance School Culture (Fiore, 2001), culture development is arguably the most significant activity a school leader is involved in. This can only be done when the leader willingly reaches out to other constituents and involves them in the creation of a positive school culture.

Although Standard 3 on the surface may not appear to be too closely related to school–community relations, the importance of managing the organization and its resources effectively cannot be overstated. School leaders who reach out to businesses and civic organizations in their community find these tasks to be much easier than do their counterparts, who by default often alienate these important community members.

Standard 4 is closely related to school–community relations because it illustrates the need for principals to collaborate with families, appreciate diversity, and mobilize community resources. Again, the ability to communicate and the desire to do so purposefully is an important component of any effective school–community relations plan. Such purposeful communication is an obvious foundation of Standard 4 behaviors.

Many of the topics in this book (i.e., working with the media, dealing with a crisis, student discipline) require the school leader to act with integrity and in a fair, ethical manner. In this way, Standard 5 relates strongly to the study of school–community relations.

Because schools are susceptible to the power of many outside sources (i.e., the school district, the state department of education, the federal government), it is extremely important that the school leader keep open the lines of communication with these agencies. Schools do not exist apart from the political and social fabric of our nation.

## Exhibit 3.8. Interstate School Leaders Licensure Consortium Standards

**Standard 1**

A school administrator is an educational leader who promotes the success of all students by facilitating the development, articulation, implementation, and stewardship of a vision of learning that is shared and supported by the school community.

**Standard 2**

A school administrator is an educational leader who promotes the success of all students by advocating, nurturing, and sustaining a school culture and instructional program conducive to student learning and staff professional growth.

**Standard 3**

A school administrator is an educational leader who promotes the success of all students by ensuring management of the organization, operations, and resources for a safe, efficient, and effective learning environment.

**Standard 4**

A school administrator is an educational leader who promotes the success of all students by collaborating with families and community members, responding to diverse community interests and needs, and mobilizing community resources.

**Standard 5**

A school administrator is an educational leader who promotes the success of all students by acting with integrity, fairness, and in an ethical manner.

**Standard 6**

A school administrator is an educational leader who promotes the success of all students by understanding, responding to, and influencing the larger political, social, economic, legal, and cultural context.

Source: *Standards for School Leaders* (1996). Washington, DC: Council of Chief State School Officers.

Standard 6, in speaking of the importance of understanding and influencing the political, social, economic, legal, and cultural context, lends itself well to strong school–community relations.

Though differing in their target audiences and their intentions, all the standards are deigned to illustrate what is really most important in education. It is clear from the ISLLC standards that the ability to communicate effectively and to involve all stakeholders fairly and equitably in the educational process helps to define what an effective educational leader is. When these standards are viewed along with goals and programs from the federal government and other agencies involved with education, the need for effective school–community relations is obvious.

## The National PTA

Of similar focus, but coming from an agency with a somewhat different agenda, the National PTA has adopted standards (see Exhibit 3.9) that clearly relate to the importance of school–community relations. As an organization existing to promote parent involvement, it is no wonder that the National PTA's focus is on parents much more than it is on other aspects of the community. Nevertheless, the standards adopted by this organization in 1997 indicate the strong commitment that this large and powerful advocacy group has to impact school leadership's recognition of the significant role parents ought to play in education.

---

### Exhibit 3.9. National Standards for Parent/ Family Involvement Programs (National PTA)

---

**Standard I:** *Communicating*—Communication between home and school is regular, two-way, and meaningful.

**Standard II:** *Parenting*—Parenting skills are promoted and supported.

**Standard III:** *Student Learning*—Parents play an integral role in assisting student learning.

**Standard IV:** *Volunteering*—Parents are welcome in the school, and their support and assistance are sought.

**Standard V:** *School Decision Making and Advocacy*—Parents are full partners in the decisions that affect children and families.

**Standard VI:** *Collaborating with Community*—Community resources are used to strengthen schools, families, and student learning.

---

Since the National PTA's adoption of these standards in 1997, they have been used by many local PTAs to impact decisions made at the local school level and as a benchmark against which the effectiveness of long-term school reform efforts to involve parents/families in education have been measured.

## Community Schools

The concept of community schools, which is the foundation upon which the Coalition for Community Schools rests, is that all people in any given community can and should be given opportunities to benefit from offerings within our schools. Related to our discussions of school–community relations, the Coalition for Community Schools seeks to expand the concept to include the many ways communities can utilize our schools' resources to benefit all members.

Thus, without focusing attention merely on how the school and community can work together to accomplish goals for the students, the concept of community schools includes the benefits that all citizens, whether formal students or not, can and should receive from our local, neighborhood schools. There are many partner agencies associated with the Coalition for Community Schools. The majority of these organizations have adopted standards of their own that speak to the importance of the school and the community working harmoniously for the benefit of all citizens. The list of partners includes:

- American Association of School Administrators
- American Federation of Teachers
- Collaborative for Integrated School Services
- Council of Chief State School Officers
- National Association of Elementary School Principals
- National Association of Secondary School Principals
- National Association of State Boards of Education
- National Coalition for Parent Involvement in Education
- National Community Education Association
- National Education Association
- National School Boards Association
- Corporation for National Service
  - Learn and Serve America
- U.S. Department of Education
  - National School-to-Work Office
  - Office of Education, Research and Improvement

- Office Elementary and Secondary Education
- Office of the Secretary
- Office of Special Education Programs
- Safe and Drug-Free Schools Program
- U.S. Department of Health and Human Services
  - Administration for Children and Families
  - Centers for Disease Control and Prevention
  - Office of Adolescent Health
  - Office of Assistant Secretary for Planning and Evaluation
- U.S. Department of Housing and Urban Development
  - Office of University Partnerships
- U.S. Department of Justice
  - Office of Juvenile Justice and Delinquency Prevention

If nothing else, the above list demonstrates the significance seen by many national organizations of bringing our schools and our communities together. The list further illustrates that resources for arriving at standards and for planning programs are plentiful for the school leader who seeks them. What is required first, however, is a commitment to establishing strong school–community relations.

This chapter has focused on the roles and responsibilities many key individuals play in establishing meaningful plans of school–community relations. It has demonstrated that, regardless of the size or location of any individual school system, school–community relations is not handled by one person. Rather, every member of the school community has a responsibility to ensure that a school's relationship with its community is solid and inclusive. In fulfilling this responsibility, all school employees must recognize that the support from outside of the school does exist. Although agendas may differ, organizational standards and plans exist in many agencies that can assist the school leader in being a leader who recognizes the importance of school–community relations.

## Chapter Summary

- The superintendent is usually the most influential member of the certificated staff. As a result, his/her vision for school–community relations is critical.
- Superintendents must be assisted in avoiding some of the common pitfalls, such as failure to consult with other members of the school system staff.

- The role of the district-level Director of School–Community Relations has changed, with much less focus on pure public relations skills.

- Principals have tremendous influence over the culture of their schools and the ways in which staff members interact with members of the community.

- One of the most important responsibilities of the principal is to ensure that all staff members recognize the valuable role they play in the school–community relations plan.

- The government and many prominent organizations are increasingly recognizing the importance of strong relationships between schools and communities.

# Case Study Analysis

## The Balancing Act

When Principal Wes Berry was summoned to Superintendent Elliott's office, he feared the worse. In the four years he had worked for the Rockmart County Schools, he had been called to the superintendent's office on only one other occasion. That other occasion was not for him to receive a pat on the back.

Superintendent Elliott began, "Wes, you know that I believe there are two sides to every story. In fact, that's why I've called you here. I want to hear your side. Yesterday, I received a very disturbing telephone call from a Mr. Patterson. He claims that the newsletter you sent home last week contained no less than five spelling errors. His concern is the example this is showing to kids. Now Wes, I don't need to tell you that this Mr. Patterson is the husband of Sharon Patterson, the lady sure to be elected to the school board in three weeks. Though I haven't seen your newsletter, Mr. Patterson needs to be made happy. Do I make my point clearly?"

Many thoughts ran through Wes Berry's mind, but none of them seemed appropriate to share. "Yes, sir," was all he said. With that, the meeting was over, and Wes was on his way back to his school.

## Questions for Analysis

1. Can you identify any of the commonly made errors that Superintendent Elliott has made in this situation?

2. Aside from the Superintendent's behavior, what are some other school district problems you can identify that hinder strong school–community relations?

3. What should Wes Berry do to avoid situations like this in the future? Where should he turn for assistance?

# 4

---

# Communicating Effectively: Everybody's Job

Clearly, one of the hallmarks of effective relationships is the ability to communicate. Likewise, a hallmark of rocky relationships is a lack of such ability. This is true in relationships on all levels, and it is especially pertinent to effective school–community relations. When problems exist in school–community relations, they usually exist more because of a breakdown in communication than they do for any other reason. In other words, most school leaders understand the importance of establishing and maintaining positive relationships with stakeholders. What they often fail to understand is the complexity of communication as a skill.

To understand why this is so, an examination of the many steps in the communication process is in order. Each of these steps is vital to effective communication. A breakdown in any one of them can, and usually does, lead to miscommunication.

---

## Showcase

Public hearings are great places to practice your communication skills. The first time that I recommended changes to several high school attendance zones, more than a thousand patrons showed up to defend their right to be eagles, panthers, rebels, tigers, and warriors for life. I first asked the group to remember that effigy meant symbolically hanging the person making the proposal, not literally stringing him up. The laughter lasted for a nanosecond and was followed by a rapid return to the declared positions. Hearings are about listening, and people want no less the opportunity to be heard than the actual chance to speak. Try not having a hearing on a critical issue. If only ten people show up then they still feel good about having been afforded the opportunity. Hearings are not places to argue with presenters. It is their turn to talk, and they expect the board and administration to look like they are interested in their ideas. Public hearings are seldom places where decisions are made, but they are always places where public perceptions are *forged*.

*Dr. William C. Bosher, former Superintendent, Chesterfield County Schools, Chesterfield, VA, now Director of the Commonwealth Educational Policy Institute, Richmond, VA*

---

# The Communication Process

Many of us recall playing a game when we were children that required one person to tell a story to another person who subsequently passed the story on to a third person. As the game progressed and the story moved from one person to the next, it became somewhat distorted. At the end of the game, the story bore little resemblance to the original tale. The lesson we learned is that communication can be difficult. Communication, too often thought of as a single act, is best understood as a complex process. The process is not complex because it challenges our cognitive abilities, but it gains its complexity by virtue of the significance of each individual step. A problem with any one of the steps can often lead to devastating outcomes. Consider the following illustration:

> As principal of XYZ Middle School, you believe that the faculty should consider changing the time of day scheduled for the upcoming open house. Instead of hosting the open house from 4:00 PM to 6:00 PM as has traditionally been the norm, you believe that more families would be served by the event being scheduled between the hours of 6:00 PM and 8:00 PM. Understanding the steps to effective communication can help you avoid an unnecessarily unpleasant situation when you share these feelings with your faculty.

## Idea Formation

Idea formation is the first step in the communication process. This step is largely internal and only involves the constitution of the speaker. It is at this initial stage of communication where the speaker generates the idea he or she intends to communicate. In the above example, idea formation occurred when the principal began thinking about the upcoming open house. The principal in this example examined what had previously been practiced, and evaluated it within his/her own experiences. A judgment was made, and the necessity to communicate this idea to others was established.

Idea formation, it must be understood, is an important step and is one in which mistakes can certainly be made. If, for example, the judgment of the principal is incorrect, then there is an increased likelihood that the idea generated will be flawed. Suppose, for example, there are logical reasons why Open House is scheduled between 4:00 PM and 6:00 PM. If the principal is unaware of these reasons, then he/she will draw an incorrect conclusion regarding whether the schedule should be changed. The good news is that idea formation is generally internal. As a result, there is time to correct the idea before it is released to everybody else. In essence, a key to idea formation is to consider many alternatives and keep as open a mind as possible.

## Idea Encoding

Idea encoding is the process by which the idea is put into language (words and symbols) that is appropriate for conveying the intended message. Again, this step is largely internal. As such, it seems difficult to imagine any problem with this step. In fact, many communication problems have their roots deeply planted in idea encoding. Consider, once again, our example of the principal of XYZ Middle School. This principal has a vast array of options for encoding the idea about changing the open house schedule. If the idea is communicated verbally, there are choices to be made in regards to words, intonations, and body language that must be considered. If the idea is to be communicated in writing, though body language is no longer an issue, there is even greater emphasis placed on word choice.

The opportunities for a communication breakdown are great at this stage of communication. Unless the principal's actions and attitudes are already clearly understood by the faculty, the words chosen to communicate the above idea become crucial. If the principal chooses to communicate this message in a one-way manner, then far greater importance gets placed on the encoding. Exhibits 4.1 and 4.2. illustrate two examples of how this idea could have been encoded. Without knowing the biases of the faculty these messages were intended for, consider how you would receive the two of them.

The intended message in both of these examples is the same. In fact, there are honestly few variations between them. Which one would you receive more positively, though? Which one is more inclusive and appears the most welcoming? The way in which an idea is encoded is vitally important to the success of any communications process.

## Communication Channel

The method by which an individual communicates an idea is referred to as the communication channel. In the example from XYZ Middle School, as an illustration, the principal has a vast array of options for communicating the idea about changing the open house schedule. The message could be delivered in writing, which would clearly only allow for one-way communication. The message could also be delivered verbally, maybe at a faculty meeting. This two-way communication would give others an opportunity to give an immediate response, which would inform the principal about the accuracy and merit of the original idea.

---

## Exhibit 4.1. Negatively Encoded Message

---

Staff,

It has come to my attention that the annual XYZ Open House has been scheduled between the hours of 4:00 and 6:00 PM. This strikes me as a bit absurd. If we truly want Open House to provide parents with an opportunity to visit our school and learn of our goals, then we must schedule it at a more convenient time. Therefore, this year's Open House will begin at 6:00 PM and conclude at 8:00 PM.

---

## Exhibit 4.2. Positively Encoded Message

---

Staff,

In keeping with our goals of welcoming parents and of being sensitive to their needs, I think we need to reexamine our XYZ Open House schedule. My understanding is that this annual event has traditionally been held between the hours of 4:00 and 6:00 PM. Given the demanding work schedules inflicting many of our parents, I believe that we would be most accommodating if we held this year's event from 6:00 PM until 8:00 PM. Your feedback, as always, is most welcome.

---

The concept of a communication channel implies the timeliness of communication as well. If the open house schedule is important, for example, then even if the principal chooses the best words and attitudes to communicate the idea, it better be perceived by others to have been done in a timely fashion. Telling the faculty the morning of the open house that a schedule change is being considered, as an illustration, will certainly lead to a breakdown in communication. In fact, with an event as important as the annual open house, even one week's notice may be too little. Inherent in decisions about the best way or channel in which to communicate an idea is the necessity of understanding the situations of those you are communicating with. Parents have many obligations to consider in planning such events. Childcare is an obvious example. By failing to allow enough time to communicate information about the open house, you run the risk of causing negative feelings among the very group you are trying to develop positive relationships with.

## Receiver Decoding

The final step in the communication process is called receiver decoding. At this point, the responsibility for communication has temporarily shifted from the individual who originated the thought to the person who is receiving the information. It is at this stage that problems are encountered time and time again. If you have ever been in a situation where you thought you said one thing, but people heard something different, then you may have experienced a breakdown in receiver decoding.

Because receiver decoding does not take place internally to the person who originated the idea, it is difficult for that person to control. I may consider my idea very carefully. I may choose the most appropriate words and symbols for communicating it, as well. Finally, the communication channel I use might be the best one in this circumstance and might afford you the best opportunity to ask for clarification. If, however, you do not perceive my message in the way I intended, then a communication breakdown outside of my control will have occurred. This can be extremely frustrating and can lead to accusations such as, "You weren't listening to what I said." These accusations, as we know, are often incorrect.

There are many factors that affect whether or not receiver decoding is accurate, as intended. While the most obvious factors are within our control (i.e., idea formation, idea encoding, communication channel), there are others that are far more difficult to plan for. There may be a language barrier, a cultural difference, a difference in the reading level if the message was sent in writing, or a temporarily poor attitude on the part of the receiver. At XYZ Middle School, for example, if the principal had just delivered news to the faculty that angered them, then their ability to accurately decode the message about the XYZ Open House may surely be affected by their attitude. Consistent, positive communication and providing ready accessibility to information are ways to reduce the inaccuracy of receiver decoding. This is why a contemporary body of research states that school leaders ought to be visible and ought to communicate on a regular and consistent basis (Fiore 1999; Whitaker 1997; Stolp 1996).

There are, as mentioned, so many opportunities for miscommunication to occur anywhere along the continuum of the communication process. If our goal is to develop and nurture positive communication with all stakeholders within the school community, then we must understand this process and constantly examine our effectiveness in using it. We will not eliminate all communication breakdowns. We can, however, minimize them by paying attention to the process and understanding the specifics of how breakdowns in communication typically occur.

## Nonverbal Communication:
## It's Not What You Said, But How You Said It

If only communication problems were limited to a misunderstanding of the communication process. If only we needed to concern ourselves solely with the words we chose and the way in which we chose to use them. Unfortunately, it is not nearly that simple. We communicate so many of our ideas without ever saying a word. Our nonverbal communication is often far more powerful than our verbal communication.

Assume, for instance, that you and I are talking and that I observe that you are sitting with your arms tightly folded across your chest. I also notice that your legs are tightly crossed, and I become a bit uneasy. To myself, I begin examining the nature of our conversation. Am I upsetting you? Have the words I have chosen to communicate, in some way, offended you? Are you unwilling to speak with me, and would you have preferred that I wrote you a note or called you on the telephone? Is there something wrong with you that has caused you to misinterpret what I am saying?

All of these questions race through my mind because of my perception of your nonverbal communication. Your arms tightly folded and legs tightly crossed tell me that you are angry or unreceptive to what I am saying. Though it certainly was not my intent to do so, I am certain that I have somehow offended or bothered you. Not being able to stand it any longer, I ask you what I have done and why you are upset. When you reply that you are not at all upset, I inform you of the negative vibes I am picking up from your body language, or nonverbal communication. Your reply to me is simple. "Doug, it's freezing in here." Imagine the snowball effect that may have taken place if I had been uncomfortable or unwilling to confront my perceptions of your nonverbal behavior. This sort of misunderstanding routinely occurs in our interactions with others.

There are probably as many incorrect interpretations made about nonverbal communication as there are correct ones. In the above example, while it is true that tightly crossed arms and legs often signify resistance, anger, or upsetness, they also signify being cold. My failure to consider that possibility caused a real breakdown in communication. Exhibit 4.3 illustrates some of the more common interpretations of an individual's body language.

There clearly are other examples of nonverbal communication that we tend to associate with particular feelings or attitudes. It is vital that we remember, though, that the exhibition of a certain behavior does not necessarily mean that we have the associated attitudes or feelings at the moment we are gesturing. I am reminded of an example that recently happened to me. For the purpose of illustration, allow this personal, nontechnical example to serve as another way of understanding the power of nonverbal communication. As a young boy growing up, a summertime reward I experienced was to go to work with my father from time to time. My father was an executive in a New York City company, and he worked in a high-rise office building. Since these experiences always occurred in the summertime when school was not in session for me, there was always at least one empty office, which was vacated by an employee who was taking his or her summer vacation. Since Dad was busy most of the day, I would sit in the vacant office imagining that I was a businessperson. As all children do, I had learned to act like I thought a businessperson should act by observing a businessperson, namely Dad. Well, Dad, as I observed, had a habit whenever he was in a high-powered meeting of holding his hands out in front of him with his fingertips of his left hand touching the fingertips of his right hand in a gesture resembling a church steeple. This, I reasoned was "the business posture." Consequently, I learned at a relatively young age "the business posture."

Though I never entered the business world but became an educator instead, images of my father as a working man always stayed with me. Years later, when I was working at my first institution of higher education, a colleague rather bluntly said to me, "Fiore, do you realize that you steeple?" Not only did I fail to realize it, but I also had no idea what it meant to steeple. This colleague of mine bluntly explained that steepling, or holding my hands out in front of myself with the fingertips of my left hand touching the fingertips of my right hand in a gesture resembling a church steeple, meant that I thought I was superior to all others. I must assure you that I do not feel that way at all. To the contrary, I am in awe of most other people. I also realize, however, that I have adopted many of my father's mannerisms as a tribute to his memory.

## Exhibit 4.3. Examples of Nonverbal Communication

| *Interpretation* | *Nonverbal Communication* |
|---|---|
| When people are feeling nervous, they are often likely to: | ♦ Clear their throat<br>♦ Avoid eye contact<br>♦ Perspire<br>♦ Fidget<br>♦ Rapidly move their leg up and down<br>♦ Speak faster than normal<br>♦ Swallow frequently |
| When people are feeling annoyed or frustrated, they are often likely to: | ♦ Clench their hands<br>♦ Clench their jaw<br>♦ Place their hands on their hips<br>♦ Shake their head from side to side<br>♦ Breathe deeply and exhale forcefully |
| When people are feeling insecure around somebody, they are often likely to: | ♦ Avoid eye contact<br>♦ Place their hands in their pockets<br>♦ Bite their nails<br>♦ Tug at their clothing |
| When people are feeling confident, they are often likely to: | ♦ Exhibit good posture<br>♦ Sit back in their chair<br>♦ Clasp their hands behind their back<br>♦ Make frequent eye contact<br>♦ Rest their hands comfortably on a desk or table |

The point is that nonverbal behaviors can tell us an awful lot about how people are feeling at a given moment. For this reason, it is wise for anybody concerned with human relations to be conscious of their own nonverbal behaviors as well as the nonverbal behaviors of others. Theses behaviors can be misleading, though. I sincerely steeple subconsciously, without the associated attitude that my colleague suspected. People really do cross their arms from time to time to signify that they are feeling cold. Some individuals swallow frequently, not because they are nervous but because they have a sore throat.

# Communication Barriers

Because there are so many steps to effective communication, there are so many more opportunities for miscommunication. As mentioned, failure at any one of the steps can lead to a total communication breakdown. These barriers to communication do not occur only because of failures during the communication process. They are, likewise, not all caused by misinterpretations of people's nonverbal communication. Instead, there are other barriers to communication that school leaders must be cognizant of. Understanding these barriers and recognizing when you are facing them, can cure many ills of miscommunication.

## Language Barriers

This more obvious communication barrier seemed less significant twenty years ago than it is today. This is because an increasingly large number of families with children in our schools do not speak or read English at a level of functional literacy.

In fact, according to the 1990 census, people who do not speak English as their first language inhabit 13.8 percent of U.S. households. Whereas it could once be assumed that this 13.8 percent lived in urban areas, this is increasingly not the case. Children from homes in which English is never spoken or is spoken as a secondary language represent one of the fastest growing segments of our school populations. This is true in almost all areas of the United States. The parents of these children, just like the parents of English speaking children, must be communicated with.

Given these facts, school leaders must be aware that non-English proficient families live in virtually every corner of the United States. Though the influx of non-English proficients is certainly greater in larger cities like New York and Los Angeles, smaller communities continue to be affected by this trend at an ever-increasing rate. Consequently, school administrators ought to closely examine whether or not the personnel are in place to facilitate communication with stakeholders who are not proficient in English. Beyond that, the best school leaders, who recognize their community role, are well served to make themselves more skilled at communicating with people in languages other than English.

## Cultural Barriers

Because so much communication takes place nonverbally, it is imperative that school administrators recognize the different cultural interpretations of body language and space. I am reminded here of an exhibit that I once saw in a museum. This exhibit was designed to illustrate the differences that exist in spatial proximity between communicants in various cultures. By standing on footprints strategically placed on the floor of this exhibit, two people could mimic the distance that would be customary to have between them during a conversation if they were from different cultures. This illustrated the fact that people clearly differ in their tolerance for personal space; some prefer very close communication distances, while others prefer farther distances (O'Hair & Ropo, 1994). Four zones (Hall, 1969) in which all communication takes place consist of the intimate zone (skin contact to 18 inches), the personal zone (18 inches to 4 feet), the social zone (4 to 12 feet), and the public zone (12 feet and beyond). It is imperative that school leaders understand the tremendous barrier erected when they violate an individual's rule of personal space.

Additionally, think back for a moment to Exhibit 4.3. The typical interpretations of nonverbal communications illustrated there are representative of the American culture. In other cultures represented by families in our schools, these interpretations would be much different. For example, consider the cultural differences noted in whether or not individuals gaze into a speaker's eyes when they are listening to them (Burgoon, Buller, & Woodall, 1989). Anglos are socialized to gaze directly at the speaker's face when they are listening; Japanese-Americans avoid eye contact when listening by focusing on the speaker's neck so as not to appear rude; African-Americans and Native Americans rarely look directly into the eyes of an authority figure. These cultural differences must be appreciated so that school leaders do not misinterpret them. Otherwise, unnecessary barriers to effective communication are created.

## Barriers Inherent in Specific Physical Disabilities

An often forgotten and frequently underrepresented group of stakeholders are those individuals with physical disabilities. Dependent upon the limitations of the individual, their communication requirements may be the same as individuals without disabilities, or they may be profoundly different. Think, for example, of a person who is legally blind. This individual will not be able to pick up on subtle facial gestures to the same degree as a person who is not blind. Consequently, school personnel must be sensitive to the degree to which their messages are typically delivered through facial gestures. An increased effort to verbally articulate points without the reliance on nonverbal gestures may certainly be in order. Along these same lines, consider the limitations that might face a person who relies on lip reading to "hear" what is being communicated. It may be that this person is a better "listener" than somebody who has full use of his or her ears for this purpose. It also may be, however, that the rate at which we speak should be altered for this individual. Again, school personnel, particularly the leaders, must be sensitive to these differences.

## Barriers Related to Time

As a result of the frenetic pace at which our schools often operate, the time necessary for meaningful communication is often unavailable. In fact, conversations with school principals consistently lead to frank discussions about the lack of time available for the human relations that these leaders find to be integral components of successfully performing their duties.

It is really a simple fact. Communication takes time. Too often, school leaders are unable or unwilling to devote the time necessary for proper communication. This failure leads to criticisms being levied, which question the concern, commitment, and fairness of the leader. It also leads to school administrators who feel forced to use quick communication techniques (i.e., e-mail, memos, announcements) instead of the more time-consuming techniques (i.e., telephone conversations, face-to-face meetings). These time-related issues lead to a great communication paradox. The mistakes that so often occur when individuals rush through the communication process often lead to their having to take more time to fix problems caused by their hurrying in the first place. Taking the time to communicate purposefully and carefully in the beginning saves time in the long run.

# Overcoming Communication Barriers

As a disclaimer, it must be accepted that communication barriers will exist as long as people continue to openly communicate their innermost concerns, values, feelings, joys, loves, and frustrations. The human dimension, so prevalent in communication, necessitates that misunderstandings and barriers will always be present. There are techniques, though, that when properly employed can greatly reduce many of the more common communication barriers we all experience. As is the case with all new skills, these techniques must be practiced until they become automatic parts, or habits, of our behavior.

## Perception Checking

Recall the earlier example of our fictitious conversation in which you had your arms tightly folded across your chest. Remember how I was unnerved by your body language? Recall, if you will, the struggle I had in understanding just what it was I said that offended you. Most importantly, remember how incorrect my assumption of your body language was. You were not angry or unwilling to listen. You were, in fact, cold.

Had I checked my perception of your body language with you, I could have avoided a great deal of my confusion and concern regarding your feelings. I could have found out early on that you were not unhappy with me, but were instead cold. I could have perhaps offered you a blanket to warm you up and then proceeded with our conversation.

Using the skill of perception checking requires that you ask the person you are communicating with whether or not you are correctly perceiving their feelings. It does not imply any judgment of these feelings, but rather affords you an opportunity to see if you have perceived them correctly. In our example, it would sound something like this: "I notice that you are crossing your arms. Are you unhappy with something I said?" Your reply would have been simple. "No, Doug, I'm just cold." Failure to use perception checking may have led to a conversation sounding more like this: "When you sit there with your arms folded and your angry, closed-minded attitude, I just can't stand being around you." Your potential reply in this example may be best left unsaid.

## Communicating Regularly

Communication that occurs with a regular pattern can become predictable. This predictability is often helpful as people come to expect it and are consequently ready to receive it. The mere fact that they are ready can greatly reduce the chance that they will misinterpret the communication that they are expecting. Of additional consideration is the degree to which this regular communication is positive. If an individual can rely on receiving some positive communication on a regular basis, then he or she will look with more favorable anticipation on any communication that he or she receives. Basically, the individual will receive the communication with the anticipation that it will be positive. Consider the following situations as examples:

> **Situation 1**: You are principal of Sparrow Elementary School. It has long been a practice in your school to communicate often with parents. This communication comes from teachers, support staff, and the main office, and it occurs when good things happen, as well as when bad things occur. Your staff sends home notes touting positive student behaviors, makes five positive telephone calls per week, and hosts a monthly tea for all parents whose children had been "caught being good" during that month.

> **Situation 2**: You are principal of Crow Elementary School. With student discipline being a major concern, teachers, support staff, and office staff make numerous telephone calls daily to parents of children who misbehave. Additionally, a note is drafted in the main office that goes home with every student who breaks a rule. It is expected that this note, signed by both you and the staff member reporting the offense, be returned to

the office within 48 hours complete with a parent's signature. As a result of this, you do communicate with at least a few parents on a daily basis.

Now, in both situations, communication occurs on a regular basis. Therefore, as Principal of either Sparrow or Crow, you are to be commended for creating a pattern of predictability. Had you failed to communicate regularly with parents, you would have discovered that your occasional communication attempts might have been met with some skepticism. Regular communication sharply reduces this negative response.

That being said, the situation at Sparrow Elementary School is far more appealing because communication occurs in both good and bad times. Because there is such a strong effort on behalf of the school staff to communicate positive things to parents, the occasions requiring negative news to be delivered are much easier to handle. Crow Elementary School parents, on the other hand, are used to receiving only news that is negative in nature. Though this communication is regular, parents receiving it are conditioned to expect the worst. In fact, when a note comes home from school or a telephone message from the school is left on the family answering machine, I am certain that it is received with negative anticipation. Sparrow parents, on the other hand, receive their messages from the school with a much grater degree of hope.

## Communicating Purposefully

Whenever teachers claim that they do not like staff meetings, they hate to see the principal walking toward them to speak with them, or they rarely read memos from the office, I invariably ask them, "Why?" Though there are a wide variety of responses given, the most common one centers on the notion that the principal is not communicating anything of importance. This leads to the idea of purposeful communication. Even if an individual fully understands the communication process, reads nonverbal cues (other's, as well as his or her own), and communicates regularly, he or she erects a giant communication barrier when the communication occurs with no apparent purpose. Schools are places of a tremendous amount of activity. Teaching is a consuming profession. Across the country, the role of many support staff members is increasing in both depth and breadth. Parents, when they can appropriately volunteer, often need to rearrange their work schedules to find the time to assist. Consequently, good school leaders need to communicate with a purpose. They do a tremendous disservice to stakeholders when they waste people's time communicating information that is irrelevant. Although it is vitally important to make communication a priority, it is equally important to do so only when there is something of value to communicate. This doesn't imply that there is a limited definition of what constitutes valuable information to communicate. There is no intention here to state that curricular issues, for example, are the only issues that are important. Instead, we must recognize that personal issues, as well as professional issues, may be equally valuable, or even more valuable to communicate in some cases. What is intended here is an understanding that the stakeholders involved must perceive the communication that occurs in a school as being important.

In research conducted in Illinois and Indiana schools with great variety in all forms of demographic profile data, Fiore (1999) found that recognizing the power of regular, purposeful, and positive communication is one way in which principals influence school culture (p. 133). Furthermore, this research created an undeniable link between the principal's ability to communicate both regularly and purposefully and the degree to which teachers viewed their school's culture positively. In some of the schools studied, a great deal of the communication provided by the principal was personal in nature. This pattern of communication was very consistent with a friendly, caring environment revealing the culture of these schools. In others, conversely, the communication was largely professional. Again, the important issue was that this communication pattern was consistent with the culture of these schools. Regardless of the school's overall culture, though, the principal played an invaluable role and made an indelible mark on sustaining the culture through the regular, purposeful communication patterns exhibited. In all cases, teachers, staff members, and parents appreciated the fact that the principal communicated regularly, and that this communication had a clearly understood purpose.

## Chapter Summary

- One of the most important aspects of positive, successful relationships is the ability to communicate effectively.
- There are many steps to the communication process. Failure or errors in any of these steps can result in a communication breakdown.
- We communicate a great deal through nonverbal means. Therefore, the ability to understand our own nonverbal idiosyncrasies becomes vitally important.
- Perception checking is a skill that allows us to ascertain the extent to which we are successfully reading another person's nonverbal messages.
- We are increasingly finding native languages to be a barrier to effective communication.
- Other barriers, such as cultural issues and physical disabilities must be understood as we evaluate our communication plans.

- Through thoughtful, intentional efforts, communication barriers can be overcome.

# Case Study Analysis

## All the News That's Fit to Print—And Then Some

Maria Rodriquez was highly respected for her leadership skills and her dedication to school improvement. During the six years in which she had been principal of Lincoln High School, the student body had experienced steady gains on standardized assessments, and parent and community support had strengthened. By most measures, Maria was an outstanding high school principal.

The day after this year's standardized achievement test results were released to the local press, Maria got an unexpected visit from a newspaper reporter who was new to the local paper. Not being very experienced, he sat down nervously in Maria's office and began asking her questions about the school's assessment results. As the conversation progressed, the reporter fidgeted in his seat, dropped his pencil several times, and was perspiring profusely. The situation was compounded by the frequent interruptions on the telephone and with discipline referrals arriving at Maria's office. After about 30 minutes and countless interruption, the two ended their conversation and the reporter left the school building to begin writing his story.

Maria Rodriquez was furious when she read the front-page story in the next morning's newspaper. Several facts about the school's test performance were misrepresented and Maria felt that many of her comments were taken out of context and made her appear apathetic to the importance of good test results. She vowed never to speak with that incompetent reporter again and began plotting how she would explain the facts in this newspaper story to her superintendent.

## Questions for Analysis

1. What effect, if any, did nonverbal communication have on the conversation between Maria Rodriquez and the reporter?

2. Were there any steps that Maria could have taken to reduce communication barriers that were present?

3. What are some issues relative to the communication process that Maria needs to consider before speaking with the superintendent?

4. If you were Maria, how would you handle future situations with the press?

# 5

## Opening Up to Your Internal Publics

Having positive, productive relationships with a school's publics requires, first and foremost, that school leaders understand who all of these publics are. It is amazing how many administrators, while trying to foster positive relationships, forget or leave out important school stakeholders. Equally surprising to many is the number of school administrators who mistakenly believe that all members of their school's community require the same efforts in relationship formation. There is an incorrect assumption in leadership preparation that leads people to believe in a "one size fits all model" of public relations.

These mistakes are partly the result of the lack of training school administrators receive in the area of public relations. Whereas an admirable job is done in teaching leadership theory and organizational dynamics, administrator training programs often miss out on the opportunity to teach would-be administrators the differences in communicating with two distinct stakeholder groups—those inside the organization and those outside the organization.

The needs of stakeholders who spend most of their time outside of the school's walls, referred to as the external public, will be the focus of Chapter 6. For now, it is important to note that these people are vitally important to the success of any school. In fact, there are many studies that verify that the work of the external publics (parents, businesses, community organizations and members) has a significant impact on the achievement of students. For this and other reasons, the term "outside the organization" is not meant to be at all derogatory. It is simply used to delineate differences between those who do most of their work physically outside of the school building and those who spend most of their day physically inside of the school building.

In the not too distant past, it was not at all uncommon for school systems to concern themselves exclusively with communicating with these external publics. In recent years, however, school leaders have begun paying much more attention to engaging in effective two-way communication with their employees and their students—stakeholders known as their internal publics. There are three significant reasons why this shift in focus has taken place:

1. A strong system of external communication (discussed in Chapter 6) is dependent upon it;

2. Employees and students will be more productive because they feel listened to and appreciated and have some of their human needs acknowledged and met; and

3. Because school leaders are actually communicating with and listening to them, these internal stakeholders will make constructive suggestions that may have otherwise remained unexplored.

The best administrators, as this chapter will explore, engage in this internal communication through some more obvious, formal means of communication. They also do it through less overt actions, such as modeling positive and enthusiastic behaviors.

## The Principal as Role Model

According to a research study completed in 1999, many school principals fail to see themselves as role models for students. Although principals, by and large, see teachers in this capacity, there is a failure by many to understand that the behaviors and attitudes they exhibit on a daily basis have a direct impact on students, teachers, and staff members. As such, these principals miss out on opportunities to regularly communicate their beliefs and values to their school's internal publics. Worse than that, they often contradict their written and verbal messages by the behaviors and attitudes they exhibit on a regular basis. If they understood that their every move was being noticed and that they really did serve as role models, then perhaps these principals would focus much more heavily on the messages they inadvertently sent to their internal publics.

When school administrators understand that they are role models, they deliberately exhibit behaviors that are consistent with the mission and vision of their school. They begin, in essence, to "walk the talk." This modeling, research has shown, has a dramatic and immediate positive effect on the internal public of a school. It forces school leaders to focus less on their management responsibilities and more on their ability to lead. As we know, strong leadership involves modeling appropriate behavior. This occurs at a much higher level than merely giving directives and expecting them to be adhered to.

Scarnati (1994) listed nine behavioral rules for administrators that are most likely to promote success. They are:

1. Practice honesty and integrity.

2. Work to eliminate fear.

3.  Demonstrate care and understanding.
4.  Accept responsibility.
5.  Develop a service mentality.
6.  Develop loyalty.
7.  Be flexible and adaptable.
8.  Develop listening skills.
9.  Practice humility.

These qualities are echoed in prominent research on leadership effectiveness. As Mark McCormack (1989) stated, "Few things in the world impress me as much as someone who does what he says he will do. Likewise, few things depress me more than someone who doesn't keep his word." Principal preparation programs often miss the opportunity to inform future administrators that these honorable character traits are essential to effective leadership. The principal as role model is a concept that is too often overlooked.

Buell (1992), who indicated the need for principals to develop further shared vision, referred to the need for school leaders to be seen as role models. As the author states, "For schools to be effective, they need effective leaders who express their values. These individual values must become shared goals so that the entire school community shares a vision." (p. 88)

It is impossible, therefore, for school administrators to avoid serving as role models to their internal publics. The individuals who constitute the internal public of a school, because of their positions on the inside of the school's walls, see the principal and interpret his/her body language, attitudes, words, and actions regularly. Failure to understand this concept is nothing less than failure to understand communication and the powerful influence it has on the effectiveness and success of the principalship. The facts are inescapable. Principals and other school administrators are role models, whether or not they wish to be thought of as such.

## Visibility Is the Key

To model appropriate behaviors, to be seen as the keeper of the vision, and to communicate regularly and purposefully, school leaders must be visible to the internal publics of their school. Many administrators have interpreted this message to mean that principals ought to leave their office doors open to appear accessible. Having an "open door policy" helps, but it is clearly not enough. Expecting people to find the leader by walking through an open door, though better than asking them to pick the lock of a closed one, still leaves the responsibility for communication and relationship formation with the other people. School administrators, as role models, cannot afford to be so reactive. Being visible requires that the administrator walk through the open door out into the world where the internal public does its work. The best school leaders utilize this visibility to their advantage by checking on problem students, conferring with teachers and staff, and monitoring the work of all members of their internal public. In this regard, visibility is not "one more thing to do." Instead, it becomes a means to an end. If the journey of a thousand miles begins with a single step, then this step is arguably the most important one for the school administrator to take. In short, to build relationships with students, teachers, and staff members, you have got to first get out of the office. This may be difficult at first, but it is an essential step of relationship building.

## The Need for Effective Human Relations Skills

As school administrator preparation programs improve, there is an increased focus on the need for school leaders to understand and utilize human relations skills known to improve employee satisfaction. This increased focus, it is hoped, will lead to the prevention of an all too common mistake school administrators traditionally make: namely, the assumption that the factors known to contribute to job satisfaction are the same ones that contribute to job dissatisfaction.

Frederick Herzberg (1975), founder of the Hygiene-Motivation Theory reminds leaders that job satisfiers and dissatisfiers are two separate sets of factors. The job satisfiers, or those that fall under the category of motivational factors, include achievement, recognition, the work itself, responsibility, advancement, and growth. When these factors are present in the work environment, then there is an increased chance that employees will be satisfied. From a leadership perspective, this tells school administrators that they must recognize the work of their staffs and students. Additionally, they must match the skills and talents of these individuals with the tasks at hand so that they may achieve, grow, and possibly advance. This will ultimately increase morale and improve the culture of the school as a result of the higher degree of satisfaction felt by the stakeholders.

On the other hand, Herzberg identifies job dissatisfiers, or hygienic factors. These include salary, working conditions, policy, status, security, and supervision. When these factors are present in the work environment, then employee dissatisfaction is prevented. These factors alone do not create job satisfaction. However, they lead to job dissatisfaction when they are absent. Again, from a leadership perspective, leaders need to focus their energy on fostering and enhancing the job satisfiers. This will create the best opportunity for the leader to improve morale. Though the dissatisfiers are important, improving them will not, by itself, make people enjoy their work more. A teacher is more apt to become satisfied at work when the principal recognizes her efforts, gives her appropriate responsibility, and assigns her work that she finds rewarding than when the leader increases the teacher's salary while ignoring these other motivational factors.

## The Student as an Internal Public

Among the many groups that make up a school's internal public, perhaps none is as important as the students. Yet, in our efforts at school improvement and educational reform, we often fail to consider the students in our decision making. For example, consider the increased emphasis many administrators and teachers are placing on effectively involving parents in the educational process. School staffs are going to great lengths to discover ways that they can bring parents into their school and utilize them for the improvement of student learning. These efforts are often little more than glorified public relations efforts, but in other instances they are important elements of the goals and action plans of many of our nation's schools. Do they ignore the students, though?

There is an inescapable fact that is often forgotten in our quest to build parents' support for our educational efforts: namely, the best way to get parents on your side is to get their children on your side. This concept, profound in its simplicity, seems to escape many school administrators. In an effort to focus exclusively on parent involvement they ignore the children, though the children are the best sources for increasing parent excitement and pleasure with the school. When students find school rewarding and when they believe that the adults working in the school building truly care about them as individuals, then they share this information and this enthusiasm with their parents. The reverse is also true, however. Students who do not find satisfaction or needs fulfillment at school tend to go home and complain about education. This can lead to a loss of parental support even before you have made any conscious effort to earn it. Somehow, school administrators need to become much more cognizant of the invaluable role that students play in advancing a school's mission. Students really are our most important stakeholders. We need leaders who can remember this and utilize this knowledge for educational improvement.

Although it is widely recognized that the students represent the most important group among the internal publics, there are many school leaders who fail to understand how to appropriately involve and communicate with them. Too often students are seen as passive recipients of a school's goals, and not as members of a two-way communication process. They "listen" to announcements administrators make on public address systems, "read" memos written by counselors, school nurses, and administrators, and "write" notes based on their teachers' classroom lectures. While students may need to do all of these things to be successful, they may be even more successful and confident if they have a voice that is heard from time to time as well. Visible leaders, it is worth noting, hear these voices much more readily than do those who find themselves chained to their desks. The same idea holds true for all school stakeholders. As a teacher, is it not more satisfying to know that the principal, superintendent, and/or board of education members give you a voice? Does this not lead to a greater sense of pride and ownership in decisions?

One of the ways for students' voices to be heard is through the formation of and participation in a Student Advisory Council. These councils, though their specific roles and functions vary from school to school, essentially create an opportunity for elected members of the student body to meet with administrators and discuss issues of concern to them. At a deeper level, they do even more than that. They empower students to assist in the governance of the school. Whether the issues they assist in governing are of major consequence or not is not nearly as important as the fact that the students are, at least, involved in the process. They have a voice. More importantly, they have a voice on issues that are generally of importance to them. Most importantly, this voice is not just listened to, but it is reacted to as well. The best Student Advisory Councils, therefore, give students opportunities to really participate in decision making. The worst ones, ones that often do more damage than good, are the ones that pay lip service to the idea of shared governance and are really little more than opportunities for the principal to listen to the students and then carry out the decision he or she intended to carry out from the very beginning.

---

## Showcase

Parkview Elementary has had a Student Council in existence for over a decade, which has proven to be an excellent avenue for maintaining good relationships with the immediate community. Student Council projects include a yearly fund raising activity benefiting Riley Childrens' Hospital in Indianapolis. We also ring the bell each year for the Salvation Army. We clean up the school grounds, design our own Student Council T-Shirts that are worn to our projects, and have a pizza party at the end of each year to celebrate our accomplishments. Being involved in activities of this nature helps children develop a sense of social responsibility. In addition, our interaction with the community helps cast our school in a positive light.

*Greg Karas, Fourth Grade Teacher, Parkview*
*Elementary School, Valparaiso, IN*

---

Of perhaps even more importance are the steps that school leaders take to involve students and make them feel welcomed when they are new to a school building. These efforts are most notably used when students make the transition from one school to the next within a particular school district (i.e. the transition from middle school to high school) and when students are new to a particular school as the result of a move or family relocation. Times such as these provide great opportunities for school leaders to communicate with students and set a positive tone for their learning experiences. These are opportunities that the thoughtful administrator never wastes.

Exhibit 5.1 illustrates an invitation to a transition program that a high school may engage in to welcome all incoming freshmen. Note the encouraging language and the use of door prizes as two methods that really aim to encourage students' attendance.

## Exhibit 5.1. Invitation to Incoming Freshmen

**In cooperation with the Wilson HS Student Council**

### You're Invited

**Calling all incoming freshmen! You are invited to a special event.**

**Date: 8/22/01**

**Time 9:00 AM**

**Wilson High School Cafeteria**

**Meet new friends! Familiarize yourself with new surroundings!**

**Win Exciting Prizes!**

**Welcome to Wilson High School!!**

For students who arrive at a school after the academic year has already begun, some schools provide a "welcome wagon" to greet and help familiarize them with some of the school's personnel and operations. At Parkview Elementary School in Valparaiso, Indiana, the welcome wagon is stocked with some necessary school supplies and organized and overseen by members of the school's student council. Once a new student starts school, members of the student council bring the welcome wagon to the new student's classroom, some welcoming school supplies are given to them, and they receive a tour of the facility. During this tour, they meet staff members like the school's nurse and secretary and receive instructions on issues of importance such as the lunchroom procedures and arrival/dismissal methods. Not only is this information of great benefit to the student who is new to the school, but it also empowers the student council members and provides them with a real sense of ownership and importance to the school. As we know, the students often know more about the ins and outs of daily school operations than do many of the adults who work in the school building.

## The Use of Discipline

How a school deals with student discipline says a great deal about its method for communicating with students. Although it is widely acknowledged that students must be well-disciplined and well-behaved in order to establish and maintain an effective learning environment, some teachers may take this notion to an extreme and communicate many negative messages to students.

The best educators know that students who become restless and inattentive often do not learn well and may disrupt the learning of other students. These educators regularly self-reflect and examine their own professional practices to prevent such situations from occurring. They understand that when such situations arise, the students are not always to blame. Consequently, these educators adjust their methodology to prevent discipline problems from arising.

Educators who are not so skilled make mistakes in regards to discipline that often hurt their relationships with their students. Chief among these errors is the administration of inappropriate punishments that do not prevent future occurrences of the infraction that led to their administration, but alienate students instead. As an example, consider the numerous times in our schools that students are removed from the classroom because of inappropriate or excessive talking. This removal and isolation only serves to alienate the student from his/her peers. Rarely does it prevent excessive talking the next time the student is bored or feeling disconnected. From a school–community relations perspective, such mistakes lead to apathy from students and constant criticism from parents.

It is important, therefore, for school administrators to recognize that much is communicated to students by the establishment, maintenance, and follow-through of their school staff's discipline efforts. It is not enough to think of pupil discipline as a classroom issue. Discipline plays a much larger role in the culture of a school. For this reason, administrators ought to carefully examine the ways in which they and their staff administer their discipline plans. They should help staff members understand the messages being communicated to students and their parents by the methods in which they deal with discipline.

This is not to imply that discipline ought to be weak in a school. Nor is there any intent to communicate to readers that discipline should never be firm or even severe. The real issues are the consistency with which it is administered and the match between the punishments and the infractions. Students want fairness above many other things. Even if a school takes a very hard line on an issue such as student dress codes, it is the fairness of the policy and the consistency with which it is followed that are most important.

## Teachers—The Most Important Adults in the Building

Though many believe that the principal is the most *influential* adult in the school building and is, therefore, the keeper of the vision, it is certainly commonly thought that the teachers are the most *important* adults in a school. They, more than anybody else, have direct, lasting influence on students and their achievement. As such, the responsibility that administrators have for working with, and developing, teachers is among the greatest responsibilities that they are charged with in the scope of their professional duties. Principals who understand how to communicate effectively with teachers are at a distinct advantage in this regard.

However, it is important to note that communicating effectively with teachers is only one part of the principal's job. Perhaps even more important in terms of school–community relations is the principal's ability to establish and maintain positive relationships with the entire school staff. Failure to do so can result in an unleashing of negativism that will severely damage a school's reputation as a caring, learning community. The importance of positive communication with noninstructional staff members is elaborated on later in this chapter.

Effective school leaders recognize that teachers often play a very active role in the community. For this reason, the teachers' overall opinion of the school can have a major influence on what the community learns to perceive and believe about the school. A teacher who is sitting in the stands at a little league baseball game complaining about the principal, central office administration, students, parents, or curriculum can do a great deal of damage to the image of the school. Often, the best intentions by the school administration cannot undo this damage. This adds to the importance of having a positive method of communicating with internal publics, particularly teachers. Although they do not need to like everything, if issues are communicated carefully and reasonably, there is a much better chance that teachers and the rest of the internal public will at least understand everything. This will lessen the extent to which they may complain in public about aspects of the school. In fact, in the best schools, teachers are often out in the public bragging about the school. This proves that strong internal communications can have a very positive impact on strong external communications, elaborated on in Chapter 6.

## The Friday Focus—A Tool for Positive Internal Communication

Todd Whitaker (1999) has developed a great model for communicating positive information to a school's internal publics. The *Friday Focus*, a weekly memo that is placed in all teachers' mailboxes before they arrive at school on Friday mornings, is designed with the following goals in mind:

- ♦ It should communicate important logistical information about upcoming events in the school. This allows staff meetings to be much more productive.
- ♦ It should be used as a staff development or inservice tool by consistently keeping the beliefs and vision of the school in front of the staff.
- ♦ It should be used as a motivational tool by mentioning good, positive things about the school.
- ♦ It can assist with planning. Because of the important logistical information contained in *Friday Focus*, staff members can be more organized and prepared about upcoming events.

The positive nature of the Friday Focus makes it a great motivational and modeling tool that the staff begins to look forward to each Friday morning. It gives the school leader an opportunity to communicate regularly, purposefully, and positively with members of the internal public in a way that keeps them motivated. Exhibit 5.2 is an example of a Friday Focus from an elementary school.

**Exhibit 5.2. Friday Focus**

# Friday Focus

### March 19, 2001

♦ Kudos to Jim, Sheila, and Karen. This school has been impeccably clean lately. Though we all play a part in that, these three individuals have worked extra hard. Thanks for being so important to our school.

♦ I visited Brenda's classroom on Tuesday to watch her class perform their original play. The creativity these students displayed was inspirational. It couldn't have happened without the hard work and dedication of a great teacher. Thank you, Brenda!

♦ At a recent Annual Case Review the following comment was made to me by a parent, "The main reason my daughter has been so successful is the dedicated Elliott staff." Can you imagine how proud I was? Thank you all for the work you do on behalf of kids.

♦ Did anybody else go by the library yesterday morning? Sue's class was engaging in their third annual Teddy Bear picnic. I had never attended one before. Boy was it fun! Your students are fortunate to have you, Sue.

♦ A heartfelt "Welcome Back" to Patti. Not only are we glad you're feeling better, but we've also realized how important you are to our school. Please don't get sick anymore.

♦ I hope each and every one of you has a relaxing Spring Break! You've all worked so hard this year and are deserving of some quality time with your families. You'll be in my thoughts.

## Positive Relationships with Noninstructional Staff

It is very easy for school administrators to forget sometimes that noninstructional staff members are often even more visible in the community than are instructional faculty members. As such, regular, positive communication with them is of utmost importance. Equally important is making sure that these valuable members of your school community are recognized and feel appreciated for the work that they do.

Members of a school's noninstructional staff want to be acknowledged and praised just as much as teachers do. Unfortunately, in many schools this does not occur. Instead, teachers often treat noninstructional staff members, such as secretaries, teaching assistants, custodians, and cooks, as though they are socially inferior. It is up to the principal and administrative team to make sure that friendly, caring attitudes are shown to these staff members and that treatment as social inferiors is eliminated. This can be accomplished through activities such as including all staff members in faculty meetings, placing noninstructional staff members on important committees for which they have a stake in the outcome and possess some expertise in the issue, and providing social situations that involve the entire school staff.

In reality, the human relations needs of all staff members are similar. Whether one is a teacher, a secretary, or a custodian has little to do with the innate wants that people have in their work environment. The concern is that many leaders misunderstand these wants and, consequently, cannot meet them in work situations. Exhibit 5.3 represents a compilation of ideas taken from interview accounts with school staff and relying heavily on the motivation-hygiene theory, as described by Frederick Herzberg. Similar studies have been done in a variety of work environments, all of which produced very similar results. As shown, employer perceptions do not match employee desires. This is one major reason why some people in our schools do not feel satisfied at work.

It is clear from this illustration that school leaders do not always understand what it is that their staff members want to get from the work environment. As Frederick Herzberg identified, the things that lead to job satisfaction (motivational factors) are often not what we would expect. If school administrators, therefore, continue to believe that staff members want pay, promotion, and working conditions in order to feel satisfied with their work, then they will miss out on opportunities to provide the interesting work and appreciation that the staff members really desire. Additionally, administrators who lack this understanding will become very upset, believing that they have given the staff everything they could possibly want. In reality, as the staff members would surely feel, the administrator has given them absolutely nothing of real value.

---

## Exhibit 5.3. What Employees Want

| Workers say these things are important: | Employers think these things are important: |
| --- | --- |
| 1. Interesting and engaging work | 1. Good pay |
| 2. Appreciation for a job well done | 2. Job security |
| 3. Feeling that they are "insiders" | 3. Opportunities for growth |
| 4. Job security | 4. Good working conditions |
| 5. Good pay | 5. Interesting and engaging work |
| 6. Opportunities for growth | 6. Loyalty |
| 7. Good working conditions | 7. Appreciation for a job well done |
| 8. Loyalty | 8. Feelings that they are "insiders |

---

# Other Members of the Internal Public

## Substitute Teachers

Substitute teachers, though providing an invaluable service when they are at the school, are often overlooked in a school–community relations program. There is a misguided assumption that these individuals are not part of the internal public, since they are not at the school on a regular, consistent basis. However, as the best administrators know, substitute teachers can also carry the message about their perceptions of a school out into the local community. Just as is the case with other employees, it is essential that the messages substitute teachers carry are accurate, positive ones about your school.

One way to ensure that substitute teachers feel like part of the school's internal public is to invite them to the school for an organizational meeting with the principal. This is best done before school opens for the year to help alleviate the difficulty that arises when they are substitute teaching in other settings. During this meeting, the substitute teachers need to be reminded of the school's mission and goals, given copies of any handbooks that outline procedures or expectations, and engaged in a question/answer session about the school and its policies. In many cases, it is wise to include other key personnel such as the secretary, counselors, and nurse who can assist by explaining their roles to the substitute teachers.

Many schools have also developed a handbook for substitute teachers. This handbook contains information that the substitute teacher will need in order to be successful, but that is often overlooked or taken for granted as common knowledge by the regular instructional staff. Exhibit 5.4 is an example of the table of contents from one such substitute teacher handbook.

---

**Exhibit 5.4. Substitute Teacher Handbook**

---

# Richdale School

*Substitute Teacher Handbook*

Table of Contents

Introduction and Welcome

Qualifications for Being a Substitute Teacher
    Application
    Certification
    Getting Your Name on the List

The School Day
    Assignment Times
    Preparing for the Day
    Reporting to Schools
    Name Tags
    Parking
    Payroll Procedures

Roles and Responsibilities
    Role and Responsibilities of the Substitute Teacher
    Role and Responsibilities of the Regular Classroom Teacher
    Role and Responsibilities of the Principal

Helpful Hints
    Map of the School
    Map of the District
    List of Staff Names and Room Assignments
    Bell Schedule
    Lunch Schedule
    Lunch Procedures

Journal Articles About the Importance of Substitute Teachers

---

## Student Teachers

Schools that are located near colleges and universities that prepare teachers usually have pre-service or student teachers in their facility to complete the field component of their teacher preparation program. Many school leaders consider this location to provide wonderful opportunities to assist beginners in their development while potentially recruiting future members of their faculty. Teachers, in many cases, view the occasion to have a student teacher positively as they, too, enjoy assisting in the development of new teachers and enjoy the extra set of hands to assist in their classrooms. As a result of the student teacher's involvement in the school on a regular basis, it becomes important that he or she is treated as a valuable member of the school's internal public.

Involving student teachers in all gatherings of the faculty is an important first step. School leaders need to remember that whether or not they hire these individuals after they complete their training, the student teachers will say a great deal that will get out into the community about their experiences in these schools to other student teachers and/or to university instructors. One of the best ways to ensure that positive things are being said is to make the student teaching experience as positive as possible for these individuals.

Orientation meetings, such as the one described for use with substitute teachers, are also excellent ways of making student teachers feel as though they are important members of the school's internal public. Additionally, these meetings give these pre-service teachers great opportunities to interact with other members of the school's internal public with whom they might not otherwise have regular contact. This, in turn, will aid in their own professional growth and development.

## The Importance of the School Secretary

School principals must always remember that the secretary is on the front line of communication. In many ways, this individual is the voice of your school. More than any other employee, the school secretary reflects the attitude of the principal to all stakeholders he/she comes in contact with. The way in which the secretary greets visitors, answers the telephone, interacts with teachers and other staff, relates with parents, and assists children is seen by many as being reflective of the principal's values. For this reason, the secretary is a major figure in any school–community relations plan.

School principals must always remember this and must regularly confer with the secretary to ensure that he/she is performing these public relations duties to the principal's satisfaction. Regular sessions dealing with topics from telephone usage to office decorating to interacting with students must be conducted to ensure that the secretary is representing the school in a positive way. Most principals believe that these human relations skills of the secretary are far more important than some of the more routine office skills. If the principals don't think this is true, you can bet that parents and community members do. A secretary with a negative attitude can cause irreparable harm to a school–community relations plan.

---

## Showcase

At our school we choose two staff members each week as our "Staff Member of the Week." These two individuals are allowed to park their vehicle in the designated "Staff Member of the Week" parking space close to the entrance door. They also receive a coupon for the week which entitles them to one of the following: (1) Leave school early one day as soon as the students leave. (2) Receive a "goody bag" (pens, Post-it Notes, candy, etc.). (3) Twenty-minute break from class with a planned activity for the students provided. (4) Free snack from the vending machine. By the end of the school year, each staff member has had the opportunity to be honored. The staff truly appreciates the special attention they get and the expression of gratitude and admiration from the administration.

*Johnna Riley, Resource Teacher, R.C. Longan Elementary School,*
*Henrico Public Schools, VA, and Graduate Student in Educational*
*Leadership, Virginia Commonwealth University*

---

## The Entire School Staff:
## The Key to Strong School–
## Community Relations

The smart school leader understands that the members of a school's internal publics are much more than simply employees. Because they live and vote in the school district as well, all of these individuals take on new importance as messengers of the good things happening in our schools. For this reason alone, all staff members must be informed of the extremely significant role they play in a school's public relations plan. Principals are well served to remind staff members at the beginning of each school year that there are many things they can do and many behaviors they can exhibit that will assist in the advancement of a positive school–community relations plan. These goals should be reviewed regularly so that all employees understand how important they are to the school's success in these endeavors. Some suggested public relations goals for all school staff members are:

- Always be friendly, courteous, and helpful to school visitors.
- Be active in community organizations and local service projects.
- Share any rumors that are being spread throughout the community about the school with the principal.
- Stay abreast of the actual facts regarding events in your school that may wind up being shared in the public.
- Share the great work that colleagues in your school are doing so that all community members you come in contact with are aware of the positive work being done on behalf of children.
- Always speak positively about your school in the community.

Consistently reminding all staff members of these goals will serve two very important purposes. First and most obvious, it will assist them in understanding how they ought to represent the school when they are living their lives out in the public. Second, it empowers them to play a significant role in the advancement of your school–community relations plan. This empowerment, more often than not, leads to an increased feeling of responsibility among the staff members. They begin understanding that the school leader recognizes their power and importance to the organization. This, as Herzberg has illustrated, often has the added benefit of leading to job satisfaction.

## Chapter Summary

- School leaders must understand and pay attention to all of their school's internal publics.
- It is vitally important for school leaders to recognize that they serve as important role models to many members of their internal publics.
- The best way to build relationships and show appreciation for people is to be visible to them on a regular, consistent basis.
- Students, often forgotten in our school–community relations plans, play a very important role in our school's success. They should be included in all of our public relations efforts.
- Teachers and other staff members carry many messages out into the community about our schools' effectiveness. School leaders must help all staff members realize this and learn how to best represent the school to other people.
- All employees of a school have similar human relations needs. As such, they must all feel important and be included in our school–community relations endeavors.

# Case Study Analysis

## "Class" Parties

The teachers of Rocky Point Middle School are members of a close-knit professional community. Many of them socialize together outside of school hours, and they all seem to get along so well during the school day. As Rocky Point's new principal, you are excited about the opportunity to share some fun and fellowship with the entire staff at Rocky Point's upcoming staff holiday party.

As the party begins, you notice many of the teachers there, having a wonderful time together. You can't help but think how lucky you are to be the leader of such a collegial, professional group. Before long you begin to notice, however, that no members of Rocky Point's noninstructional staff are in attendance. Quickly you turn to Joe Nixon, veteran teacher and president of the local teacher's association. "Joe," you ask, "wasn't this party advertised as being for the entire school staff?"

"Of course it was," comes Joe's reply. "It's always only the teachers who come, though. The rest of the staff feels a bit inferior, you know, with them not being professionals and all."

Your jaw drops in amazement. How, you wonder, could you have been so blind?

## Questions for Analysis

1. What could have caused all members of the noninstructional staff at Rocky Point Middle School to believe that they were inferior to the teachers?
2. What ramifications, if any, could these feelings of inferiority among noninstructional staff members have on the school's perception in the external community?
3. What would you do when you return to school on Monday?

# 6

# Embracing Your External Publics

The communication skills required of successful administrators are not reserved for sole use with a school's internal publics. Though it is, as we have seen, critical for successful school administrators to communicate effectively with the various stakeholders constituting a school's internal publics, it is no less important for them to utilize these communication skills as effectively with those stakeholders spending most of their time outside of the school's walls. In fact, as we witness the speed at which people have access to information during this new century, it becomes apparent that school leaders must keep all concerned members of their external publics informed. Failure to do so gives all school stakeholders opportunities to receive inaccurate information about the state of education, without any rebuttal or clarification from the leaders of our schools. Administrators must not allow this to happen.

But, who are these stakeholders referred to as external publics? What information about our schools do they need and desire? Finally, how is this information best communicated to them? This chapter focuses on answers to these questions and gives information necessary to support the notion that successful school leadership lies, at least in part, in the administrator's ability to embrace the school's external publics.

## Appropriate Parental Involvement

All professional school staff members are inundated with information regarding the importance of parental involvement and the effects it has on students' academic achievement. As all educators have learned, parent involvement certainly is one of the most significant factors influencing student achievement. Throughout the past decade, there have been numerous reports and a large body of research stating that parent involvement is a critical factor in the success of students (Benson, Buckley, & Elliott, 1980; Epstein, 1992; Rioux & Berla, 1993; Whitaker & Fiore, 2001). In addition to what this literature states, the federal government has been paying increased attention to this concept. Consider that an eighth goal dealing with parental participation was ultimately added to the now famous National Education Goals (Goals 2000). Specifically, the eighth goal is stated as: "Every school will promote partnerships that will increase parental involvement and participation in promoting the social, emotional, and academic growth of children" (Achieving the Goals, 1997). The wording of this goal, after careful analysis, acknowledges parental involvement's ability to promote social, emotional, and academic growth.

The addition of the eighth goal therefore illustrates, in large part, the federal government's acknowledgment of parents' significance in education. This significance had not previously been acknowledged so strongly by any federal agency (Whitaker and Fiore, 2001). In further acknowledging parents' important roles, the National Parent Teacher Association (PTA) devised a list of six national standards with the sole purpose of "promoting meaningful parent and family participation" in 1997 (p. 6). These standards are set forth in Chapter 3. The organization has also led many studies during recent years with the purpose of exploring the nature and intent of parents' involvement in their children's education.

## Involving Parents While They Are at School

Helping parents believe that they are important members of our school communities is a difficult goal for many school administrators to accomplish. However, it is a task of utmost importance, which is a prerequisite to any meaningful opportunities for getting and keeping parents involved. For a myriad of reasons, a large percentage of our parents simply do not believe that we, as school leaders, deem their involvement to be at all important. Worse yet, some parents believe, for a variety of reasons, that school leaders do not want them in the school at all. Therefore, it becomes imperative for all school leaders to recognize the significance of creating opportunities for parents to change their misconceptions and to understand that we do really want them and need them to be involved. Elaine McEwan, educational consultant and author, suggests structuring school projects, such as fun fairs, so that parents and teachers work together, and hosting career days in which parents "come to school and educate children about their careers." (McEwan, 1998, pp. 80–89) These structured or forced gatherings of parents and teachers help to break down the invisible wall that so many parents feel has been erected between them and the school. Moreover, when parents can share their careers and/or expertise with children in our schools, their sense of value and worth to our mission and goals is certainly heightened.

Because many states are experiencing a reduction in funding for classroom assistants, teachers are increasingly turning to parents for the instructional support that they used to receive from classified staff members. They are utilizing parents to help tutor struggling students, prepare materials for lessons and/or classroom bulletin board displays, and assist in less structured school experiences such as recess at the elementary

## Showcase

James B. Eads Learning Labs took place on a nine-week rotation during the last 50 minutes on the school day on consecutive Fridays. Three nine-week sessions were held during the school year. The courses offered included: Architecture and Land Development, Sign Language, Origami and Japanese Culture, Photography, Science Experimentation and Discovery, Writing a Newspaper Story, Spanish, The Stock Market, Environmental Awareness, and Building Complex Machines with Lego's, to name a few. The Eads staff taught some of the Labs while others tapped parents, community leaders and central office personnel. We prepared a catalogue of course offerings, which changed every nine weeks. The catalogue was sent home with the students so parents could help their children make their choices. An assessment of the program showed that parents and students absolutely adored the program. The media coverage for Learning Labs was colossal. The newspaper had a smorgasbord of stories to choose from each time Learning Labs were offered. Learning Labs was a very successful program that needs the full commitment of the staff.

*Sondra G. Estep, Ph.D., Former Principal, James B. Eads Elementary School, Munster, IN, now Professor, Governors State University, IL*

level. Though these represent wonderful opportunities for increased parental involvement, it is important for school administrators employing such techniques to consider the potential legal ramifications associated with them. This is often overlooked in the name of necessity of finding some assistance for teachers.

The mention here of potential legal ramifications is not intended to unduly alarm administrators or other school employees. However, it is worth noting that the Family Educational Rights and Privacy Act (FERPA) of 1974 provided substantive and procedural safeguards for the privacy rights of students and their parents. Essentially, this means that school officials must keep most data contained in student records confidential. Whereas school officials and teachers with a legitimate educational interest in the student are entitled to access these records, even their access must be recorded and documented. Volunteers, whether parents or nonparents, who are often tapped by schools to provide necessary tutoring, do not have the same rights in terms of accessing confidential student information.

Also of note, many school districts now require background checks of all volunteers. Although this may appear insensitive or demeaning to volunteers, a valid concern for school administrators to express, the risk of liability because of a volunteer's negligence is great. Therefore, these background checks are sound practice. More importantly, background checks on volunteers can be conducted and presented in a way that illustrates to parents and community members alike the school's unending quest to ensure student safety and well being. The smart school leader can use communication and human relations skills to turn this possible concern of appearing insensitive to volunteers into a very positive message of his or her commitment to students and their safety.

## Welcome to Our School?

An important consideration of getting and maintaining parental involvement at the school is the ways in which we greet and welcome parents when they arrive. This becomes a potential public relations nightmare when considered along with all of the valid concerns we must have in regards to school safety. School leaders all across the nation are struggling with how to keep their students safe while also maintaining a welcoming, friendly atmosphere. The greatest success in this regard is being enjoyed by those leaders who have found ways to welcome visitors openly within constraints that allow for steady monitoring of all visitors who enter the building. School leaders who mistakenly believe that restrictive entrance to a school building must be accompanied by a cold, unfriendly message, on the other hand, are experiencing failure. Consider Exhibits 6.1 and 6.2. They show examples of greetings that might be found at the entrance to some of our schools. Look at them carefully and try to assess the way in which parents and other visitors may perceive them. Exhibit 6.2. is far more friendly and inviting, yet it still delivers the same important message about student safety and visitor access.

These are actual messages that appear at the entrances of two different schools. Both of them have the same goal and were created in response to the need for keeping track of who is in our school buildings at all times. Not only is this necessary to do, but it also creates an important sense of safety, even though the messages can be ignored in many cases. In some schools, there are guards at the doors, which have a great impact on school safety. In most schools across the country, however, these messages are the only means by which access is truly restricted. So which one is more effective at accomplishing the desired goal?

Some may argue that the forceful language in the first example is necessary. Without such forcefulness, it can be argued, people would not respond and do what they are being asked to do. This position is difficult to defend, however. Others maintain that individuals who would ignore a message that says "Welcome to our school! We are so glad that you are

---

## Exhibit 6.1. Unfriendly, Cold School Greeting

"Stop! For the safety of our students, all visitors
must sign in at the office before proceeding farther."

---

## Exhibit 6.2. Friendly, Warm School Greeting

"Welcome to our school!
We are so glad that you are here!
We do ask that all visitors please sign
in at the office upon entering."

---

here. We do ask that all visitors please sign in at the office upon entering"
are also more likely to ignore a more forceful message. The vast majority
of school visitors, especially parents, are well-intentioned people who follow rules and regulations. Additionally, these people appreciate the
school's efforts at restricting visitation and creating a safe environment for
their children. By utilizing an unfriendly, more forceful message, schools
unintentionally make some of their more positive visitors feel unwelcome
in the school because of the rather unfriendly edict that greets them.

The odds are that the same people will report to the office no matter
how the message is delivered. The negative effect that the message has on
otherwise positive people is what is of great concern. School leaders must
concern themselves with student safety. There is simply no question
about that. In doing so, they must be cognizant of who has access to the
school building while children are in attendance. Messages, prominently
displayed, that urge people to sign in and be accounted for before proceeding throughout the school building, are essential. In designing such
messages, however, school leaders must be aware of the other, more subtle messages that they are delivering. These messages, which do no more
good than friendly ones, can run the serious risk of making parents and
other visitors feel unwelcome in our schools.

## Involving Parents While They Are at Home

It is in the best interests of administrators and teachers alike to recognize the important point that parents can be partners in schooling from
within the confines of their own homes. Rather than bemoaning the fact
that many parents appear unwilling or unable to come to school and be involved, school leaders must recognize that parents play a very important
educational role even while they are in the home. The entire school com-

munity must understand this, and it must be communicated to parents on a regular basis. Not only is this a welcome idea for some parents, but also it validates the fact that family needs have certainly changed over time. The National Committee for Citizens in Education backs up this notion by urging all parents to:

- Support student events and performances by helping with them (such as sewing costumes or planning scenery for a school play).
- Be part of decision-making committees dealing with school issues and problems, such as a Parent Advisory Committee (these often meet during the evening).
- Ask your child's teacher if he or she has materials that you can use to help your child at home.
- Help your child develop a homework schedule that he or she can stick to.
- Have high expectations for your child's learning and behavior, both at home and at school.
- Avoid making homework a punishment.
- Praise and encourage your child. (Whitaker & Fiore, 2001)

Many individual school districts across the United States have taken the initiative to inform parents of ways in which they can be involved with school from within their homes. Stephen Kleinsmith, assistant superintendent in Millard, Nebraska encourages faculty and staff to share the following list of parent involvement options with parents:

- Call the school staff on a regular basis, and talk with teachers before problems occur.
- Help proofread and edit the school newsletter.
- Become involved in the student's curriculum planning, and discuss academic options with your son or daughter.
- Encourage involvement in the school activities of the student's choice.
- Ask your son or daughter, "What good questions did you ask today?" or "What did you learn in school today?" Then practice good listening, a key to effective communication.
- Encourage reading, using the library, and purchasing books at a young age. (Dietz, 1997)

Many other schools have developed similar lists for parents. Though the specific content of these lists varies from one community to the next, the common theme of all of them is that there absolutely are ways in which parents can be very involved in education without having to come directly to the school building. All schools must confirm the value of these at-home tasks so that parents will begin to feel part of the educational process without any of the unintended guilt that accompanies not being able to spend time in the school.

Finally, the Parent Partnership program in Philadelphia is another example of an innovation involving parental involvement from home. This program provides reading and mathematics booklets to parents as well as a Dial-A-Teacher Assistance project for help with homework in all basic subjects. Many school systems in recent years have expanded on the Dial-A-Teacher concept to include help and assignment information via the Internet. Also used in some markets is local access cable television. These telecasts can include advice for parents on providing assistance, as well as the more traditional call-in help programs for students.

The San Diego Unified School District offers materials in both English and Spanish designed to assist in student homework. This is in recognition of the fact that many students do not live in homes that use English as the primary language for communication. As a result, many parents are not involved in their child's school because of an honest barrier to communication. Educators sometimes mistakenly assume that parents have the same command of English as do the children we work with. Often, we have discovered, this is not the case. As in San Diego, many school districts are providing information to parents in multiple languages to reduce this obvious barrier to parental involvement. (Whitaker & Fiore, 2001)

## Other Members of the External Public

Thus far, this chapter has focused on the importance of involving parents in our schools. Though there will be some more specific ways to accomplish discussed in subsequent chapters, it is essential to note that parents are not the only external public that school leaders ought to concern themselves with. Exhibit 6.3. illustrates several other external publics and briefly summarizes some of what these groups want to know about our schools. Effective, regular communication with them is essential to ensure that their needs are being met.

Exhibit 6.3. does not identify every member of a school's external publics. Additionally, there are individuals who fit into more than one of these categories. For example, a community member may have attended the school as a child, may not have children of his or her own, may be affiliated with a church, and may work in the community. Obviously, this individual would be concerned about the school on multiple levels. Similarly, an individual may belong to several of these groups but have no apparent interest in the school. School leaders ought to communicate with these groups as though everybody is interested, however.

## Exhibit 6.3. External Publics

Taxpayers

How is their money being spent? Is there evidence showing that money spent is accomplishing a desired goal?

Churches/Religious Affiliates

Is the school discriminating based on religious beliefs? Are students penalized for failing to attend in observance of a religious obligation? Does the curriculum support/counter their religious beliefs?

Legislators

What are some needs in the school that can be assisted through legislative activity? How does proposed legislation affect the learning that takes place in the schools?

School Alumni

Are school traditions still being observed? What is the school staff retention rate?

Families Without Children in Schools

How do students in this school perform in comparison with those in other schools? What ramifications does this have on property values? Are people attracted to the community because of the schools?

Businesses/Industries

Does the curriculum prepare students for the workforce? What percentage of students go to college instead of directly entering the workforce?

## Showcase

For nearly two decades Parkview Elementary School has put on a special event for students in fourth and fifth grade known as "Friday Night Live." The entire staff becomes involved in creating skits and other activities that are incredibly elaborate. Creative parents spend a great deal of time procuring decorations and other items that generally amaze the children. We have had cowboys on horseback, Olympic-level archers, professional basketball players, live tigers, yachts, limousines, ice sculptures, the mayor of the city, classic Harley Davidson motorcycles (roaring down the hallway), letters from the President's wife, and dozens of other items that people provided because they knew we were cooking up something really special for the children. Many fourth and fifth graders (years later) say it was the best thing that they were ever a part of in school. The goodwill engendered as a result is beautiful and worthwhile.

*Greg Karas, Fourth Grade Teacher, Parkview Elementary School, Valparaiso, IN*

## Establishing Key Communicators

Depending on the size and location of an individual community, it may be impossible for a school to have the resources necessary for communication with all members of the external publics. For this reason, it is important that key communicators be identified within each of these external groups. These key communicators, whom George Pawlas identifies as "the opinion leaders, the people who influence the directions and actions of the various community organizations" (1995, p. 74), ought to be representatives of these external public groups that have the greatest access to people. The editor of the local newspaper, for example, is often an excellent key communicator as a result of the access that this individual has to a large audience on a regular and consistent basis. A high-volume local realtor may also be an excellent key communicator. Like the newspaper editor, this individual has access to many people and influences, to a large degree, how people perceive the schools and the community.

In your own community, you can probably think of many people who would be excellent key communicators. They may be religious leaders, business officials, leaders in civic organizations, politicians, higher education faculty members, members of the police force, or the coordinator of the community's welcome wagon. What is important is the access they have to community members and the ability they have to communicate with, and influence, them.

These key communicators ought to be invited to the school at regularly scheduled intervals so that the school principal can share information with them and listen to their concerns. In addition, they should receive copies of the school's newsletters, and should receive telephone calls from the school principal whenever matters of importance to the community surface. To ensure that the key communicators best understand what is going on in the school, it is important that the principal answers all questions, letters, and telephone calls with a personal telephone call or letter promptly. This is essential practice for all communication that the principal engages in, but it becomes crucial when dealing with key communicators. School leaders must remember that key communicators see a great number of influential people on a regular, consistent basis. It is, therefore, imperative that they have correct information communicated to them.

## Where to Start with Key Communicators

If a school leader wishes to start a program involving key communicators in getting the word out about the school's mission and goals, then an important first step is identifying who these key communicators really ought to be. Suggestions for doing this were made in the preceding section, but they were intentionally largely generic. Successfully utilizing the right key communicators in a school community relations program necessitates involvement of many school employees. Therefore, the wise school leader should have various school employees compile independent lists of possible community members to include as key communicators. These lists should then be analyzed and evaluated. The odds are that several names will appear on multiple lists indicating, more often than not, that these individuals would be outstanding choices.

The next step that ought to be completed is for the school leader to contact individuals, informing them that they have been identified as community members who would be excellent members of the school's key communicators program. These contacts are best made through formal letters and personal telephone calls. Obviously, contacting members through both of these means increases the likelihood that they will respond favorably to the invitation.

The size of the school and some specific demographic information about the community it serves will have a great deal to do with the next step. In some communities it would be appropriate to then meet with the key communicators either one-on-one or in very small groups. During these meetings, the school leaders would explain the goals of the key communicator program and consistently remind those chosen that they have been identified because of the influential role they play in the community. This serves to increase their level of confidence and commitment to the program. In other school communities, it may be more appropriate to have one big meeting with all of the key communicators where the same goals would be accomplished. The school leaders and their most trusted advisors best determine which method is most prudent. What really matters is that this group, which can range in size from 5 to 100, understands its role in carrying the good news from the school to the community and echoing back to the school any concerns or questions that arise within the community.

## The Importance of Community Members with Grown Children

For the past 25 years, our population has been aging at its most rapid rate in modern history. This has had an impact on many decisions and directions in our country, but has sadly been ignored by many school administrators. Trained in administration years ago, these school administrators have focused their energy and attention on parents of school-age children, thereby ignoring the fastest growing segment of our population and their community. Contemporary school leaders must understand the importance of older adults as significant members of a school's external publics. Among the many reasons why this is so are the following:

♦ Approximately 75 percent of adults over the age of 65 are registered to vote in this country. Almost as many turn out to vote in national elections, despite the fact that overall voter turnout has declined in the past 25 years. Many of these older adults also turn out to vote on school budget and bond issues.

♦ Approximately 75 percent of the tax-paying households in most school districts do not have children in schools.

♦ The American Association of Retired Persons (AARP), the largest organization in the United States targeting this population, currently claims a membership in excess of 35 million members.

School leaders must reach out to this segment of their external publics. When they do, they usually find a group that is very supportive of education. Older adults want the best possible educational opportunities for America's youth. What they are lacking, in many cases, is an understanding of what local schools need to do their jobs well. It is, therefore, up to the school leaders to communicate with, and reach out to, these individuals. This must be done, furthermore, through means that are more personal than mere written communications. Though older adults in your school community ought to receive written communications from you, they should be involved in the school in more personal ways as well.

## Intergenerational Programs in Schools

There are programs involving intergenerational relationships popping up all over the country in response to the need for involving older adults in our schools. In 1986, 100 national organizations that deal with people of varying ages formed Generations United. One of the goals of this organization, which involves such groups as the national Parent-Teacher Association (PTA), the National Education Association (NEA), and the National Council on Aging (NCOA), is the establishment of strong intergenerational programs in every single state. These programs get filtered down to our schools and lead to programs that involve older adults and students in meaningful, educational ways.

It is important to note that the involvement of older adults must be more than having them attend an annual Grandparent's Day. Though Grandparent's Day is an important event at many schools and does a great deal toward bridging generation gaps and positively involving older adults, it is quite limited in both its appeal and its effects on learning. Older adults must be involved more regularly through activities such as the following:

- ◆ *Computer Activities*: As part of a class, students can tutor older adults in computer usage and applications. This assists the older adults in learning important skills, while also providing a wonderful opportunity to assess the students' computer abilities and understandings.

- ◆ *Reading Tutoring*: Older adults can serve as volunteer reading tutors for students. This does not require sophisticated teaching skills, but can be as simple as having the older adult serve as a "listener" for a student struggling in reading.

- ◆ *Vocational Training*: Older adults can share their vocational expertise with students in a variety of ways. Not only will the students benefit from the expertise that an experienced worker brings, but they will also be able to compare/contrast different methods for accomplishing the goals of a job.

- ◆ *School Safety*: Older adults can assist as doorway and hallway monitors to help keep our schools safer. Borrowing from the concept of "bargain store greeter," this is a great opportunity for a retiree to be involved in the schools, while also giving the school another set of eyes to ensure that visitors are following appropriate school safety guidelines.

By following these and other suggestions, school leaders will earn the support of a very important segment of their external publics. At the same time, they will be providing their students with rich learning opportunities that they cannot get from a textbook.

# Presenting Students to the Community

It seems that every time members of the community watch students perform, read student publications, or view student creations they express delight and surprise that children can do things so well. More often than not, these people communicate their delight and surprise to other members of the community through word of mouth. Therefore, if schools provide more opportunities for members of the community to see the wonderful work students do, then there will be an increase in the amount of "good gossip" being spread throughout the community. This can do a great deal toward securing the kind of support and commitment from external publics that schools need and deserve.

Unfortunately, many school leaders squander opportunities to involve members of their school's external publics in presentations and exhibitions by students. They fail to understand the dividends paid by including and inviting all members of the community to such events as plays, musicals, athletic events, recitals, debates, art shows, and academic competitions. Community attendance at these events can show a great deal about a school's strengths, while also increasing the number of people attending in support of the children.

## Athletics

Athletic competitions provide many citizens with the only contact they are likely to have with the school. Attendance at athletic events in most communities is far greater than at any other singular school event, with the possible exception of commencement activities. Because of this, resources are often poured into athletic programs at a rate that troubles people involved in other student activities. However, because athletics have proven to be important to local communities, it behooves school leaders to pay attention to how they greet and treat the public at these events. Clean, comfortable athletic facilities, accessible concessions, and reasonable prices for the community are all important matters that school administrators must consider in evaluating how they present student athletic competitions to the public. Since public opinion of a school's athletic programs, fairly or not, often transfers to their opinion of the rest of the school, it is important that athletic teams look good, have presentable uniforms, and play with an acceptable code of conduct. A well-disciplined team often leads the public to assume that the student body is well-disciplined at school. A poorly disciplined team can leave members of the external publics believing that the school is a poorly disciplined place for students to learn.

## Plays

Dramatic productions and musical plays draw tremendous numbers of people to school in many communities. As is the case with other forms of student productions, the audience is often amazed by the quality of the productions put on by students. This is true of the performances themselves, but also extends to the quality of scenery and set design, and the creation of costumes. Students enjoy being involved in these types of theater productions because of the versatility of talents required. Students can participate in the creation of the program, in technical capacities such as sound and lighting, in various other production roles, or as performers.

Additionally, these productions provide wonderful opportunities to involve members of the community as more than mere spectators. Many productions allow opportunities for citizens to participate in making costumes, properties, and stage sets. The bottom line in evaluating plays as methods of involving and embracing external publics lies in the versatility of student skills they demonstrate and in their ability to involve members of the external publics in their creations.

## Other Artistic Endeavors

Many schools showcase student artwork, either as separate events or in conjunction with artistic endeavors like dramatic or musical productions. Once again, these opportunities often lead community members to feelings of awe and wonderment at the abilities of students. There is an assumption by many that if students can express themselves through their artwork, then there probably is at least some degree of transference to their academic work. In other words, to many spectators quality artwork is indicative of quality academic schoolwork.

Musical recitals and forensic exercises provide similar opportunities for students to show their talents and abilities to members of the school's external publics. In addition to generating feelings among community members that students have abilities even greater than they imagined, these opportunities provide students with the feedback necessary to increase their own sense of accomplishment and feelings of self-worth. Such opportunities really do provide win-win situations for students and community members alike.

## Academic Competitions

Events such as spelling bees, geography bees, and science fairs provide yet more opportunities to involve members of the school's external publics. Though there are shortcomings to these competitive events, they do assist in demonstrating to the public that our students are indeed academically well prepared. The risk that exists is that the students will perform poorly in front of the public, thereby unintentionally fueling any discontent that may already exist relative to the school's academic strength. However, this risk can be virtually eliminated if the school leaders have done their job communicating with the external publics on a regular, consistent basis, with honest appraisals of the strengths and weaknesses of the school's academic programs. In other words, we should be proud to showcase the academic ability of our students, even when that ability is not as great as that of a neighboring school community. As long as our students are being challenged to stretch beyond their innate abilities, then we should be proud of the results, whatever they may be.

## Be Forewarned

Although it is absolutely essential to involve members of all external public groups in school activities, school leaders must be forewarned that there is the risk of appearing to exploit children's talents in the name of public opinion. Again, the ability to understand your community is essential before delving too far into public displays of student talents. We can probably all think of school communities that rely too heavily on a winning football team. This becomes so important to the community that it outweighs all other school endeavors. Worse, when circumstances become such that the school can no longer provide a dominant, winning team, then the players become devalued. This can take a tremendous toll on a young person's psyche. It is, therefore, essential that a healthy balance exist between providing win-win opportunities for student athletes and the community to share in prideful competition and the unnecessary pressure that can be put on student athletes who feel that a victory on the field is their obligation to deliver.

The same concept holds true for all other exhibits of student talents and abilities. They must be done so that students can feel a sense of worth and can contribute in positive ways to the community. Including an audience must serve the dual purposes of providing support to students and involving the community in educational pursuits. When these ideals cease to be the goals and when students begin to be exploited for public relations gains, then school leaders must cease and desist such involvement immediately.

## Chapter Summary

♦ It is essential that school leaders identify all of the different groups that make up their school's external publics.

♦ Appropriate parental involvement has a tremendous impact on student achievement.

♦ Parents can be appropriately involved at school only if they really believe that they are welcome in the school.

- It is vitally important that school leaders do a better job of showing parents how they can be involved from within their own homes. Furthermore, all school personnel must value this type of involvement.
- There are many external public groups besides parents that require regular, purposeful communication as well.
- If school leaders identify and then involve key communicators, then they will find it much easier to engage in meaningful two-way communication with their external publics.
- Older adults, the fastest growing segment of our population, are very significant members of a school's external publics. Consequently, they ought to be communicated with and involved in school activities.
- Presenting student activities to the external publics is an important way to build understanding of and support for the school.
- There are cautions to consider before presenting students and their work to the public on a regular and consistent basis.

## Case Study Analysis

### That's Not What I Meant to Say

At the first PTO meeting in September, first-year principal Alonzo Lucas anxiously awaited the opportunity to address the parents in attendance. The first three weeks of school had gone very well, so Lucas expected a nice meeting with parents.

"I want to thank all of the parents in attendance for seeing to it that your children are prepared for school and on time each day, he began. Furthermore, I want to express my gratitude for the encouraging notes and phone calls that I have received since arriving here. This school is your school, and your voice will always be heard here. Parents are their children's first teachers, and you know what's best for your own children. Please know that I will never forget that."

The next morning, Alonzo Lucas received a phone call from Patty Thompson, president of the PTO. "Mr. Lucas," she began, "I want you to know how grateful all of us were to hear your words yesterday afternoon. As you know, a few of the teachers here are not very good, and we have always enjoyed the opportunity to let the administration know which teachers we wanted our children to have for the next school year. A few of us were concerned that you would end that policy, but after hearing you say yesterday that we know what's best for our children, we are all delighted that you seem to feel this policy ought to continue."

## Questions for Analysis

1. Should parents have a voice in who their child has for a teacher? If so, to what extent should their voice be listened to?

2. If Alonzo Lucas wishes to engage in meaningful dialogue with parents about this issue, how should he proceed?

3. Have any communication errors been made to this point? What are some potential pitfalls to anticipate in the future?

4. If you were Mr. Lucas, what would your first reply to Mrs. Thompson be?

# 7

# Improving Media Relations

"The media is only interested in reporting the bad things that happen in our schools." "Bad news sells newspapers. That's why they never write about the good things that we do in our schools." "The news media purposefully misquote us." "No matter how many times we call the newspaper to tell them of the good things we're doing, they never show up unless there's a problem." These are examples of the responses educators often give when asked about their relationship with the news media. It is clear to see that very few educators consider the news media to be their closest allies. In fact, in many cases the news media is seen as the enemy.

This chapter is designed to dispel what is often a great misconception about the news media and the important role it plays in maintaining positive, productive school–community relations. It is written to show that school leaders can help their schools in dramatic ways by refusing to adopt a defeatist attitude when dealing with members of print, audio, and video media. Finally, this chapter will demonstrate how school leaders can and should use the news media as an ally in spreading the good news about education. It all begins with a change in attitude, though. In order to cultivate positive relationships with individuals who report education news to your community, you must first accept that these individuals want to report events as accurately as possible. You must understand things from their point of view, and you must refuse to accept the negative feelings that so many educational colleagues have regarding the so-called media monster.

It may appear as though this chapter ignores those rare situations in which the media descends upon a school rapidly and in mass. These times, known as crisis situations, require even more skill and careful planning, for they do not allow educators to take time to think and craft a careful response. For this reason, they are omitted from this chapter and are, instead, the subjects of their own discussion in Chapter 10.

# All the News That's Fit to Print

Though there are some general guidelines that are applicable to relationships with a variety of news media sources, the focus here is on working with the press. Though our means of communication continue to develop and change rapidly, the newspaper business remains one of the major sources of information about schools that typical taxpayers receive. By following the communication tips suggested throughout this book, the best school leaders will give taxpayers in their communities many other means for receiving this information. However, as many studies continue to demonstrate, local newspapers remain a prime source of information about our schools. As many people believe, this will become even truer in the future as the number of taxpayers with children in our schools decreases. It is really quite simple. The astute school leader must develop skills for working with members of the print media in order to increase the likelihood that the information printed is accurate and beneficial to the community.

## When the Reporter Initiates the Contact

Being an effective school administrator is a difficult and time-consuming undertaking. As such, there are many occasions in which a newspaper reporter may contact the school leader at a very inconvenient time. This brings up a dilemma. If the busy administrator refuses to speak with the reporter, then the reporter may be forced to write a story with less than accurate information. If, on the other hand, the administrator agrees to speak with the reporter in the middle of a chaotic day, then the chance of the administrator speaking inaccurately increases as well. For this reason, it is vitally important that the administrator be open and honest in confronting this dilemma. Comments such as, "Gee Hannah, you caught me in the middle of several things that are demanding my immediate attention. Could I call you back later this afternoon?" are very appropriate and far better than saying, "I'm too busy to speak with you now." Although both comments deliver the message that the reporter caught you at a very inconvenient time, the first one demonstrates far more commitment to the importance of the reporter's questions than does the second one. It is perfectly acceptable to let news reporters know that you are extremely busy and unable to speak with them at the moment. It is unacceptable and unwise, however, to lead reporters to conclude that you do not think their questions are important.

After all, news reporters have legal rights to much of the information they ask for. Because school districts rely on public funds for support, newspapers have as much of a right to report news relative to schools as they do to report about any other government agency. Failing to recognize this and give reporters the information they desire has caused many school administrators unnecessary grief. In addition to the harm they have caused to the relationship between their school and the newspaper, these administrators have shown the public that they are dishonest and that they have some information to hide.

Sometimes, honestly telling a reporter that you are extremely busy at the moment but that you will call back later is not enough to delay the conversation, as you would like to. Again, it is important to try and understand the reporter's dilemma before rushing to judgment. The reporter may be facing a deadline and may, therefore, be in need of an immediate response. However, the question he or she needs a response to may be one that you want to ponder for a moment to ensure that you give the best response possible. This creates our second dilemma.

Because I am not overly astute at giving accurate, thoughtful answers off the top of my head, when I was a school principal I always liked to have a couple of minutes to formulate my response to a reporter's questions. Knowing that in virtually every instance the reporter's deadline was not so imminent that he/she could not afford me a few minutes, but that he/she rarely recognized this, I always instructed the office staff to respond to a reporter's telephone call in a manner similar to this: "I'm sure the principal would be pleased to speak with you. Though he is unavailable at the moment, I will give him this message and I assure you that he will call you back within a few minutes if at all possible. Could I tell him what your call is in reference to?"

Notice the polite tone of that response. It lets reporters know that the principal considers their telephone calls to be important. It promises reporters that returning their telephone calls is a top priority. Furthermore, and arguably of greatest importance, a response such as the one in the example above gives the principal time to thoughtfully formulate a response to the reporters' questions. Then, when the principal does return the telephone call, he/she is in much more control of the conversation than he/she would be if they had been caught off guard. The principal is now much more likely to give an accurate response and, except in the most extreme circumstances, the reporter is also likely to meet the imposed deadline.

An important caveat in being open and honest is to be sure that you deliver on what you promise. With this in mind, it is critical to remember that office staff members should be strongly admonished not to promise a return telephone call if the principal is expected to be occupied for a prolonged period of time. Making such a promise but then failing to follow through can be far more damaging to the school's relationship with the media than simply stating up front that the principal will be unavailable for a prolonged period of time. Simply put, if you or one of your staff members say you will return the telephone call, then you must do as you have promised.

A third dilemma that educators often find themselves in involves a newspaper reporter asking them a question to which they do not know the answer. This is obviously damaging in a situation in which the educator ought to know the answer, such as an incident involving a student injury while the educator in question was in charge. Sometimes however, the educator does not know the answer to the reporter's question because the reporter is asking the wrong person the question. An example would be if a reporter contacted a school principal to discuss the results of recent statewide standardized testing, but the principal had not yet received the scores. In some school districts there may be a delay between the time in which the central office administration receives information such as test scores and the time in which such information is passed on to the building-level administration. In a situation like this one, the building-level administrator could not possibly comment on the scores. This does not mean that the administrator should hide from the reporter's question. Instead, he/she must choose between a couple of options, all of which necessitate honesty and openness. Either the administrator can tell the reporter that they have not yet seen the scores but they will call the reporter as soon as they do, or the administrator can refer the reporter to an appropriate person at the central office who has already seen the scores. The specific response given depends largely on the school system's organizational structure, the wishes of the superintendent and board, and whether or not the communications plan is centralized, decentralized, or coordinated as discussed in Chapter 1. The significant thing to remember is that the reporter is entitled to a response.

## When the School Leader Initiates the Contact

Being proactive, that is taking initiative and not first reacting to situations, is almost always preferred over being reactive. Although it is obvious that many situations require a reaction from the school leader, many reactions can be avoided if the school leader is aware of everything that is going on around him or her and is proactive in dealing with situations before somebody else brings them forward. This concept or paradigm is obviously applicable in dealing with members of the news media. Of particular focus here, let us once again examine our dealings with newspaper reporters.

When asked to give advice to new or aspiring school administrators, I always instruct them to make contacts with local newspaper reporters and to learn their names so that they may be addressed in familiar, friendly terms. Remember, as mentioned earlier, all school leaders must begin looking at members of the media as friends. Local newspaper reporters perform a valuable service to your school's community. Additionally, because they have the power to reach so many people in the community with their words, it is more than reasonable to assume that everybody wants the reporter's words to be accurate. By establishing a friendship with reporters, the school leader is offering to assist them in making their words about the school as accurate and informative as possible. This requires a high degree of proactivity. A savvy school leader cannot afford to wait for the newspaper reporters to initiate contact so that they may be assisted in reporting accurate information. Because in many cases, school leaders do not treat the reporters as friends, reporters are not likely to call just to ensure that their information is as accurate as possible. Instead, if school leaders wish to have some influence over the information reporters have printed in the newspaper, then they must be proactive in communicating with reporters on a regular basis.

As mentioned earlier, many educators regularly complain that newspapers are only interested in publishing bad news. Additionally, these educators bemoan, newspapers never give coverage to the good things happening in our schools, even after we initiate the contact and inform them of positive events. Although there is some truth to the fact that bad news often helps sell newspapers, it is both inaccurate and unproductive to take strongly the position that newspapers are not interested in our good news. Instead of taking such a position, which is not likely to increase our schools' positive news coverage anyway, school leaders are well served once again to try and understand the position that reporters are in and the highly competitive business of selling newspapers.

With these points in mind, school administrators need to be proactive and contact their local newspaper every time something is happening in the school that they believe warrants press coverage. We must all understand that the media will be unable and perhaps unwilling to give news coverage to all of these events. However, by contacting them every time something newsworthy is happening in their school, administrators can dramatically increase the odds that their school will at least receive some positive media coverage.

## Involving Staff Members in the Process

With all of the tasks that school leaders must attend to, is it really possible to contact the media every time something newsworthy is happening in our schools? The answer to this question would most likely be "No" if the school leader were responsible for uncovering all of the newsworthy events and single-handedly communicating them to newspaper reporters. This is not the case if the school leader involves other members of the school community in this important aspect of creating positive school–community relations.

Teachers can be involved in this plan in the following way. Each month, the principal could pass out a form (see Exhibit 7.1) to teachers that asks them to list upcoming newsworthy events in their classroom. This form should then be returned to the principal by the specified date so it can subsequently be forwarded to local newspaper contacts. Depending on the arrangements made with the newspaper reporters, the principal or his/her designee may need to prioritize all forms received before sending them to the reporters. However, in my experiences, reporters are quite happy to receive the information in any way the school will provide it. These people really do want to write newsworthy stories. Newspapers with blank pages rarely stay in business!

---

### Exhibit 7.1. Newsworthy Events Reporting Form

Please list any events taking place in your classroom during the next month that you feel deserve local newspaper coverage. Include a brief description of the activity, the location, date, and time it will be taking place, and contact information so the reporter can easily reach you.

1. Event:

_____

_____

_____

2. Location:

_____

_____

3. Date and Time:

_____

4. Contact Information:

_____

---

A similar form could be given to other members of the school community. The kitchen staff could report such events as nutrition month, special menus designed by students, or human-interest stories highlighting one of the cafeteria staff members. The custodial staff could report on maintenance upgrades or students caught doing their part to keep the school clean and attractive. Finally parents, who are usually community members themselves and consequently read the local paper, can highlight upcoming PTO, PTA, or Parent Advisory meetings. The sky is the limit!

If it is up to the school principal to generate all of the information, as it is in many of our schools, then it is easy to see why such information does not get communicated to the news media. When the principal involves all members of the school community, then so much more information can be collected. People responsible for certain areas in the school think of news-worthy events that the principal may otherwise miss. Additionally, the responsibility for collecting information is shared among all stakeholders. This helps reinforce the point that school–community relations are everybody's responsibility. Finally, the news media will be flooded with more information than they can possibly print. This leaves them in control of reporting on events based on their newspaper space availability. They are much more likely to fill in a small part of a page with a nice picture and a caption if you have informed them in advance of the opportunity than they would be if they needed to discover it on their own. They are likewise more likely to devote a major section of their newspaper to an event that you informed them of in advance.

A key point not to be missed here is that this information should be sent to the newspaper at regularly scheduled intervals. Whether it is once a month or every other week is not as important as the fact that the newspaper reporters can anticipate the arrival of your information when planned. Nothing is more reassuring to the local education reporter than knowing there is a school they can count on regularly to send in newsworthy information. The early bird, as the proverb goes, gets the worm. Therefore, it is equally important to communicate events that your school has planned before other schools in your community send such information to the newspaper. Examples of occasions when this is important are the annual red ribbon campaign events and holiday concerts and pageants.

## The News Release

Another important tool in an administrator's school–community relations arsenal is the news release. News releases give newspaper editors all of the facts they need in a concise page that is easy and quick to read. As is the case with the form depicted in Exhibit 7.1, a goal of an effective news release is to make it as easy as possible for the reporter or editor to include the information you sent in an upcoming issue of their newspaper. Therefore, the news release should be written to include only the necessary information. Who, What, Where, When, Why, and How should all be addressed in the initial paragraph. Contact information, should the reporter or editor need to gather further information, should be clear and apparent.

For specific information about how the newspapers in your local community like news releases to look, don't be afraid to ask the editor. Usually, the editorial staff of a newspaper is more than happy to discuss information with school officials that will create a better match between what the school system sends to the paper and how the editors like newspaper copy to look. The following are a few generally acceptable rules:

♦ The story should be prepared on white or light paper, 8.5 by 11 inches in size.

♦ News releases should be typed, double or triple spaced, on one side of the paper.

- The date that the release is being sent and the date you wish it to be published should appear at the top of the page.
- The name of the person sending the news release, the person to contact for more information, and the school name, address, and telephone number should appear at the top of the first page.
- Copy should begin about one-third of the way down the page so that enough space is available for the editor to write in a headline.
- The news release should be limited to two pages unless unusual circumstances are present.

Exhibits 7.2 and 7.3 are examples of news releases. Notice how in both of these examples, all pertinent information relative to the event being discussed is shared in the initial paragraph. This serves the same purpose as the form in Exhibit 7.1, in that it gives the newspaper reporter enough information to decide if coverage of the event is warranted. It also serves other purposes, though. If written well, the news release can stand alone as a short filler, or it can be accompanied by a photograph for an even larger human-interest story.

## Communicating Through Local Radio

In many communities across this country, there are local radio stations. Whenever I travel, I like to tune in to these stations to learn something about the community I am visiting. When I do this, I rarely hear anything being broadcast about local schools in the area. The main exception to this is the advertisement of local high school sports competitions. One reason this may be so is that school leaders are often unaware of the methods for communicating via this exciting, widely tuned in to medium.

Listening to the radio does not require a very heightened level of attentiveness. Many people actually use the radio as a background device, similar to what is known as white noise. Reading the newspaper, on the other hand, does require a bit more consciousness on the part of the reader. In Chapter 8, the concept of three different kinds of readers, ranging from those who read every word at one end of the spectrum to those who briefly skim through pictures and headlines on the other, will be explored in greater depth. For now, let us suffice it to say that newspaper reading, for many individuals, requires more of the participant than does listening to the radio. Although it is true that most people listen to the

*(Text continues on page 130.)*

**Exhibit 7.2. News Release—Upcoming Event**

## "Home of the Lions"

# Rome Free Academy

500 Roaming Lane
Pride, PA 14352
(315) 336-0071
(315) 338-4260

Mr. Roaralot, Principal
Mrs. Kingofthejungle,
Asst. Principal
Mr. Wanna Playagame,
Activities Director

February 27, 2001

TO: Daily News Editor
FROM: Usta Roaralot, Principal
RE: News Release

Mr. Jeffrey Simba s sixth grade technology class will launch the rockets they have built Wednesday, March 14, to celebrate the completion of their unit on rocket science. The explosion of fun will take place on the school s football field from 1:30 PM until 3:15 PM

If you are interested in obtaining more information regarding this special event please contact me, either at school (315) 336-0071 or at home (315) 337-8235. You may also contact Mr. Jeffery Simba at school between 8:00 AM and 10:15 AM.

## Exhibit 7.3. News Release—Past Event

# Clover Middle School
2358 Flower Lane
Daisy, VA 25316
(804) 569-8590 fax (804) 569-8591
rosedaily@pasturek12.org

DATE: January 22, 2002
TO:     Media
FROM:     Rose Daily
RE: Media Release—Breakfast with Dr. Carnation
    For immediate broadcast/publication

Dr. Robert Carnation, superintendent of Pasture County Schools, served breakfast to the teachers and staff of Clover Middle School on Monday, January 21, to celebrate Clover's 100% participation in the county's United Way campaign. This is the fourth year in a row that Clover has had 100% participation.

Breakfast fare included eggs, bacon, fresh fruit, freshly baked cinnamon rolls, juice, and coffee. Dr. Carnation was assisted in the kitchen by other central office personnel.

\* \* \* \* \* \* \* \* \* \* \* \* \* \* \* \* \* \* \* \* \* \* \* \* \* \* \* \* \* \* \* \* \* \* \* \* \* \* \* \* \* \* \* \* \* \* \* \* \* \* \* \*

For verification or additional information, please contact Rose Daily during school hours, 7:30 AM to 3:30 PM.

radio with a different level of awareness than they employ when they read newspapers, the fact is a vast majority of Americans tune in to radio broadcasts on a daily basis. For this reason alone, radio is a medium for communication that school leaders ought to pay attention to.

## Spreading the Good News

One way in which school leaders utilize the power of radio is as a means for sharing upcoming school events with the community. Holiday concerts, schoolwide fundraisers, academic fairs, and athletic competitions are just some of the events that can be broadcast through radio. Most radio station program directors are more than willing to air announcements of these events at no cost to the school district. This is particularly so with radio stations that market themselves as being voices of the community. Check with your local radio station program director regarding their particular policies for airing these announcements.

## Public Service Announcements

Public service announcements, similar in their intent to commercials, are short pieces designed to inform and sometimes persuade the public to feel or act in a particular way. Most radio stations, much like they do with less formal announcements like those mentioned in the preceding section, will air public service announcements written by local school districts free of charge.

Public Serve Announcements (PSAs) can be used for the following purposes:

- To inform the audience about a particular idea or belief of the school community
- To conduct a campaign to generate understanding and/or support of a project requiring community support or participation
- To advertise an event honoring educators, such as American Education Week
- To highlight a school program or series of programs

When writing a PSA, it is important that it be written exactly the way it should be broadcast. Because the radio announcer will most likely be reading the PSA over the air in the precise way it was written, it is wise to read PSAs you have written yourself to see how they sound. Practicing with an audience, even if it consists of one loyal advisor, is excellent advice. PSAs are rarely edited by radio station personnel before they are read over the air.

PSAs are similar to news releases in that they contain pertinent information (Who, What, Where, When, Why, and How). It is not as critical that these things are addressed at the very beginning though, as is the case with a news release. This is because the tone of a PSA should be conversational. A conversational tone permits the writer to exercise a little bit more poetic license, making the PSA sound more like it is part of a conversation than a quick, to-the-point news release.

The most effective PSAs are written in simple sentences, free of jargon. The most important information, such as dates, times, and contact people, should be repeated more than once in the announcement. It is also wise to write more than one PSA about the same event, each one of a different length than the other one. Giving a radio station a 10-second PSA and a 30-second PSA about the same event, for example, increases the likelihood that they will have an opportunity to use at least one of them. Only sending them a 30-second announcement greatly diminishes your chances of having it read, particularly if the station has only 20 seconds of free air-time in which to make the announcement. To assist in determining the length of your PSAs as you begin writing them, use these approximate numbers of words:

- 10-second PSA: 25 words
- 20-second PSA: 45 to 50 words
- 30-second PSA: 55 to 75 words
- 60-second PSA: 130 to 150 words

Exhibits 7.4 and 7.5 are examples of PSAs of varying length. Notice that both of these examples are double-spaced, typed in all uppercase letters. This is one additional step that makes PSAs easier for the radio announcer to read.

## Exhibit 7.4. 10-Second PSA

ON WEDNESDAY, DECEMBER 11, AT 7:30 PM, HARRISON

ELEMENTARY SCHOOL, LOCATED ON SYCAMORE

STREET, WILL PRESENT ITS ANNUAL HOLIDAY PRO-

GRAM. THE EVENT IS OPEN TO ALL COMMUNITY MEM-

BERS.

**Exhibit 7.5. 30-Second PSA**

ON WEDNESDAY, DECEMBER 11, AT 7:30 PM, THE STU-
DENTS OF HARRISON ELEMENTARY SCHOOL WILL PER-
FORM THEIR ANNUAL HOLIDAY PROGRAM. THIS
YEAR'S PROGRAM, ENTITLED "THIS IS OUR STORY,"
WILL INCLUDE A SPECIAL VISIT FROM SANTA CLAUS.
THE EVENT, SURE TO PUT ALL WHO ATTEND IN THE
HOLIDAY SPIRIT, IS OPEN TO ALL MEMBERS OF THE
COMMUNITY. HARRISON ELEMENTARY SCHOOL IS LO-
CATED AT 4562 SYCAMORE STREET, BETWEEN 2ND AND
3RD AVENUES.

## Lights, Camera, Action!

Though television is not routinely utilized in all communities, many school leaders have known the benefits of television for delivering messages to their constituents for some time now. These individuals have utilized the television medium for public service announcements, much like those broadcast via radio and for more personalized opportunities to be interviewed on the air. For the latter purpose, television cannot only be a powerful communication tool, but can also be one that requires careful preparation and attention as well. Unlike with radio and print media, in which all that is important are your words, on television, appearance is significant as well.

To enhance this point, consider what we already know about nonverbal communication. As discussed in Chapter 4, most of what we communicate is done through nonverbal means. Therefore, it is critical that school leaders are highly aware of their nonverbal behaviors during a television interview. Though the message you are attempting to communicate may be a good and worthwhile one, negative nonverbal communication can severely inhibit its communication. This is especially true if the television personality conducting the interview is respected and admired by the public. In these cases, establishing positive rapport with the interviewer and appearing comfortable in his/her presence is critical. Because viewers trust the interviewer, they are much more likely to trust and be receptive to somebody whom they see as a friend of the interviewer.

Maintaining an open posture, as discussed in Chapter 4, will help to create the appearance that you are open and honest. Again, this is not suggested as a gimmick. You probably are a very open and honest person. Because so much is communicated through nonverbal means and because so many television viewers may not be at all familiar with you before they see you on the air, the suggestions made by your nonverbal gestures become that much more important.

Consider for a moment the presidential debates from the 2000 presidential election. Much of the public opinion about the two candidates generated by these debates was based, at least in part, on their nonverbal behavior. These behaviors became the parody of many late night comedians and comedy shows, such as Saturday Night Live. Al Gore was depicted as being smug and condescending, whereas President George W. Bush was shown to be confused. These descriptions of the two candidates may have been entirely unfair. However, in the television arena it's not just what you say, but how you say it that matters.

It is equally important, as is the case with PSAs, that the tone of your responses appear conversational. To calm nerves, many people decide that it would be best for them to read prepared statements. However, to the television viewer, this is considered impersonal. Television is a very personal medium. It is best to find other ways for relaxing and to respond to questions in a conversational tone. This is not to imply that it is unwise to prepare responses to questions that you expect to be asked. The reverse is actually the best advice. Just do not read your response verbatim; this will enable a conversational, less formal tone to be maintained.

When considering the tone of your response, do not ignore your vocal tone and intonations. A monotone voice will almost guarantee that viewers will tune out. A voice with enthusiasm and appropriate vocal inflections, on the other hand, will be far more likely to hold the viewer's interest. When you add some volume behind your voice, it gives the impression that you really believe in, and mean, what you are saying. This dramatically increases the likelihood that other people will believe in your message.

The old saying that you never get a second chance to make a first impression is worth acknowledging here. The first impression television viewers have of you will often be their lasting impression. Therefore, when asked a question, make sure that you are able to get to the main point of your response within 15 seconds, or preferably within 10 seconds. That is often all the time the viewer will allow you before deciding that you really do not know what you are talking about. Continuing along the lines of making a positive first impression, consider very carefully what you wear for a television appearance or interview.

## You Look Marvelous

Although it may not be fair to judge a book by the appearance of its cover, many television viewers will judge you, at least in part, based on your personal appearance. Consider the following advice, offered by the National Association of Broadcasters:

- Wear suits or dresses of soft, medium colors. Avoid sharply contrasting patterns and colors.
- Keep jewelry simple and uncluttered.
- Men may require a little powder on a bald head, or if their skin is exceptionally oily.
- Women should avoid heavy makeup and the overuse of lipstick.
- To relax throat muscles and nerves before going on air, participants should yawn or stretch their body as they would if they were tired.
- Avoid unnecessary movements or gestures. These may attract the attention of the viewer and distract from what is being said or done.
- Move more slowly than normal—quick hand and body movements are difficult for the camera to follow.
- Also look, listen, and speak to the person conducting the interview. An exception would be if you have a key point to say directly to the viewing audience. In that case, it is appropriate to look directly into the camera.
- Resist the temptation to look at yourself on the TV monitor in the studio. This can be very distracting to the viewer.

While fashions may change and what is out of style one day may be all the rage the next, the suggestions above are far more timeless. Though it is perfectly acceptable to acquiesce a bit to current fashions, it is unwise to deviate much from what is customarily acceptable as a more conservative form of dress. It is important to note also that it wise to get additional information about what types of clothing are appropriate for the market in your area from the program director of the television station conducting your interview or coordinating your appearance. Exhibit 7.6 summarizes key points to remember when making television appearances.

---
**Exhibit 7.6. Eight Keys for
Successful Television Appearances**

---

1. Dress neatly and in soft, medium colors.
2. Sit up straight and do not squirm in the chair.
3. Enunciate clearly; do not hurry through your responses.
4. Avoid all educational jargon.
5. Speak in simple, straightforward words and sentences.
6. Look directly at the person interviewing you unless you look at the camera to make a point directly to the audience.
7. Be enthusiastic, pleasant, and positive.
8. Act naturally. Remember, you are not playing a role.

---

## Do Not Feed the Monsters

Far more often than not, the media is not the enemy. Instead, they are a collection of responsible individuals charged with keeping the community informed about our schools. Since we all care so deeply about our schools, we probably want the public to be very well informed about what we do and how we do it. Remember this always when dealing with the media and you will find your dealings to be far more pleasant than if you approach the media adversarially.

This being said, there are certainly times in which members of the media do not behave well and act as the monsters many educators claim them to be. Because it is difficult to ever completely change another person's behavior, we are wise to simply learn how to deal with this monstrous demeanor. In attempting to do so, ask yourself the following question: "How can I tame the media monster so that my school and its accomplishments are represented fairly and accurately to the community?"

### Be Proactive

When thinking of the role proactivity plays in successful school–community relations, we often focus on concepts such as "taking initiative," "not reacting," and "being forward thinking." Each and every one of these ideas is a powerful and important aspect of proactive behavior. As such, school leaders are prudent to incorporate them into their daily interactions with the media and with everybody else in their school communities. However, being proactive in all of its forms involves even more than these ideas. Being fully proactive, that is, devoting ourselves to a true manifestation of the meaning of proactive, does so much more in assisting educators who are forced to deal with the occasionally monstrous media.

In *The 7 Habits of Highly Effective Families,* Stephen Covey speaks of a time many years ago, when he came upon a paragraph that profoundly influenced his understanding of the concept of proactivity:

> Between stimulus and response, there is a space. In that space lies our freedom and power to choose our response. In our response lies our growth and our happiness. (Covey, 1997, p. 27)

If we examine this paragraph in light of the stress created when we are forced to deal with monstrous media members, it ought to become clear that the resulting stress we experience is a direct product of the choices we make. So, in order to deal effectively with the media and tame the monster when it rears its ugly head, educators must make good use of the *space* that Covey refers to.

Educators cannot control the attitudes and behaviors of the people they encounter on a regular basis. Nor can they control the ill-timed questions that may come from the media. They have complete control, however, of how they choose to respond to these stimuli. The freedom created by this choice ought to empower educators, not stifle them. For those who aspire to educational positions of leadership, as readers of this text most likely do, the imperative to be empowered is that much greater.

There is an old saying that you attract more flies with honey than you do with vinegar. When the media is behaving in a monstrous way, it may appear as though vinegar is running through their veins. Remembering that you have the choice to respond with honey and not the vinegar you have been fed is one more example of the power of proactivity.

Finally, to conclude the sermon about proactivity, a sermon that ought not be taken lightly, I ask you to examine one more reason why proactivity is a great aid in taming the media monster. As a school leader, you will undoubtedly experience moments where you will feel as though you have truly been attacked. Some of these moments, though we expect them to be less frequent, may come at the hands of the media. In their quest for a story, the media may lash out at you and bite like a snake. The human impulse in such instances is often to bite back. A proactive person resists this temptation, because he or she knows that biting back will only make matters worse. Remember, it isn't the snake bite that does the serious damage; it's chasing the snake that drives the poison to the heart. Therefore, do not chase after individuals who cause you to feel angry. Take the bite, and move on.

## We All Make Mistakes

Despite the best efforts of the members of the media and the school administration, there will be times when errors are made in news reports.

These are not opportunities to say, "I knew those media people were out to get me"! They are, instead, times to contact the errant reporter and inform him/her of the mistake that was made. Good news reporters do not like mistakes to appear in their news stories any more than we like mistakes in our work. By making a personal contact to inform the reporter of the error, the wise administrator increases the likelihood that the error will be corrected and that future errors will be avoided at all costs.

---

## Showcase

Following a school board meeting, the local newspaper introduced its article with a header that stated: "Haney looking to curb summer school classes." A review of the tape recording of the meeting verified that my report to the school board emphasized the need to complete an assessment of the summer programs to determine if some summer school programs were having a negative impact on enrollment during the regular school year. After consulting with the school board president, the determination was made to use the opportunity to strengthen relations with the editor of the newspaper rather than belittle the staff writer. We also shared the official minutes with the editor of the newspaper who acknowledged that the headline could leave the wrong impression. He asked me what I wanted him to do, and my response was to inform the reporters that they could call me at the office or at home to seek clarification or obtain additional information whenever the need arose. The decision to act in a positive manner paid off. Relations between the school district and newspaper strengthened; numerous times after that incident the editor wrote editorials supporting school board decisions.

*David W. Haney, former Superintendent, Jamestown, ND, now,*
*Assistant Professor,*
*North Dakota State University*

---

## Parting Shots

The media, regardless of the demographics of your particular school community, are important parts of your community as a whole. This is true whether we enjoy positive relationships with them or not. Therefore, the best advice, followed by thousands of positive, proactive school leaders across this country, is to embrace the media. Getting along with, respecting, and valuing the media can take school leaders far toward their quest to communicate positive things about their schools to the rest of their community. This is not to say that the media should not be admonished when they behave inappropriately. To the contrary, as leaders in the community, educators, particularly administrators, have an obligation to inform the media when they are out of line and are failing to accurately assess situations and provide the community with factual information. It is imperative, however, that school leaders perform this role in a manner that builds bridges and strengthens relationships. There are communication techniques and directives throughout this text that, if taken to heart, will assist educators greatly in this regard.

Understand that different types of media require different techniques and methods for successful communication. Although all media in your community share a common obligation to serve the community as providers of information, the differences between print, radio, and television are great. As such, school leaders need to practice unfamiliar tasks like writing news releases, crafting PSAs, and preparing for interviews. Honing your skills in these areas will benefit you greatly as you ascend to even greater leadership roles within education. Do so while employing and adopting an attitude that the media is an ally. This is arguably the single best piece of advice in taming the media monster.

Finally, consider the dozen helpful tips from Ordovensky and Marx (1993). These 12 tips are alluded to throughout this section. Enumerated here, they underscore many significant points to remember. School leaders who utilize these tips will certainly enhance their school's relationship with the media.

1. Get to know the members of the media on a first name basis.
2. Be readily available to reporters. Return telephone calls promptly.
3. Be honest, sincere, and straight in giving reporters the facts. Protect your credibility.
4. Extend reporters the same courtesies as you do other visitors.
5. Avoid educational jargon.
6. Be helpful, but don't suggest how the reporter should report the story.
7. Make the faculty, staff, and students available to reporters. (If students' names or photographs are to be used, be sure to obtain the parents' permission first.)
8. Give the media advance notice of newsworthy events.
9. Piggyback stories when possible. Pointing out another story besides the one the media are there to cover may pay off in an additional story being reported.
10. Nothing is ever "off the record."
11. Never ask the reporter to show you the story before it is published.

12. Take the time to say "Thank You" when your school gets good coverage.

## Chapter Summary

♦ The idea that the media, as a whole, is only interested in communicating negative news about our schools is a grave misconception.

♦ A paradigm shift is needed to allow educational leaders to begin viewing members of the media as allies.

♦ In dealing with newspaper reporters, honesty really is the best policy.

♦ Much of the information that reporters request about our schools is information that they are entitled to have by law.

♦ Regularly sending information about school events to the newspaper in forms such as news releases can dramatically increase the likelihood that your school will receive increased press coverage.

♦ Communicating via radio is a rarely used, valuable tool for informing the community about your school.

♦ As with news releases, writing public service announcements requires skills that any educator can strengthen through practice.

♦ It is vitally important to consider body language, dress, and appearance while being interviewed for television.

♦ Educators must be proactive in dealing with any members of the media.

♦ Sometimes the media can be like a monster. Strong human relations skills and increased proactivity can tame this media monster.

# Case Study Analysis

### I Think It's True What They Say About the Squeaky Wheel

"You're just going to have to face it," teacher Sandra Miller said. "Even if you are the greatest principal in the state, you can't perform miracles. Locust Valley Elementary School has always gotten more press coverage than we have. There's no reason to think it will ever change."

As principal of Brownsville Elementary School, you fear that Ms. Miller may be right. For the past four years, you have tried diligently to lead Brownsville to greatness. Test scores had improved each year, parent involvement was at an all-time high, and your staff and students seemed more than content. Why hadn't the press noticed?

As you ponder this, Superintendent Shirley appears in your office doorway. Superintendent Shirley never visits the schools. "What is he doing here, and what have I done wrong," you wonder. The superintendent breaks the silence.

"I want to begin by telling you how pleased I am with the progress you and your staff have made here at Brownsville. You all should be very proud of your accomplishments. I am concerned however," Superintendent Shirley continues, "about the public perception of this school. It seems that every morning when I pick up the newspaper, I see a story about Locust Valley. Why can't I see a picture of a Brownsville student staring back at me each morning? Then maybe the rest of the community would know what a good place you've got here. Do you realize how important it is that we look good to the community?"

## Questions for Analysis

1. What would be your initial response to Superintendent Shirley?
2. Describe steps you would take to increase the media coverage at Brownsville Elementary School.
3. What role could teacher Sandra Miller play in your plan for improving media coverage?
4. Would Superintendent Shirley have a role?
5. How would you assess the degree to which your plan was successful? How would the success become known to Superintendent Shirley?

# 8

# Putting It All on Paper

As previous chapters have illustrated, a great deal of written communication is essential in all successful school–community relations plans. Because of the size of some schools and/or school districts, and as a result of the busy, often hectic schedules of many school employees and constituents, much of what is communicated is done so in writing. An important skill for a good school administrator, therefore, is the ability to clearly articulate one's thoughts through the written medium.

However, a pitfall that school administrators can fall into exists because of the many audiences that comprise a school's internal and external publics. Great attention was paid to the importance of communicating internally and externally in Chapters 5 and 6. The focus here, therefore, is on writing for all of these different audiences. Because so much is communicated through writing, it is absolutely essential that the school administrator develop the skills to distinguish between the abilities and interests of these various audiences. The result of such skill development will be communication that reaches the intended audience in a manner appropriate for their understanding.

## Three Kinds of Readers

Essentially, we can classify people that read our written communications into three groups. Although variations certainly exist among those grouped into the same classification, the general behavior characteristics apply. It is important that these three kinds of readers are considered whenever we craft any written communication for distribution. Although specific attention will be paid to particular design elements of our written communications later in the chapter, the focus here is on the essential components for reaching all three kinds of readers.

### The 20-Second Reader

The 20-second reader devotes less than one-half minute to reading our written communication. Unless this individual is a graduate of Evelyn Wood's speed reading course, he/she will never be able to read everything in a several-page school newsletter. Because of this, the newsletter or other school publication must be designed to maximize the 20 seconds that we have this reader's attention.

The 20-second reader looks at no more than headings, titles, and pictures. With this in mind, care must be taken to develop headings, titles, and pictures that capture the essential ingredients of the story. Additionally, attention must be paid to the font, size, and style in which headings and titles are written. They must appear to jump off of the page to prevent the 20-second reader from having to spend time searching for them. Twenty seconds can go by quickly. We cannot afford to lose any of that precious time as the reader searches for headings and titles.

With pictures or other graphics, they too must clearly depict that which we intend to be depicted. Far away group photographs, for example, take too long to process. Pictures and graphics must, therefore, be kept simple while also doing a good job of representing the main ideas of the story.

## The Newspaper Reader

The newspaper reader goes through our written communications in much the same way as the typical person reads his or her morning or evening newspaper. That is, this reader glances at titles and pictures and then reads a little bit of some stories and all of those that really interest him/her.

For this reader, many of the same design elements necessary for the 20-second reader also apply. This reader also does not like to search for information. Because this reader does tend to glance at each story, it is important that the opening paragraph of each item grabs the reader's interest. Remember, this person will read the full text of some of our articles. The title, opening paragraph, and accompanying picture(s) will do a lot to determine which stories this reader chooses to pay close attention to.

With this reader in mind, those stories or reports that you want read the most must be made the most interesting. Though this seems obvious, positioning these stories in prominent locations, such as the left hand column on the front page, will help draw attention to them. It is essential to write the stories with an irresistible opening that leaves readers needing to read on to get the information they need.

## The Novel Reader

The novel reader will devour our written communications in much the same way as he/she devours a favorite novel. That is, this reader will proceed through the newsletter or other school publication from cover to cover. This person wants to miss nothing so, in many ways, he/she becomes the easiest audience to write for.

This is not to say that the novel reader is not influenced by design elements, though. Quite the contrary, this individual, though he/she may read every word, will determine the importance of a newsletter story based on the prominence it appears to be given in the publication. This reader will also look at pictures and will make determinations of the quality of the school publication based on these and other design features.

Because the novel reader will read every word of your written communication, this reader may, in some cases, become your biggest critic. A mistake may slip past the 20-second or newspaper reader. Mistakes are unlikely to elude the watchful eye of the novel reader, however.

## Does Impressive Language Make the Impression You Desire?

A major complaint that many parents have about the written communication they receive from their child's school is the overuse of educational jargon. Too many educators flood their writing with this professional jargon that is unclear and unimpressive to the targeted audience. This is done for the wrong reason, in many instances. Though there are certainly times to appropriately use professional educational terminology, too many educators are using it to show their professionalism to a public that they think already questions it. In thinking back to the results of polls like those illustrated in Chapter 1, this fear that the public fails to see us as professionals is largely unfounded. Nevertheless, many educators refuse to believe this, and, thus, they mistakenly believe that by using educational jargon with the public, they will get the professional respect they yearn for.

School administrators have an obligation to demonstrate to their staffs that respect is earned through actions and behaviors. The overuse of terminology that is unknown to the public creates an image that the educator is unapproachable and unable to communicate effectively. Regularly communicating with the public in terms that are appropriate to the audience will have the opposite effect. The school leader must demonstrate this understanding by creating written communications that are free of jargon and appropriate to their intended audience. In this way, they are more apt to earn the respect they desire because of the public's perceptions that they are approachable and skilled in communications.

## Showcase

Principals are incredibly busy people. Probably no one in the school system is more overburdened than the building administrators. Their tasks are myriad and diverse. They are constantly on center stage. Everything they say, do, and write is observed, reacted to, and scrutinized by their public .While their actions and statements are always subject to public response and analysis, only their written documents become part of a very public record. Principals need to do all they can to guarantee that they have done all they can to prevent their writing from coming back to haunt them at a later time. Principals cannot avoid writing, so they must make sure that their writing will present them in the best possible light. Writing clearly, simply, concisely, and correctly should enable the principal to communicate with authority, humanity, and pride.

*Dr. India Podsen, former Assistant Principal, Lindle Middle School, Smyrna, GA, now Associate Professor, North Georgia College and State University, and author of Written Expression: The Principal's Survival Guide*

## The School Newsletter

One of the most frequently used forms of written communication created by school administrators is the school newsletter. Though the frequency of distribution may vary from one situation to the next, it is a wise idea for all school principals to publish newsletters on a regular basis.

When properly written, the school newsletter becomes an essential public relations tool. Not only is this so because of the information a newsletter provides, but also because the school newsletter can serve as a great source of goodwill. The principal, through the newsletter, provides information about school events that parents will find essential. As a goodwill gesture, the principal can also use the newsletter as a forum for parent organizations, business partners, community groups, and media outlets to provide information relative to their work within the school community. Not only does this create feelings of goodwill, but it also increases the likelihood that members of such groups will regularly read the newsletter. The first objective of any written communication ought to be that the intended audience reads it. Any steps that can be taken to ensure that newsletters are read, therefore, should be attended to.

Because the school newsletter is such an important information instrument for parents, great care must be taken in its design. The first step in such designing is for the school administrator to understand the many uses of the newsletter in order to maximize its effectiveness. Many school leaders agree that the school newsletter is an important instrument to:

- Build support for the school and its programs
- Give all stakeholders accurate information
- Increase parental and community involvement, participation, and attendance at school functions
- Inform all community members of the important role that the school has in improving the overall community
- Showcase the many educational endeavors that students and staff are engaged in at the school
- Give parents advice and assistance regarding how to best help their children academically

There are many other reasons for using a school newsletter, as well. Probably the most significant one is that a regularly scheduled newsletter is, in many instances, the only recurring communication that the school principal has with many parents. Although the more difficult parents may be frequent visitors to the principal's office, the majority of parents never speak in person with the school principal. This majority comes to depend on the school newsletter as an opportunity to get to know the principal.

Further, as most parents do view the principal as the educational leader of their child's school, the newsletter becomes the leader's way of saying what the most important information about the school is. With students having contact with different teachers and varying school subjects and programs throughout the course of a school day, the information coming home to parents may, in some cases, become overwhelming. It may be difficult for some parents to sort out what is most important. When the principal sends home a newsletter, however, then parents can believe that the information contained in this publication is the most important information that the school has to communicate with them.

The above paragraph leaves a great deal of responsibility at the feet of the principal in designing a newsletter. Therefore, a carefully planned, well thought out, appropriately written newsletter is one of the most important ways that a principal communicates with the public. Care must obviously be taken in creating one.

The first thing to consider after deciding to write a newsletter is how your messages will be communicated with the three kinds of readers discussed earlier. This will surely lead to an examination of the newsletter's layout. The number of columns of type, the font used, the positioning of pictures or other graphics, the wording of headlines, and the paper size are some of the decisions to be made. The variables in each of these are discussed below.

## Columns of Type

Most school newsletters are produced on 8.5- by 11-inch paper and use only one column of type which extends across the entire page. The reason for producing the newsletter in this manner has little to do with a belief that it may be the most appealing way and a great deal to do with ease of creation. However, for the most professional appearance, school leaders should strongly consider adding a second column. A single column that extends across an entire page is considered by many to be too wide for people's eyes to follow comfortably.

## Font Size and Style

Generally, the minimum font size used should be 10-point. While 11-point and 12-point are easier to read and enjoyed by many people, 10-point font obviously allows more words to fit on a page, thereby reducing production expenses. Once the font size falls below 10-points, however, the message becomes difficult for some constituents to read. Ignoring this can put the newsletter creator at risk of producing something that nobody is able to read. While it is acceptable to use a boldface type style to accentuate important words or headings, italics should be used sparingly, if at all. While italics do look attractive, as is the case with small font size, italicized print is too difficult for many constituents to read.

## Pictures and Graphics

The primary reasons for using pictures and graphics in school newsletters are to give information at a glance to the 20-second readers and to attract people to a particular story. With these reasons in mind, it is important to choose pictures and graphics with care to accomplish these goals. Careful placement of these items on the page is another important consideration. To make the newsletter more attractive, clear photographs and/or sharply produced graphics should be placed in a way that enhances a story while breaking up otherwise large blocks of text. A rule to remember here is to examine each page with the "dollar bill test." Simply put, if you lay a dollar bill in any manner across the newsletter page, it should always touch a picture, graphic, or headline. If this is not the case, then your text runs the risk of not being read in its entirety.

## Headline Wording

If we wish to create newsletters that people actually read, then they ought to be created with headlines that really "grab" the readers' attention. This does not mean that the wording needs to always be dramatic. In fact, the most important concept in headline wording is that it is accurate. Some stories lend themselves to exciting titles. For others, the significance of the headline lies in its ability to actually convey what the text is all about. In addition to the importance of using words that grab attention, the headlines should use a larger type size and should be placed in a manner that aids them in standing out.

## Paper Size

As cost invariably is an issue with newsletter production, typically school newsletters will use standard sized paper (generally 8.5 by 11 inches). In certain instances, such as those of great importance, using a non-standard paper size will increase the likelihood that the newsletter will be seen and read. Using different colored paper, though typically not advisable, also has a place for those newsletters that carry greater importance than those typically produced by the school administration.

# Newsletter Topics

There is no end to the list of topics that can be included in a school newsletter. As long as it is written in a style comfortable to most readers, the newsletter can be a forum for sharing a variety of thoughts and ideas. Exhibit 8.1 gives some examples.

---

### Exhibit 8.1. Topics to Include in Newsletters

---

- School activities, especially classroom activities.
- Opportunities for parents and others to help at school.
- Personality sketches of staff members.
- How staff development programs on early release days better prepare teachers—what specific activities they participate in on those days.
- Awards and special recognition of students.
- How the instructional program is meeting individual needs of students.
- Brief summaries of parent group business.
- Reminders—arrival and departure times, breakfast and lunch prices.
- Thoughts for the day.
- Poems or inspirational messages.

---

Exhibit 8.2 was created to give even more specific ideas for newsletter stories. These have been divided by months so that the school administrator can have ideas for each individual month while also being able to see the big picture in planning stories for the entire school year. As you can see from reading the list, there is certainly flexibility possible in moving story ideas from one month to another.

Although Exhibit 8.2 was created to give administrators a ready list of newsletter ideas, school leaders would be well served to adapt this list or create their own list to suit their school's uniqueness. Creating such a list during the summer months, before students and teachers arrive, is an excellent idea. In this way, the less hectic months for school administrators are used in preparation or planning for the busier months from September through May.

Again, it is important to remember that Exhibit 8.2 provides a framework to build upon. The school administrator could utilize the faculty and staff to generate ideas specific to a particular setting. It is amazing what a time saver it can be to have a list like this available when the school year begins. Though important events will happen on the spur of themoment and pieces of information will need to be communicated with little warning, the items on this list work very well for those times when there just does not appear to be any news.

## The Use of Technology

Without question, technology has changed and continues to alter the manner in which we communicate with our publics, both internal and external. Many administrators see technology as a blessing, as it has provided easy assistance to many publication tasks through the advent of better hardware and software. Other administrators curse the use of technology as it also has caused the bar to be raised in regard to the quality of publications that some people have come to expect. It has also troubled some administrators because of their own confusion and/or apprehension about utilizing technology to their advantage. For this reason, all school districts need to examine carefully the quality of any staff development or in-service training efforts they employ to assist all educators in taking advantage of technology's many benefits.

Invariably, written communication is easier in the twenty-first century than it was previously. The addition of software packages that virtually create professional-looking publications by themselves has made the task of designing newsletters with high visual appeal much easier than it used to be. Moreover, little technological proficiency is required to produce professional-quality publications. The ability to type and to access the desktop publishing program is about all that is required. Because the computer will do the rest, there really is no excuse for newsletters that fail to have visual appeal.

Technology assists educators in many other ways as well. In many communities, newsletter are no longer printed on paper and sent home.

## Exhibit 8.2. Newsletters: What to Include and When to Include It

**August**
New programs to be introduced
Summer maintenance

**September**
New employee profiles
School lunch nutritional information

**October**
Homecoming plans
November holiday plans

**November**
American Education Week plans
Capital improvements planned or underway

**December**
Holiday programs
Cold weather school closing information

**January**
Long-range planning activities

**February**
February holiday reminders
Spotlight on history curriculum (e.g., Black History Month)

**March**
Spotlight on Special Education
Budget needs for next year

**April**
Spotlight on school secretary
Bike safety tips

**May**
Graduation plans
Volunteer Appreciation

Instead, they are posted on the school's Web site for community members to access at their convenience. This is a tremendous cost-saving idea that also appeals to people who want to access school information at their own convenience. It backfires from a school–community relations viewpoint, however, if all members of the community do not have ready access to the school's Web site. Therefore, this is one more area in which school leaders must know their own school community and must make these decisions accordingly.

School Web sites are also very useful for staff members desiring to post important information to be viewed by masses. Many teachers post homework assignments, study guides, and other pertinent classroom news. Media specialists highlight special book selections and/or reading incentives. Food service specialists post menu changes and nutritional information. There is really no end to the uses of technology for communicating information that would otherwise be written the traditional way. Though the cost savings and freedom of access are benefits, many community members still rely on being kept informed through more traditional means. These people cannot be forgotten in our school–community relations plans. Instead, school administrators must ensure that they and their staff members communicate with community members through a variety of forums.

## The Student Report Card

Rarely thought of when we focus conversations on written communications from the school is the student report card. Ironically, however, it is the report card that is the most widely recognized and read communication that ever leaves our schools. Despite this fact, a large number of school administrators fail to consider the design of their school's student report card as an essential component of their written communication plan.

Poorly designed student report cards give very little written communication outside of a checklist of accomplished skills. Although checklists are far easier for teachers to complete than are narratives, the best report cards allow for some narration from the teacher. Knowing that a child recognizes numbers from 1 to 100 may be important for parents, but most parents also wish to know how their child performs, behaves, and adapts in the teacher's own words. This gives a greater sense of the child being important to the teacher than does a mark on a checklist.

However, in certain situations, such as those in which teachers must give report cards to 150 or more students, suggesting written comments accompany each one may seem unfair. There are other ways to accomplish providing more personal, specific information, though. By examining the design of the report card, school leaders may find that there are no places on the card that report assessments of study skills or interpersonal behavior, and these items can be added. Even when written comments are not possible or practical, adding items to an already existing checklist can be helpful.

Regardless, all school leaders ought to regularly examine their student report cards in light of one simple question: "As a parent, would I be satisfied with the depth and breadth of information this report provides?"

## A Personal Letter from the Principal

In addition to regularly scheduled newsletters, school principals are often required to write personal letters to parents, business leaders, or community members that inform, persuade, or thank them for some service or donation. Although few people enter the profession of school administration because of a desire to write, these written communications are important opportunities for principals to show professionalism and care or, on the other hand, amateurism and carelessness.

Though principals are finding themselves to be increasingly busy, it is essential that they, or somebody they trust, carefully proofread any written communications that leave the principal's office. Though there are mistakes that happen to everybody, spelling and/or grammatical errors imply a rushed, unprofessional job. Such work is probably not part of the image that the principal intends to portray.

The layout of the letter is another very important element that the principal must consider. Laying the letter out professionally, particularly if such layouts are taught as part of the school's curriculum, is essential. If the principal were unsure of proper layout, he/she would be wise to consult with teachers charged with teaching this skill. It would be very damaging to a principal's image if in the crafting of a letter he or she made habitual mistakes that students of the school knew better than to make. Beyond the issue of image, a letter that is laid out properly is much easier and more accessible to read than is a poorly designed one.

Exhibits 8.3 and 8.4 are two admirable sample letters from school principals. Exhibit 8.3 is a letter to parents that intends to inform the parents of improvements that their child has made academically. Exhibit 8.4 is written to the owner of a local business, thanking her for sponsoring a school dance.

It is important to note that teachers who send home personal notes to parents when appropriate also enjoy more positive relationships with them. Although newsletters from teachers are important means for regularly communicating with parents, as will be illustrated later in this chapter, a personal note goes a long way towards establishing bonds with parents.

*(Text continues on page 154.)*

**Exhibit 8.3. Letter to Parents**

# Woodview School

123 Woodview Lane
Anytown, USA

**Ima Goodfellow, Principal**
**Susie Sunshine, Administrative Assistant**

Mr. and Mrs. George Gray
456 Guardian Drive
Anytown, USA 12345

Dear Mr. and Mrs. Gray,

It is with great pleasure that I write to inform you that Clara has been making steady progress in Algebra class over the past four weeks. This is indicative, I believe, of Clara's increased focus and effort, your support and encouragement from home, and some great teaching from Mrs. Parker. If this great work continues, Clara will finish this academic marking period with a much-improved Algebra grade.

I am particularly pleased with Clara's attitude in class, as reported to me by Mrs. Parker. Mrs. Parker has told me on several occasions that Clara is attentive in class and willing to take risks at a much greater rate then was previously the case. I attribute this to Clara's newfound confidence and to the support system that she has come to count on. I extend my thanks to both of you for being such integral parts of that support system.

Please share your reactions to this letter with Clara. She has obviously benefited from your support thus far. My sense is that this support will continue to be important to Clara's future academic progress.

Sincerely,


Ima Goodfellow
Principal

---

**Exhibit 8.4. Letter of
Gratitude to a Local Business**

---

# Woodview School

123 Woodview Lane
Anytown, USA

**Ima Goodfellow, Principal**
**Susie Sunshine,Administrative Assistant**

Ms. Allison Brown, Proprietor
United Beverage Distribution
1127 3rd Avenue
Anytown, USA 12345

Dear Ms. Brown,

On behalf of the students, staff, and parents at Woodview School, I wish to express deep gratitude for your generous donation of 16 soft drink cases for last week's Homecoming Dance. Without the support of generous merchants like you, our students would not enjoy as many quality extracurricular experiences as they deserve. I can assure you that there are many people in this community who recognize this fact and appreciate your support.

The dance was a huge success. Over 300 students were in attendance and, I am happy to report, none of them went thirsty. In fact, the many bodies huddled together in our gymnasium raised the temperature a bit and caused your soft drinks to be an increased relief for all.

Thank you again for your continued support of our school. Your generosity will be acknowledged in our upcoming newsletter. As you may be aware, this newsletter is distributed to all residents within our school's boundaries. It is my sincere hope that this acknowledgment gives you the increased business you so richly deserve.

Sincerely,


Ima Goodfellow
Principal

---

## Words or Phrases to Avoid

Thus far, it has been clearly established that great care and thought must go into the design and creation of all written communications. This is true whether the communication is intended for a one-person audience or for mass distribution. The written word has lasting power. Although the spoken word is powerful in its own right, words that are written down can last much longer. Weeks after initially reading something you wrote, an individual can revisit your written communication, which is something he or she cannot do with verbal dialogue. For this reason, the specific wording must be carefully crafted to ensure that you are communicating as accurately and as effectively as you intend to.

Now, this can create an overwhelming feeling of responsibility that leads some school administrators to avoid writing things at all costs. However, because of the power of written communication, it is important that administrators do as much of it as possible. Many people feel that written words are more sincere. Still, other individuals, particularly those who recognize the importance of correctly wording something, understand that more time is often put into a written communication than is the case with verbal communication. Finally, because the audiences school administrators often find themselves communicating with can be difficult to reach via telephone or face-to-face communication, written communication is often the most efficient means we have at our disposal. It is also one of the best ways to reach large audiences.

If the responsibility of correctly crafting a written piece of communication seems daunting, then preplanning and practice become essential steps. Just as we instruct students to begin with thoughts, then to connect the thoughts with proper sentence and paragraph structure, and then to reread and share their writing with other people to avoid choosing inappropriate or ambiguous words, so should school leaders engage in the writing process.

Although using correct grammar, spelling, and punctuation is important, it is more important that the language used is not offensive to the audience. Many educators, usually with good intentions, have discovered the challenges created by choosing inappropriate and unflattering words to describe children and their behaviors. Although the message these educators attempted to communicate was important and accurate, choosing words that parents were offended by caused the messages to get lost. Exhibit 8.5 seeks to assist educators in avoiding some of these more common wording errors.

## Exhibit 8.5. Negative and Positive Expressions Helpful in Reviewing School Correspondence

| *Negative Expressions* | *More Positive Expressions* |
| --- | --- |
| Unclean | Exhibits poor hygiene habits |
| Bashful | Reserved |
| Troublemaker | Disturbs other students |
| Stupid | Can do better with help |
| Poor quality work | Below his or her usual standard |
| Liar | Tends to stretch the truth |
| Must | Ought to |
| Impertinent | Discourteous |
| Urgent problem | Lost opportunity |
| Failed | Failed to meet requirements |
| Show-off | Tries too hard to get attention |
| Profane | Uses inappropriate language |
| Uncooperative | Needs to learn to work with others |
| Steals | Takes without permission |
| Will fail | Has chance of passing, if… |
| Cheats | Depends on others to do his or her work |
| Doesn't care | Seems unmotivated |
| Dumb | Capable of doing better |
| Selfish | Seldom shares with others |
| Stubborn | Overly self-confident |
| Insolent | Outspoken |
| Below average | Working at his or her own ability level |
| Disinterested | Complacent |
| Clumsy | Awkward |
| Wastes time | Could make better use of time |
| Lazy | Gives inconsistent effort |
| Mean | Difficulty in getting along with others |
| Truant | Absent without permission |
| Messy | Could do neater work |
| Dubious | Uncertain |
| Rude | Often inconsiderate |
| Time and time again | Usually |

# Written Communication from the Classroom

If a school principal heeds all the advice in this chapter and regularly, purposefully, and accurately uses written communications with all stakeholders, only one step toward positive and productive school–community relations will have been taken. Although the principal may be the most influential adult in the school, it is the teachers and staff who are the most important. Therefore, these employees must understand all that the principal understands about written communication. This will only happen if the principal makes such understanding a schoolwide priority.

Partly through staff development, but mostly through modeling, the school principal must demonstrate to all employees that written communication is important. Beyond this, the principal must also ensure that staff members understand the different types of readers and the efforts that must go into written communications to appeal to all stakeholders.

Teachers, regardless of the grade level(s) or subject(s) they teach, should also have a plan for regular written communication with parents. Just as is the case with schoolwide communications, parents need to be able to count on the teacher to keep them informed. Many teachers, in a response to this edict, have developed their own classroom newsletters. Though teachers of primary grades tend to design these newsletters on their own, teachers of older children often enlist the help of the students in the newsletter's creation. In many high school classes, the newsletters are entirely student-created, with the teacher serving as editor-in-chief. Also common practice in many high schools are newsletters from grade-level sponsors or chairpersons of large departments.

Exhibits 8.6 and 8.7 illustrate two different classroom newsletters created by elementary grade teachers. The simplicity of the design shown in 8.6 allows the teacher to update it weekly with very little effort. The newsletter depicted in Exhibit 8.7 requires a bit more time and effort, but looks rather professional. For less frequent updates, this model would make a better impression. However, as a weekly newsletter, Exhibit 8.6 does an excellent job.

The newsletters teachers create can be very beneficial to parents, because they often contain information that children may inadvertently forget to communicate. In this regard, teacher-created newsletters also deliver the unspoken message that the school staff understands the importance of keeping parents informed. They further demonstrate that teachers believe so strongly in parent involvement that they are willing to devote the necessary time to creating these newsletters. This is a powerful message to parents who may otherwise believe that the school is not interested in their involvement.

*(Text continues on page 159.)*

**Exhibit 8.6. Weekly Classroom Newsletter**

# Watkin's Words

November 2, 2001

**Math:** The children are doing well with their multiplication facts. Please remember the weekly timed tests.

**Science:** Our classroom is spinning with planets. Come in and visit our hand made solar system.

**Language:** Please remind your children to keep up on their Read It! books. The whole class is working hard on winning the pizza party.

A big THANK YOU to all of the parents who helped make our Halloween Haunt a success. Nobody could believe the transformation of the school gym.

**DATES TO REMEMBER:**
Nov. 22–23 Thanksgiving Break
Dec. 4 Winter Concert

## Exhibit 8.7. Detailed Classroom Newsletter

May 11, 2001

# McCoy's News

**May is Filled with Many Exciting Events!!**

*Excellent!*

### Technology Night Tuesday, May 22, 2001
**6:00–8:00 PM**

As you know, next Tuesday is Our First Ever Technology Night. Please plan to attend for updates of the exciting things that have been happening in our building! There will be many displays of student learning through technology. Plus, you could be the winner of the FREE Dell Computer!! See attached registration form to volunteer your child's services as one of our class's docents. I need approximately 12 children to work in our classroom to highlight the learning that has taken place.

### Field Day Friday, May 25, 2001

Calling all volunteers! By now, you may be familiar with this routine. We need at least 4 parent volunteers to run stations on Field Day. Like always, this year promises to be filled with great activities. If you are unable to attend, we could still use your help in other ways. Donations of lemonade or juice, paper cups, peanut butter sandwich crackers and ice would be greatly appreciated. Thanks in advance for doing your part to make this a great year.

## Awards and Accomplishments

### Readers of the Year

Susie Blake and David Silva

### Most Improved Reader of the Year

Denia Grates

### Writer of the Year

Samantha Latke

**Reading Your Child's Accelerated Reader Student Record Report**

There are some key areas to watch on your child's weekly Accelerated Reader **Student Record Report**. The report should be **dated for the prior week**. It will list the **title**, the **percent correct**, the **points possible** and **points earned** for each book your child tested on that week. **Your child should check out, read, and test on enough books during the six weeks to meet his/her point goal. Use the weekly point goal as a guide.** Longer books may take more than a week to complete.

Newsletters, whether created by principals, teachers, or other staff members are essential components of a successful school–community relations plan. If regularly scheduled newsletters do not currently come from your school, then you would be well served to change this behavior promptly. Do not be concerned if your writing and publishing skills will limit the initial quality of your newsletter efforts. Most principals and teachers readily admit that the style of their newsletters has evolved over time. By heeding the suggestions in this chapter, anybody can produce a top quality newsletter for parents. Though you will improve with practice, the parents of the students you serve will appreciate your initial offering. The time to start is now.

## Communicating Via the World Wide Web

The use of the World Wide Web (Web) for academic pursuits has been understood since the infancy of the Internet. All across America, students are now connected to the Internet and are using it for a variety of purposes. Among those purposes are the following:

- To communicate with another class through e-mail
- To communicate with an expert or a significant person
- To gather data for use in a class project
- To follow an online expedition or trip
- To read works written by other children
- To read for information about current events
- To take a virtual field trip with their class
- To join an existing online project
- To create their own online project

As schools have increasingly infused usage of the Web into their curricula, they have begun to realize that the Internet can provide even more uses than purely academic ones. School leaders understand with increased frequency that the Internet can also be a powerful communication tool. As recently as 1990, the idea of schools communicating with stakeholders via the Internet was considered futuristic thinking. By 1995, there were still many schools lacking the capability and the staff to effectively use the Web for communicating with parents and the larger community. As this book goes to press, however, the Internet represents one of the most widely used methods school leaders employ for keeping all stakeholders informed and connected to the business of their schools.

According to a May, 2001, report from the United States Department of Education's National Center for Education Statistics, 98 percent of all public K-12 schools are connected to the Internet. This compares to 35 percent of K-12 schools that enjoyed Internet access back in 1994 (Cattagni &

## Showcase

I publish the Manteno Magic E-Mail Newsletter for the parents, students, and fans of our show choir Program. I started in 1998 with just 35 e-mail addresses from our students. The students without E-mail were partnered with an on-line student who would print a hard copy of the newsletter for them. Today, more than 85 percent of my families have access to e-mail, and parents are just as likely as students to read it. Teachers from across the country are also among the subscribers. When we compete, the judges record their oral comments onto audio tape. I summarized the judges' remarks and sent them in the newsletter. I try to explain what a judge has said and how it relates to our show concept. I also publish some of our press releases in the newsletter. I've even written short articles that answer frequent questions from parents or students.

*David Conrad, Music Director,*
*Manteno School District, Manteno, IL*

Farris, 2001). Although this data verifies the tremendous increase in connectivity experienced in our schools, it does not give an indication of how the schools are actually using this technology. What is clear though, is the fact that almost all school administrators now have at their disposal a very effective means of sharing information about their school with any and all of their publics.

One way in which school staff members use the connectivity of technology is by sending and receiving e-mail. It is common practice in many schools for teachers and administrators to use email as an internal communication tool. It is also becoming increasingly common for e-mail to be an external communication tool. The downside to this trend is that some school staff members forget to regularly check their e-mail accounts for messages. Although it has long been a habit to check for telephone messages, new users of technology often forget to be as diligent in checking e-mail. The result can be a frustrated public that is not getting answers as quickly as they should. A rule of thumb, therefore, should be to not advertise e-mail as a means to communicate with you if you are unwilling or unaccustomed to regularly check for and respond to messages.

School leaders who understand the need to provide information to their publics in as accessible a format as possible are using the Internet with increasing frequency. By creating a school Web site and updating it regularly, school leaders can, in effect, leave important information available for stakeholders to read and view at their convenience. As the American workforce evolves to include both parents often working different shifts, the ability to access school information at any time of the day via the Web becomes increasingly attractive. School Web sites have grown to be efficient sources for posting school calendars, lunch menus, important dates of school events, and stories, pictures, and audio/video clips of classroom activities.

## Points to Consider

Many of the same considerations for writing any materials that will be circulated to a school's publics are applicable to the creation of school Web sites. School leaders must again be cognizant and respectful of the reading styles and abilities of those who will be visiting the Web site. With this in mind, reminders for parents should be free of unnecessary jargon and should be designed with pertinent information easy to find. The different ways in which people read newsletters may also have applicability to the way in which people read the contents of a Web page. Headlines and pictures should, therefore, be chosen carefully and purposefully. Font size, style, and color should all be chosen with creating minimal distractions to readers as a primary goal.

Another point that is easy to overlook is the speed with which the user's computer will be able to access and download information from the school's Web site. For many home users, these speeds are far less than the speed with which the school's computers access the Web. Without having received a great degree of technological training, many school leaders mistakenly assume that the more photographs, videos, or multimedia elements they place on their school's Web site, the more attractive it will be to the viewing public. What happens instead, in many instances, is that the viewing public does not own computer hardware with the capability of opening these graphic-intensive Web pages in an efficient, timely manner. The result is often a public that is frustrated at the thought of ever accessing the school's Web site again. Therefore, it is of paramount importance that school Web sites be designed in a manner that increases, not decreases, their accessibility. In many cases this means that the school leader must opt for a simpler design. School leaders would always benefit from consulting individuals with expertise in Web page design before embarking on such a project alone. Many school districts have such people on staff for just this purpose.

Still another issue that is often overlooked is the fact that many school stakeholders do not have Internet access in their homes. Studies completed around the turn of this century (NUA Surveys, 1999; The Wirthlin Report, 1999) indicate that anywhere from 35 percent to 45 percent of U.S. households have Internet access at any given time. Trends indicate that this figure continues to rise, but it appears safe to assume that roughly half of the population in any given community is unable to access school information on the World Wide Web from the comforts of their home. Although this does not mean that school leaders should feel reluctance about using the Internet to inform their publics, they must remember that it is only one way to do so. The Internet provides a wonderful opportunity to inform people all over the world about the wonderful things happening in our schools. It is not poised to replace newsletters, telephone conversations, and most importantly, face-to-face encounters though.

## Chapter Summary

- In creating written communications, it is essential that you recognize the different types of readers likely to receive what you have written.
- The 20-Second Reader will glance at headings, titles, and pictures. Therefore, these items must be carefully placed and worded to convey essential information.
- The Newspaper Reader will treat your writing as he/she treats the newspaper. That is, this individual will glance at titles and read all or part of stories that interest him or her.
- The Novel Reader will read your communication from front to back. For this reader, your writing must contain minimal flaws.
- Principals and teachers ought to recognize the benefits associated with producing regularly scheduled newsletters.
- There are suggestions of topics to include in newsletters for any time in the school year. These should be interspersed with ideas and offerings unique to your school setting.
- Written communication should be free of the educational jargon that often turns many readers off.
- Student report cards are an often-overlooked form of written communication. Report cards should be examined to see if they communicate the information we intend in a clear manner.
- Principals and teachers ought to also remember the power of personal letters. Time spent writing personal letters can pay large dividends in the long run.
- The proliferation of new technologies in our schools enhances our abilities to create professional-looking, errorless publications. School leaders should, therefore, embrace these new technologies as powerful communication aids.

- Web sites and e-mail are quickly becoming normal, routine ways for schools to communicate with constituents. Care must be taken when utilizing these or any technologies.

# Case Study Analysis

## The Write Stuff

Having been chairperson of the high school English department for the past seven years, Cynthia Walker knew that written communication would be her strength as a principal. In fact, Cynthia had become so disgusted with the previous principal's lack of writing skill that she pledged to make quality written communication her trademark.

Cynthia got off to a great start in her new position. Teachers appreciated her understanding of the difficulties inherent in their jobs, students loved her, and parents were impressed by her organization and work ethic. The only negative comments Cynthia had received during her first semester as principal came from the few parents and staff members who stated that they missed the previous principal's frequent handwritten notes of praise.

As the year progressed, more complaints began to surface. Several parents stopped reading the principal's newsletters, claiming that the publications used language that was clearly meant to impress. These parents liked to be told things in terminology that they were familiar with. As one father put it, "We don't need to be reading news about the school that requires us to pull out a dictionary first." Cynthia dismissed comments like these as representative of the few individuals who had never learned to write properly. Pride in written communication, she reasoned, was something that this school needed.

It was Jean Harbison, new chair of the English department and one of Cynthia's closest friends, who finally came to Cynthia to give her guidance. "Cynthia," she began, "I think many of the teachers miss getting quick notes in their mailboxes, praising them for good efforts. Also, you ought to keep in mind that notes you send home are not candidates for the Pulitzer Prize. I think you need to lighten up, my friend. Some people are becoming a bit intimidated by your writing."

## Questions for Analysis

1. What do you think of Cynthia Walker's desire to improve the quality of written communication that comes from the principal's office?

2. Should principals and teachers create newsletters that meet the needs of the community or that set good examples? How does one arrive at the happy medium?

3. Is Cynthia failing to understand elements of praise and motivation? If so, how would you help her to understand them better?
4. If you were in Cynthia Walker's position, what next steps would you take to enhance written communication with your publics?

# 9

# Saying What You Mean– Meaning What You Say

A great deal of what constitutes school–community relations involves the spoken word and the internalization of it by other people. Earlier chapters have focused on the communication process and all of the potential for breakdowns at any point in the process. These chapters have also paid attention to the many different groups that constitute a school's publics. Some of the groups are considered "internal" groups because they spend the majority of their time within the school's walls. Still others constitute those publics that are "external" because most of their time is spent outside of the school's walls. These chapters have also focused on ways in which our writing can communicate effectively with groups and individuals, and on how important clear writing is to effective school–community relations.

The focus of this chapter is on the spoken word. As a great deal of the administrator's time is spent in spoken conversation, it is essential that administrators have a sense of behaviors and techniques that will enhance their ability to speak publicly. These behaviors will be useful in both individual conversations and in large group presentations.

## Telephone Etiquette

Though research (Fiore, 1999; Whitaker, 1997) does indeed support the notion that the most effective principals are out of their offices regularly, a fact of school administration is that there are many telephone calls that must be taken or returned. Oftentimes, we know, these telephone calls occur at very inconvenient times for the administrator. The way in which the administrator responds to the telephone calls, convenient or inconvenient, tells a great deal about his or her understanding of school–community relations.

As a rule of thumb, all incoming telephone calls must be taken courteously. This is one reason why school secretaries must undergo training in proper telephone etiquette. They must be taught to answer the telephone in a cheerful voice, identifying the school, and asking the caller how they can be of assistance. Secretaries who fail to do this are undermining severely the administrator's efforts at good school–community relations.

Although the secretary, as the first voice people hear when calling the school, is important; all other staff members must use the same courtesy when receiving telephone calls. This is particularly true of the principal, given the nature of many of the telephone calls he or she receives.

If, for example, a concerned parent calls to speak with the principal, the principal should take the call courteously and with a genuine desire to assist the parent. This courteous tone does not mean that the principal necessarily ought to be on the parent's side regarding the issue being discussed. The tone and manner of the principal's voice must demonstrate a desire to help, though.

The tone also becomes important if a member of the media is calling to get information from the principal. Although the principal may not wish to discuss all of the issues in question, the tone of the principal's voice ought to demonstrate a cooperative nature.

As a final example, consider a telephone call to the principal from an administrator in the central office. This call is being made to request information from the principal that is not readily available or convenient for the principal to get. Again, a courteous, helpful tone is in order.

The two questions immediately raised by these examples are "Why?" and "How?" Why is this tone so important, and how can it be achieved? Let's examine responses to these questions below.

A courteous tone is important because principals must remember that one of their primary responsibilities is to serve the public. In fact, the concept of servant leadership (Greenleaf, 1977) is widely referred to as a model for school leadership. True greatness as a leader is often thought to come from the leader's desire and capacity for serving those who are lead. When visiting a fine restaurant, a rushed greeting by wait staff desirous to take our order quickly so they can move on to other tables rarely elicits a high tip for service. We tend to expect those who are serving us to be courteous, friendly, and willing to devote time to our needs. Individuals calling to speak to the school principal have a right to the same expectations.

The tone is further important because of our desire to have people deal with us in a courteous and friendly way. The implication is that people will be more attracted to you, and thus more courteous, if they are treated courteously by you. Therefore, for selfish reasons, school administrators who are courteous on the telephone are more likely to receive courteous treatment themselves.

Finally, a courteous tone is important because of the principals' role as the "tone setter" of the school. In recognition of the important roles all staff members play in a schools' success, the principal is the most influential member of the school staff. People look to the principal for guidance and leadership. How he or she deals with other people, therefore, determines the public's perception of how the entire school deals with people. The responsibility of so strongly representing the tone and climate of the school is one more important reason why school administrators must receive telephone calls courteously.

There are times in the workdays of all principals where courteous telephone calls become difficult to take. For this reason, a good secretary takes messages courteously, and then gives the caller an approximate time to expect a telephone call to be returned by the principal. While people who call want their calls to be taken immediately, they are much more forgiving of a promptly returned telephone call that is courteous than they are of a rude, curt, rushed answer. Administrators ought not feel as though they are held hostage by the telephone. They should not believe that they must be available to courteously receive all telephone calls. To do so, in addition to being mentally challenging, would prevent the administrator from being visible in the school, a behavior supported by research as being essential to a positive school culture (Fiore, 1999). What administrators should realize, instead, is that it is important to good school–community relations that they return all telephone calls not taken within a reasonable time.

## Telephone Calls From the Principal

Whether a principal is returning a telephone call or placing one on his or her own volition, there are some key elements that must be kept in mind.

- *Be courteous.* As already discussed, it is essential that the principal place the telephone call in a courteous and friendly tone.

- *Avoid interruptions.* Though difficult to avoid entirely, it is important that telephone calls be placed at a time less likely to involve outside interruptions. If, for example, the principal has one minute between appointments, this is likely not a good time to be returning a telephone call to a concerned parent who may need several minutes to speak.

- *Have a script.* Although it is impractical to develop a script for every telephone call in its entirety, having a script for the beginning of a telephone call is a good idea for the sake of consistency. Beginning all telephone calls with the same greeting, whether the call is for good news or bad news, illustrates the principal's fairness and desire to always be familiar.

- *Prepare relevant data.* If a telephone call is being made to discuss a student discipline referral with a parent, then it stands to reason that the principal ought to be familiar with the incident before placing the call. Likewise, if the telephone call is being made to a newspaper reporter wanting to discuss standardized test data, then the principal may want to have the data available before placing the call.

   ◆ *Anticipate questions.* Similar to preparing a script, the principal ought to anticipate questions likely to be asked by the recipient of the call. Rehearsing some of these beforehand will allow the principal to be more confident in his or her response once the questions have actually been asked.

In essence, it is vitally important that principals and other school officials take some time to prepare for telephone calls. Though any individual call may seem insignificant to the principal placing it, the individual on the receiving end may be speaking with the principal for the first and only time. As such, this person will base many judgments on this seemingly insignificant call. Remembering this, although not intended to make individuals nervous, may serve the purpose of ensuring that principals take their telephone presence seriously.

## Face-to-Face Conversations

There are numerous opportunities for face-to-face conversations to occur throughout the typical school day. Some of these are informal and occur in hallways or on sidewalks, whereas others represent scheduled appointments and occur in more formally arranged settings. Though these differences in location impact the nature of the face-to-face conversations somewhat, there are some general rules that should be kept in mind for portraying the desired communication.

In Chapter 4, the importance of nonverbal communication was discussed at length. Paying attention to the nonverbal communication that is a part of your own communication patterns is essential. Not being overly sensitive to other people's nonverbal cues and checking your perceptions of them when they do concern you are other concepts that were discussed. Here, the focus is more on your spoken language, as it was in the section about telephone etiquette.

When given the opportunity to engage in a face-to-face conversation with any school stakeholder, a school principal should remember to speak clearly and deliberately. Practicing clear speech in all aspects of the principal's personal and professional life will make this a natural speech pattern. Feeling and behaving naturally is especially easy if the principal is comfortable with the person whom he or she is communicating with. However, though hopefully occurring less frequently, there may be times in which the principal is not comfortable in a face-to-face conversation. These situations require some special skills.

There should be a careful tone of confidence in the principal's voice at all times. Though certain individual conversations may make the principal more uneasy than will other conversations, this uneasiness should be absent from the principal's voice if at all possible. Not showing uneasy feelings can be accomplished in three ways.

1. *Close the gap.* Oftentimes, an angry or aggressive individual expects us to back away when they express anger with us. If you think of the stereotypical playground bully, this is precisely the response that person usually receives. In our mental images of bullies, we probably see them moving aggressively towards the individual they are bullying, while that person backs away scared. This gives the bully the upper hand he or she desires in confrontational conversations. The best way to overcome this is to do exactly the opposite of what the bully expects. Therefore, in difficult conversations that make the principal uncomfortable, the best advice is to gradually close the gap. It's important to note that this should be done deliberately, but very gradually. This will make the angry, aggressive person a bit uneasy, and may give the principal some needed confidence.

2. *Maintain eye contact.* It is often difficult to look somebody in the eye when they are angry with us. However, that is exactly what a principal should do in a conversation with an angry or aggressive person. Looking the person squarely in the eye accomplishes several goals. First, it shows the other person that the principal is not intimidated by their anger. Second, it makes it more difficult for the angry person to continue expressing anger, as they are not used to people looking them in the eye when they do so. Third, it restores some of the principal's own confidence. Again, this must be done deliberately to demonstrate the confidence that the principal has in his or her position, even if the principal is not feeling overly confident inside.

3. *Lower your voice.* When involved in a face-to-face conversation with a loud, aggressive person, it is important for a principal to maintain a soft, quiet vocal tone. Although the impulse may be to raise our own voice in response to another's loud voice, the opposite strategy has a more profound effect. Lowering his or her voice will allow the principal to maintain a rational, calm, and confident demeanor. It will also make the other person's inappropriate demeanor seem even more inappropriate in comparison. This, in turn, may lead the other person to become self-conscious of his or her behavior. Any time the principal can cause the angry, aggressive individual to fo-

cus on his or her own inappropriate behavior, there will be a new opportunity to gain the upper hand in the conversation.

The primary point to remember is that these techniques are useful in uncomfortable conversations with difficult people. A strong school–community relations plan, based on positive frequent interactions with stakeholders, will severely lessen the extent to which these suggestions will be needed. The principal should remember that a courteous demeanor and clear, deliberate communication will best prepare him or her for face-to-face conversations.

Although the focus here has been on the school administrator's behavior, the same techniques discussed are applicable to teachers and staff members. A courteous demeanor and clear, deliberate communication from any school staff member will lead to a multitude of more pleasant face-to-face conversations.

---

## Showcase

Last spring we had a community forum to discuss moving from traditional one-grade classes to multiage classes. As the meeting started I reviewed the issues and asked if anyone had more to add to make sure we addressed all concerns. Teachers presented the process and the plan. I then followed up by addressing questions. I made sure I addressed the tough questions. This is the power of knowing your community. It was easy to know which people would have issues. I did this to model how being positive and respectful with responses carries so much more weight than being defensive. This experience reminded me of how the power of being positive, relaxed, and nondefensive, carries over to not only the other presenters but to the entire audience. The simple questions I ask myself when preparing for these type of events are: "If I were in the audience, what would I want to get out of this meeting? And how do I want to feel?" With that in mind the rest takes care of itself.

*Dr.Dale Lumpa, Principal,*
*Charles Hay Elementary, Englewood, CO*

---

## Speaking to a Large Group

There are many occasions during which a school administrator may be called upon to speak before a large audience. Several of these are outlined in Chapter 11 as opportunities for a school to make a favorable impression on the public. Accordingly, the administrator's ability to respond with a thoughtfully presented speech takes on relative importance. Though most members of the public do not expect school administrators to be highly skilled public speakers, an administrator who appears comfortably at ease speaking to large groups of people is often perceived more favorably than is one who becomes nervous and perhaps confused in like situations.

One of the best groups to practice speaking in front of is the school faculty. A principal who can effectively and succinctly make points to the faculty during a meeting is able to move a meeting along at a productive pace. Teachers tend to enjoy and look forward to faculty meetings if the principal is able to lead conversations and make points effectively (Whitaker, 1997). This enjoyment is enhanced when the principal involves faculty members in discussions, often serving as facilitator of those discussions (Fiore, 1999; Whitaker, 1997).

Because many school faculties are quite large, these meetings can be excellent opportunities for the principal to hone his or her public speaking skills. Being aware of nonverbal messages being sent while speaking and utilizing appropriate vocal volume and inflection are two skills that principals can practice during the meeting. The principal can then ask certain faculty members for feedback regarding the skills and techniques being practiced.

There are several places that principals and other administrators can turn to for suggestions to improve their public speaking abilities. The first and most convenient place is to administrative colleagues that the principal trusts and respects. Having a cadre of fellow administrators to bounce ideas off of is an essential component of many administrators' successes. These administrative colleagues can best understand some of the job's frustrations and can often provide very helpful feedback for colleagues desiring improvement. Many seasoned administrators have tales to tell of some of their own early career miscues regarding public speaking. Because speaking before large groups is a skill that is improved over time, many of these colleagues can share their personal accounts of specific steps they have taken to improve their abilities. This can be of great benefit to fellow administrators.

Another place that school administrators can turn to is an organization like Toastmasters International (www.toastmasters.org). This organization, with chapters in over 70 countries worldwide, provides instruction and support for giving speeches in public. Their members include professional, stay-at-home parents, students, and retirees. Among the advice Toastmasters gives is the following, posted on their Web site (www.toastmasters.org/tips.htm):

- *Know the room.* Be familiar with the place in which you will speak. Arrive early, walk around the speaking area and practice using the microphone and any visual aids.

- *Know the audience.* Greet some of the audience as they arrive. It's easier to speak to a group of friends than to a group of strangers.
- *Know your material.* If you're not familiar with your material or are uncomfortable with it, your nervousness will increase. Practice your speech and revise it if necessary.
- *Relax.* Ease tension by doing exercises.
- *Visualize yourself giving your speech.* Imagine yourself speaking, your voice loud, clear, and assured. When you visualize yourself as successful, you will be successful.
- *Realize that people want you to succeed.* Audiences want you to be interesting, stimulating, informative, and entertaining. They don't want you to fail.
- *Don't apologize.* If you mention your nervousness or apologize for any problems you think you have with your speech, you may be calling the audience's attention to something they hadn't noticed. Keep silent.
- *Concentrate on the message—not the medium.* Focus your attention away from your own anxieties, and outwardly toward your message and your audience. Your nervousness will dissipate.
- *Turn nervousness into positive energy.* Harness your nervous energy and transform it into vitality and enthusiasm.
- *Gain experience.* Experience builds confidence, which is the key to effective speaking. A Toastmasters club can provide the experience you need.

By heeding this advice, school administrators will be able to improve their presentation skills. Occasions, such as open houses and school board presentations, will become easier for the school administrator to manage and will result in much more fluid, organized speeches being delivered. As with all things, the school administrator must recognize the need for enhancing oral communication skills and then must learn and practice skills and techniques for acquiring them.

## Communicating During a Campaign

It was during campaigns, designed to produce votes or support of an educational idea, that school administrators of old conducted much of what they considered to be school–community relations. As is sadly the case with some contemporary administrators, when the campaign was over and the issue had been resolved, they stopped communicating with any members of the school's external publics. The next time support was needed; the administrators put their friendly faces back on and went out again to communicate with stakeholders in the community.

This level of school–community relations leads to skepticism in the community. The end result of communicating with people only when you need their support to put a construction project or curricular adjustment through is often a public that mistrusts you and comes to doubt your sincerity regarding communication. For this reason, school–community relations in the twenty-first century demands that school leaders communicate regularly and purposefully with all stakeholder groups. This communication, as has been discussed, must be two-way, with the school leader listening as much as, or more often than, he or she speaks.

However, it is still vitally important that school administrators understand how to communicate effectively during a campaign. This involves an understanding of specific language and delivery systems that will lead to the community's acceptance of the new idea being promoted. Today, more than anytime in public education's history, it is imperative that school administrators successfully communicate with their publics in all financial matters. With Census Bureau data and public opinion polls showing less than 50 percent of American families having school-age children in their home, improvements and construction projects can rarely happen without voter support at the polls. An administrator who communicates effectively during a campaign has a much easier time getting the public to support buildings and innovations that his or her students need.

An administrator desirous of community support for an educational innovation must understand how typical people come to make decisions regarding innovative ideas. Without such knowledge, the administrator may end up throwing his or her hands up in the air, exclaiming that there is no way to convince people. Understanding the mental process people endure and the types of communication most effective at each stage in the process will be a tremendous asset to the administrator.

Rogers and Shoemaker (1971) developed a model of this process containing four steps:

1. *Knowledge*—This occurs when the individual first hears of the innovation and begins developing an understanding of it.

2. *Persuasion*—At this step, the individual forms their attitude about the innovation.

3. *Decision*—During this step, the individual engages in thoughts, dialogues, or activities that lead him or her to accept or reject the innovation.

4. *Confirmation*—This occurs as the individual seeks reinforcement for his or her decision. The decisions can be reversed if enough conflicting messages about the innovation are presented.

Examining these four steps and beginning to understand their implications points administrators toward certain communication techniques for each step. Because it is impossible to engage in face-to-face, two-way communication with each individual stakeholder, understanding at which step such communication is particularly useful provides the administrator with some very useful knowledge.

Consider people's needs during the knowledge step, as an example. Oftentimes, the way that members of the public first become aware of an issue is through one-way communication. They read a news release published in the local paper, or they hear a local radio announcement urging them to attend an informational session about a proposed educational innovation. If they have children in the schools, then the community members may hear of the proposal through a school newsletter.

Following Rogers and Shoemaker's model, it is during the next two steps that most people form their decisions. With this knowledge in mind, school administrators can ensure that as many people as possible are reached face-to face during these two steps. It is perfectly adequate to first inform people of the innovation through a one-way mass communication effort. Then, before people have had a great deal of time to ponder the idea, the school administrator ought to meet and greet as many of them as possible to persuade them to adopt the innovation as an educational necessity.

The meeting and greeting of thousands of people cannot, obviously, be accomplished without careful planning and organization. For this reason, a member of the school district's administrative team ought to serve as the lead individual for scheduling and organization. This individual, not always the superintendent, should schedule opportunities for key administrators to meet with local civic, government, and business organizations. Many influential community members are parts of these organizations. Speaking before the organization while allowing time for personal, informal conversation afterward, gives the administrative team an opportunity to make their case before people who often have a great deal of influence in the community.

A mistake often made during a campaign occurs when many people are at step four in their decision-making process. School leaders have traditionally overlooked the necessity people have for confirming the decisions they have made. These leaders mistakenly assume that once people have made up their mind they ought to be left alone.

The reality is that some people, as Rogers and Shoemaker's model explains, change their minds after being given new information by another party. Community members who were persuaded and convinced by school officials to vote favorably toward a bond issue may, in fact, change their minds after being confronted by friends, neighbors, colleagues, or business leaders who offer a different perspective on the project's need. It is thought by some school leaders with impeccable records during campaigns that step four is the step at which people need to hear from school leaders the most.

School leaders also want to be careful not to alienate people after receiving their support. This can lead people to feel used, which will make it much less likely that they will support the school's ideas in the future. Instead, people ought to receive confirming news from the school after the decision has been made to show that the innovation was necessary. A school district I am familiar with, for example, sought community support to receive funding to hire additional school nurses. After the nurses were hired, news releases were regularly sent by the school to the local newspaper touting the benefits of these nurses and telling stories of the good work being done for the community's children.

---

## Showcase

As superintendent I was involved in many bond referenda but few like the "winner of 96." Several proposals had been voted down in the state and with 264 "modular classrooms" we were about to propose a $173 million bond issue to the voters. Because public funds could not be used to promote bond referenda, a citizen group was selected to organize support. The elected officials were supportive and the needs were obvious, but the reality loomed that only 30 percent of the homes had school-age children. Realizing that parents alone would never have the clout to prevail, we took the case to the "owners." Senior citizens, small businesses, churches and synagogues all provide a forum through which they could be reached. People typically do not vote for money, they vote for their beliefs. In this case, the owners spoke and passed the bond in every precinct with 83.3 percent of all voters in support. You may have the right message, but you need to get it to the right people.

*Dr. William C. Bosher, former Superintendent Chesterfield County Schools, Chesterfield, VA, now Director of the Commonwealth Education Policy Institute, Richmond, VA*

---

## Communicating with a Citizen's Advisory Committee

The general rules to follow during a campaign ought to offer no surprises to individuals already cognizant of how to establish and maintain strong school–community relations. The key is a concerted effort toward understanding the community's needs and utilizing appropriate communication techniques to demonstrate the need that the school believes is present.

As presented in Chapter 6, understanding the community's needs and/or perceptions can be a very difficult process for school administrators, particularly for those who are new to their communities. Many of the issues that have taken place through the years in a community have created perceptions that may remain hidden from the view of even the best communicating school administrator. This is one reason why Chapter 6 strongly advocated for the use of key communicators. Because it is impossible to always gain the opinions of the community firsthand, school administrators must rely on other people to represent different parts of the community.

A citizen's advisory committee serves the same purpose during a campaign. This important group can help the school administration establish the need for their proposed curricular or facility change. The advisory committee is also of great value in determining how the message ought to be delivered to the community. Finally, the citizen's advisory committee can provide the school administration with assistance in both delivering the message and evaluating its effectiveness. This is all true if care goes into choosing the membership of the committee, that is.

If a school district is located in a larger community (over 20,000 residents), then the membership of the citizen's advisory committee ought to number somewhere between 20 and 100 members. The larger the community, the more members there ought to be. Size alone does not constitute a good committee, though. Instead, representation should come from every subgroup (socioeconomic, racial, ethnic, religious) known to dwell in the community. Among some of the "interest" groups that ought to be represented are parent–teacher associations, religious leaders, taxpayers' associations, business people, realtors, mass media representatives, members of the school staff, students, labor unions, veterans' groups, service clubs, and the local Chamber of Commerce.

As size cannot determine a groups' effectiveness by itself, the actual composition of the group cannot do so, either. This is where the communication skills of the leader are so important. Whether the group is lead by the superintendent or his/her designee from the administrative team ought to be determined by several factors. These factors include:

- The individual's knowledge of the proposed innovation.
- The individual's experiences working with large groups.
- The individual's availability when group members need to confer.
- The individual's skill in all aspects of communication.

To effectively lead a citizen's advisory committee and to be successful in a campaign effort, the leader must be able to communicate effectively with all types of people. Because the citizen's advisory committee is composed of individuals from all walks of life, their perceptions and goals may differ greatly. A skilled listener ensures that all people are heard during a discussion. An individual who is aware of nonverbal communication has a much better sense of people's inner feelings than does somebody not adept in this regard. Finally, a persuasive speaker can take the viewpoints he or she has listened to and respectfully combine them into one idea that is explained well.

If a citizen's advisory committee is lead by an administrator without strong communication skills, two pitfalls are likely. The first one involves the chaos that is almost certain to break out in the group. Because this committee is usually comprised of people with their own leadership abilities, conversations can get heated. The leader with strong communication skills often senses conflict before it erupts and takes steps to squelch it. This leader also listens carefully to what people are saying, including what they are saying with their body language, and can restate it in a safe, nonthreatening manner. A good listener can often be an effective mediator in a potentially volatile situation.

The other pitfall of having an advisory committee lead by a weak communicator occurs when the leader tries to represent the groups' thinking in his/her speaking or writing. Failure to accurately communicate group consensus leads group members to believe that the leader already had a preconceived agenda and was not really listening to other viewpoints. The ability to communicate the group's consensus, even when some individual viewpoints are not represented, is a skill that is learned over time and perfected with experience leading diverse groups.

## The Campaign's Conclusion

The ability to orally communicate effectively is often demonstrated by school administrators after a campaign has concluded, regardless of the outcome. Because campaigns for facility upgrades, new buildings, or curricular innovations can often be somewhat divisive, the school administrators can count on addressing questions regarding the outcome for some time. The ability to address these questions, utilizing many of the skills presented in this chapter, will define a good part of the administrators' leadership in the eyes of many people.

School administrators also ought to be prepared to include details of the campaign's success or failure in public addresses they may be called on to deliver. If a large high school has experienced a campaign for building a new athletic facility, for example, this will be a discussion point for quite some time, regardless of the outcome. If the campaign resulted in a new facility, then the school administrators will need to reinforce the value of this facility in their speeches. If the campaign was defeated, then a continuing case for the need of the facility likely will be included in speeches.

If the campaign issue was particularly divisive, then the school administrators must use skill and care in bringing the issue to closure. In the heat of the battle, many people mistakenly place too much emphasis on the issue the battle is fought over. Because schools are complex organizations charged with important tasks (education of youth) for which there are far-reaching consequences, the school administrators involved must be keepers of the whole vision and help people put the divisive issue into the proper perspective. Leadership from the school administrators is vital to place the community's focus back on other educational issues. Again, the ability to communicate effectively will be tested in this regard.

Exhibit 9.1 is a letter written by a principal after a local campaign resulted in an addition to the school facility being scheduled for building. Because the community was divided over the necessity and cost of such an addition, the letter is written to bring some closure to the issue.

## Chapter Summary

+ All school staff members, particularly administrators, must remember to be courteous in all telephone conversations.

+ As "tone setter" for the school, the administrator's telephone manner helps people form an opinion about the friendliness of the school.

+ It is a good idea for the administrator to have a script or outline ready before placing an important telephone call.

+ There are techniques administrators can employ to avoid appearing uncomfortable during some face-to-face conversations.

+ Administrators should develop skills for speaking before large groups.

+ Campaigns are situations that require particular care in communicating with stakeholders.

+ Understanding how people reach decisions about change issues will help administrators determine techniques for communicating effectively with them.

+ A citizen's advisory committee provides great assistance in communicating with the larger community during a campaign.

+ Strong communication skills are required of administrators who lead advisory committees.

+ The school administrator must bring closure to a campaign through effective communication with stakeholders.

## Exhibit 9.1. Closure Letter
## at a Campaign's Conclusion

### Woodview School
123 Woodview Lane
Anytown, USA

**Ima Goodfellow, Principal**
**Susie Sunshine, Administrative Assistant**

May 29, 2001

Dear Parents,

As many of you already know, the school board voted last night to accept the bid from Reynolds and Harper, Inc., to begin expansion of the north side of our school building. Because this approval was the final step in an ideological and fiscal discussion this community endured throughout the past 18 months, let me take this opportunity to thank you all for sharing your concerns and to urge you to join me in moving our school forward.

Whereas many of you supported this addition, which will begin on June 20, there are others of you who did not. Months of discussion ended with this division of opinions still apparent. If we continue to focus on the issues that divide us, I fear that we will create an obstacle to our primary purpose for joining together; namely the education of your children. To that extent, allow me to inform you of some exciting ideas we plan to implement when the next school year begins:

- All of our classrooms will experience technological enhancements, as 3 new Dell computers per class will be installed on the network during the summer months.

- With the addition of a part-time Art teacher, who will be hired shortly, all classes will now have the opportunity to be visited weekly by Ms. Zamboni. Her collaboration with your child's classroom teacher will result in terrific, integrated Art projects to enhance instruction.

- Our dedicated staff members, who truly care about your children, will all be returning.

Further updates regarding the construction will be forthcoming. For now, let me thank you again for the support you consistently show us here at Woodview. Together, we will continue to create opportunities for all children to succeed and reach their full potential.

Sincerely,

Ima Goodfellow
Principal

# Case Study Analysis

## Pass the Antiperspirant

When Reggie Thomas first mentioned the need for a new baseball field to the superintendent two years earlier, he never imagined it would be the cause of so many sleepless nights. Reggie didn't even really like baseball, but as he attended the games during his first year as Clarksville Middle School's principal, it was apparent that Clarksville's field looked terrible in comparison with the rest of the area's fields. Who knew that by asking for a new field, he would become part of a bitter community battle over taxpayer dollars being used to fund a multitude of school improvements? The high school needed an auditorium, modernization of its eight science labs, and a cafeteria expansion. Two of the elementary schools needed new roofs and parking lots, and his school's baseball field were now part of a multimillion dollar package.

As Reggie sat in his office awaiting the arrival of six angry parents, his stomach ached. Mrs. Jones was representing the Band Boosters, angry because the band room looked worse than the baseball field did. Mr. Green was representing the Swim Club, upset because the pool facility lacked appropriate diving boards. Dr. Harris was representing the basketball team, unhappy about the condition of the boy's locker room. Three other parents were going to be there as well, though Reggie had no idea what their complaints were.

Reggie felt himself sweating, as he wondered why he hadn't noticed the need for these improvements sooner. He wondered if he had done an adequate job informing parents of his perception that the baseball field needed serious renovation. He was concerned about having to address questions about how these multimillion dollar proposals were made, because he did not recall being informed that any of his school's parents were involved in any meetings at all. Was he guilty of being part of a team that "railroaded" ideas through the community?

Reggie's' thoughts were interrupted by his secretary's voice. "Mr. Thomas, there are some parents here to see you."

## Questions for Analysis

1. Was Reggie wrong for informing the superintendent of the need for a new baseball field two years ago?
2. Analyze Reggie's communication skills since speaking with the superintendent two years ago. Are there glaring errors? Should he have handled things differently? If so, what should he have done?

3. Has this school district done a good job gaining public support for the improvements? Why/Why not?
4. How should Reggie handle his meeting with the six parents? What are some particular steps he should take?

# 10

# In Crisis Situations, You Must Have a Plan

Crises can arise anyplace and at any time. This is what makes them so frightening to millions of people. There is a degree of unpredictability about crises that goes against the comfort all of us find in having things happen according to our plan or our schedule. This lack of predictability, often more than the event itself, is what distinguishes a crisis situation from what may otherwise simply be an unpleasant one. This, and the fact that in many situations we define as crises, things take place that have no business happening in safe places like our schools.

As the heads of their schools, administrators must have plans for dealing with these crisis situations. They must be prepared to respond to the variety of stakeholders whose lives are affected by crises at school. A crisis at a school, even more so than a crisis at home, requires special attention and specialized communication efforts. What is meant by the term crisis situation? Does it refer only to tragic occurrences, such as that of Columbine High School in 1999?

A crisis may include criminal acts or serious threats of criminal acts such as shootings, knifings, bombings, bomb threats, arson, kidnaping, or rape. A crisis situation may instead involve natural disasters such as blizzards, tornadoes, hurricanes, earthquakes, or floods. Finally, the term crisis situation can be used to refer to employee problems like strikes, student disturbances, or other situations like power outages and water contamination that can lead to the rapid shutdown of the school or school system. Although all of these things are crises, they are not all created equal. They share one common element, however. That is, the only way to successfully deal with these crisis situations is to have a plan in place before the situation arises.

## The Importance of Planning

Every school district and every school within every school district must have a plan for responding to crisis situations. The key word is "every." If you had an opportunity to interview the administrators at any of the schools across this country that have experienced a crisis within the past decade, you would find a unanimous claim that the administrators never expected such crises to happen at their school. None of us expect a crisis to occur in our school. Thankfully, this expectation is correct, as most readers of this text will probably not experience a major crisis while they are in charge of a school. But rather than playing the odds and assuming that such tragedies as those experienced at other schools will never happen at ours, all educators must be prepared to respond efficiently and effectively to crisis situations. The responsibility is the greatest with school administrators.

An essential consideration in designing a crisis management plan is that the plan be highly structured. Lack of structure could lead an otherwise manageable crisis situation to become chaotic. Whenever the public views our efforts as loose and chaotic, then we run a great risk of losing the credibility we have worked so hard to achieve. Worse yet, a loosely managed crisis could lead to harm to students, teachers, or staff. Although a structured plan cannot hope to address each and every conceivable specific crisis that can develop, the structure of the plan should be such that it accounts for nearly every type of problem. Some flexibility and adaptations will always be necessary, but a structured crisis management plan specifies the who, what, where, when, why, and how to the greatest extent possible. Exhibit 10.1 illustrates critical components of any crisis management plan. Addressing these components virtually assures that the crisis management plan will be a structured one.

---

## Exhibit 10.1. Designing a Crisis Management Plan

A comprehensive plan should:

- Select individuals to serve on crisis response and aftercare teams.
- Establish a headquarters for the crisis response and aftercare teams.
- Select an individual to be the official spokesperson during a crisis.
- Establish a procedure for activating community support services.
- Establish a procedure for developing channels of communication.
- Establish a procedure for controlling rumors.
- Establish a procedure for assessing the crisis management system.
- Establish a procedure for bringing closure to the crisis.

---

All of these components are general enough to be applied to virtually all crisis situations that could arise in schools. However, the components are also specific enough to create a structured plan that will greatly assist the school staff in dealing with the situations in an effective and efficient manner. Let's examine each component separately to gain a better understanding of how each one is best understood and implemented.

## Select Individuals to Serve on Crisis Response and Aftercare Teams

Although potentially all members of the school community are affected by a crisis situation, it is both impractical and illogical for each person to play a role in responding to the crisis. That, more than anything else, would likely lead to chaos. Instead, the school administrator should select members for the crisis response and aftercare teams based on his/her knowledge of each person's strengths. Although school counselors and social workers may make excellent members of the aftercare team, a team that requires counseling and human relations skills, there are likely additional members of the school community with some of those skills. Likewise, though the school secretary may be a logical person to assign to the crisis response team, as making telephone contacts and announcements are skills necessary for this team, there are doubtless other members of the school community who would be excellent choices to carry out these duties as well.

It is important that individuals selected for these teams are aware and approve of their selection. Above all else, crisis response and aftercare teams need individuals with a desire to serve on them and an understanding of their importance. Finally, and likely obvious to most, individuals selected for these teams ought to be people who are regularly in the school or, at least, have very quick access to the school. A half-time teacher, living some 30 miles from the campus, is not a good choice for this particular assignment.

## Establish a Headquarters for the Crisis Response and Aftercare Teams

Chaos is probable if the crisis response or aftercare teams have no place to go in a crisis situation. In situations like the Columbine incident, those who are on the response and aftercare teams need a place to do their work. There must be a specific room in the building where the team meets, formulates strategy, responds to the press, and makes decisions. This must be decided upon before the crisis takes place. It would be very damaging to a school's public image, not to mention their ability to assure safety during a crisis, if members of these teams were running around bumping into each other as they searched for a place to meet. Whether it is the school media center, the cafeteria, the teachers' lounge, or someplace else, the crisis response and aftercare teams must have an established place to meet. They are also wise to have a backup place in the event that access to their normal meeting place is blocked.

## Select an Individual to be the Official Spokesperson During a Crisis

Although a high-ranking school administrator is typically chosen for this role, this does not necessarily have to be so. I have known many administrators who lacked the calmness and rationality to act as spokesperson during times of crisis. This did not make them bad administrators. It did, however, make them lousy spokespersons during a crisis situation. The person selected for this role must understand much of what was explained in Chapter 8. They must be aware of their nonverbal communication idiosyncrasies, they must have a pleasant demeanor, and they must be able to respond calmly, rationally, and assuredly during emergency situations.

Some larger school districts have hired public relations personnel to deal with issues such as these. If your school does not have access to such personnel, then it is critical that a person be selected who has the appropriate qualities. As always, this person must agree to the assignment and must understand the significance of the role he or she is agreeing to.

## Establish a Procedure for Activating Community Support Services

The more serious the crisis, the more important it will be that community support services are made available to your school family. In virtually all of the school tragedies experienced during the last decade, community support services have played a major role in assisting students with issues such as grief management, guilt, depression, fear, or even suicidal feelings. It is not only the students who benefit from these services, though. School staff members and parents often have tremendous difficulty coping with tragic events taking place in schools that they assumed were too safe for such things to happen.

As is the case with each of these components, lack of planning can really be as devastating as the crisis situation itself. Therefore, it is imperative that the plan specifies who will contact community support services, how they will be contacted, and when the contact will take place. Failure to address these concerns will increase the risk that community support services will be lost as an oversight.

It is further important that the list of support services and their contact information is kept in a secure and reliable place. The individual in charge of this list must regularly update it to ensure that contact information is as accurate as it possibly can be.

## Establish a Procedure for Developing Channels of Communication

Who contacts the superintendent and the school board? Are they contacted immediately? Who contacts police and other emergency personnel? Are the press responded to as they arrive, or are press conferences held? If there are press conferences, where are they held? How are parents notified? Who notifies them? Who tells the staff? Are students informed of the crisis in a large assembly, or is it handled individually in classrooms?

These are just some of the questions that point to the significance of developing channels for communication. It is so easy during a crisis to overlook informing somebody who really ought not be overlooked. It is equally easy to incorrectly inform individuals or to release information out of sequence or to the wrong party. Establishing channels of communication ahead of time avoids these problems. In many schools, telephone trees have been established for this very purpose. Although they tend to be more prevalent in areas that may be affected by severe weather closing school unexpectedly, telephone trees are a very traditional, simple way to keep people informed. Exhibit 10.2 is an example.

Obviously, not all of the questions above are appropriate in all crisis situations. For example, if a gunman opens fire in a crowded cafeteria, all students are likely to know about it quickly. If a staff member is killed in an accident on the way to school, however, then the issue of informing students becomes a bit more delicate.

## Establish a Procedure for Controlling Rumors

Whenever a crisis develops in a community as large and as diverse as a school, there is always a risk of rumors being developed and disseminated. Because the facts of a crisis may be delicate enough to deal with, there is no need to be forced to deal with rumors as well. Therefore, there must be a plan for keeping rumors controlled.

Part of this plan should involve the assurance of honest communication. People often start rumors, not out of cruelty, but because of a lack of correct information. Therefore, keeping people appropriately informed will help squelch some rumors from circulating. The school administrator should take the lead in requiring all staff to put an end to rumors early on. Students who may be having difficulty dealing with the crisis situation may spread rumors as a defense mechanism or as a way of suppressing the truth that they do not understand how to deal with. Staff members need to be sensitive to these possible defense mechanisms and should

## Exhibit 10.2. Telephone Tree

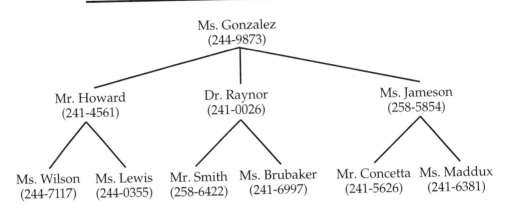

Ms. Gonzalez
(244-9873)

Mr. Howard
(241-4561)

Dr. Raynor
(241-0026)

Ms. Jameson
(258-5854)

Ms. Wilson
(244-7117)

Ms. Lewis
(244-0355)

Mr. Smith
(258-6422)

Ms. Brubaker
(241-6997)

Mr. Concetta
(241-5626)

Ms. Maddux
(241-6381)

seek out the assistance of counselors, social workers, or community service agencies when dealing with these students.

## Establish a Procedure for Assessing the Crisis Management Plan

As is the case with virtually all that we do in education, there must be methods in place for assessing our crisis management plan. This includes an assessment of the personnel in key roles and the comprehensiveness of the plan itself. As a crisis management plan is designed, there is no real concrete way for determining the extent to which it has been appropriately created. This lack of a concrete method is why, if misfortune strikes and a crisis does occur, school leaders must seize the opportunity for evaluating the plan's effectiveness.

In assessing the system, it is important that administrators ask the difficult questions. Were people properly informed? Did our plan have the necessary structure? Were grieving school community members appropriately assisted? Were key personnel able to perform their duties as we had imagined they would? Did we use space appropriately? These are just a sample of the questions that ought to be a part of your assessment system. A good piece of advice is to develop assessment questions before the plan must be implemented. This is no different than the effective teacher who often develops assessment tools before he/she completes the teaching of an instructional unit.

## Establish a Procedure for
## Bringing Closure to the Crisis

Among the greatest lessons school administrators have learned from school tragedies that have taken place before is this one: Just as in all other personal tragedies human beings may endure, closure must ultimately be brought if healing is to successfully occur. Although this does not mean that the school administrator arbitrarily chooses a date at which he/she declares the crisis and its aftermath to have ended, it does mean that at some point the school must ceremoniously end the crisis. It is important to remember that different people with differing relationships to the crisis victims will heal at dramatically different rates. School administrators must be sensitive to this and should ensure that services are available for as long as members of the school community need them.

However, in respect to these individual needs, the school administrator must ensure that the crisis is brought to closure for the entire school community. This may mean that a memorial service is held and school is cancelled for a period of time. It may mean that a monument of some sort is erected in memory of victims. It may mean, in the case of a less tragic crisis, little more than a newsletter summing up how things have been handled. The school administrator must work with the crisis management team to develop a plan for bringing closure to the crisis in a way that respects individual needs, honors what people endured during and after the crisis, but reminds everybody involved that the purpose of schooling must endure.

# Showcase

This is a condensed version of one New York school's response to the tragic events that struck our nation on Tuesday, September 11, 2001.

♦ Meetings with all students were held to discuss events and feelings on Tuesday and Wednesday. Sessions were lead by our own counseling staff (including a school psychologist who retired from Hommocks in June) and counselors from the Larchmont Mamaroneck Community Counseling Center.

♦ On Tuesday, every telephone line in the building, including the teachers' union office phones, was used to help students reach their parents if they were afraid. In many cases, these were children whose parents worked in New York City. Hallway monitors were assigned to deliver messages to students whose parents telephoned the school.

♦ During seventh, eight and ninth periods, teachers interviewed every student in the school to inquire about who took care of them after school. Approximately 100 students had two parents working in New York City. A team of teachers manned the telephones to call friends of the family and neighbors to make arrangements to have an adult open their home to each child.

♦ A special faculty meeting was held on Wednesday before school. Psychologists addressed teachers to train them to help children cope with the crisis. The counseling staff was made available to teachers who themselves needed an ear to listen and shoulder to cry on.

♦ The Crisis Response Team, comprised of teachers, counselors, the Town of Mamaroneck Youth Officer, and administrators directed the school's efforts. They met four times during the week to identify emerging needs and to make plans accordingly.

*Seth Weitzman, Principal,*
*Hommocks Middle School, Larchmont, NY*

Although it is illogical to live in fear of a potential crisis, particularly in an age when schools have taken great measures to improve the safety of all students, it is more illogical to hide our heads in the sand and insist that a crisis will never happen to us. Remember, the school communities that have experienced some of the worst American school tragedies strongly believed that such events could never happen in their schools.

Proactive school administrators use staff development opportunities to promote, practice, and perfect their crisis management plans. This is an outstanding use of these nonstudent days that helps ensure that the school community is prepared. In many school communities, these staff development days include assistance from local police and emergency personnel. These individuals, highly skilled and trained at crisis response, make excellent members of a school's crisis planning team. If you ask them, you will more than likely discover that they are happy to provide community service and assist you in designing meaningful staff development around the issues of school safety and crisis management.

In the School Town of Munster, located in Munster, Indiana, for example, Superintendent William J. Pfister held an administrative retreat devoted to crisis management. Munster, a nice, well-to-do, upper middle-class community, is not a place that one may expect a school crisis to occur. However, recognizing the need for all communities to be prepared, Superintendent Pfister invited key members of the Munster Police Department to the administrative retreat to assist administrators in understanding appropriate responses to potential crises. The police officers posed real-life scenarios to the administrators and assisted them in assessing their readiness to respond.

Opportunities such as this are excellent first steps. Building level administrators should then go to the next step, which includes designing a plan with the entire staff's involvement, rehearsing it, and then, most significantly, regularly revisiting it to keep it fresh in everybody's mind. Again, though it is not possible to be prepared for every possible crisis situation that may occur, it is probable that most schools could become more prepared than they currently are.

It is very important that school leaders take the potential for crises seriously, while not becoming stifled in fear by the mere thought of a crisis developing. This goal, too, can be assisted through staff development. Although it is desirable to have a school community that is cognizant of the dangers and warning signs of potential crises, it is critical that the school community understand how rare crises, from the highly tragic ones to simple mechanical problems, really are. School leaders can design staff development opportunities that share statistical data and trend analyses about youth violence and domestic issues in order to increase awareness. It is through staff development such as this that factual information can be shared and discussed. Members of the school community can be made aware of two dichotomous facts: whereas overall youth violence increased at the end of the last millennium, school violence decreased. Consider these statistics: The National School Safety Center reported a decline in the number of killings on school campuses. They reported 24 deaths in 1998–1999, down from 54 in 1992–1993. There have also been reports of fewer fights on campuses despite the fact that youth involvement in violent behavior outside of school is reported by many to be on the rise.

Legal issues regarding school safety, crisis response, and crisis prevention make for additional staff development topics. Too often, issues of legal consequence are not shared with school staffs. This creates an environment of uncertainty, as individuals are not sure how to set limits or what behavior will be permissible by law. Many educators would be astonished to know what our courts have recently been deciding regarding issues of school safety. For example, a 1998 court case starkly illustrates a school's duty to maintain a safe environment for students. After a boy was attacked and stabbed in his classroom, his mother brought an action against the school, alleging that nothing had been done to implement safeguards at the school, despite previous acts of violence that had occurred on campus. The court agreed with the boy's mother and found that the school district was negligent for not adopting or implementing security policies, procedures, or safeguards (Brum v. Town of Dartmouth, 690 N.E.2d 844 (Mass. App. 1998)). This example drives home the point that beyond the obvious ethical imperative, schools face a legal imperative to improve school safety where it appears to be lacking. Though not all acts of violence constitute school crises, they are often indicative that the school may not be as prepared as it ought to be for responding to a crisis situation.

## Communicating in a Time of Crisis

Two of the most important considerations when schools are faced with a crisis are deciding who to inform and how to inform them. Not only must these points be addressed in a school's crisis management plan, but they also must be points that have close attention paid to them to ensure that damage above and beyond the crisis does not occur. Failing to consider carefully how and when to inform individuals during a crisis can be a really difficult malady to survive.

Again, there are some crisis situations that are so severe that everybody in the school community becomes instantly aware. Still others may occur without the knowledge of too many people. A mechanical problem that requires heating or cooling to be shut down, and a student suicide occurring at home, are two examples. In situations like these, the school administrator is relied on to understand all the intricacies of effective communication. Exhibit 10.3 illustrates important considerations for informing the school staff during a crisis situation. Note the importance of informing staff members first and of assessing individual staff members' readiness for communicating with students regarding the crisis. This assessment is made much easier by meeting with staff face-to-face if at all possible.

When meeting face-to-face with all staff members is not a possibility, then the administrator must still avoid using the intercom at all costs. Students should never find out about a school crisis of any magnitude through such an impersonal means.

## Exhibit 10.3. Informing Staff of Crisis Situations

- Faculty and staff must be informed first so they have time to prepare.
- Never use the intercom to relay critical information.
- Try meeting with all faculty—not just representatives.
- Control rumors.
- Remind faculty of their responsibilities.
- Note which staff members are not capable of working with students due to their own emotional condition.

Exhibit 10.4 deals with considerations for informing students of a crisis. Notice here the increased focus on the emotional well-being of the students. Although different crisis situations will likely illicit different responses from students, there is always the likelihood that students will find the information more difficult to deal with than staff members will. For this reason, staff members are informed first, an assessment is made regarding which staff members are best equipped for communicating with students, and students are informed in as personal a way as possible.

## Exhibit 10.4. Informing Students of Crisis Situations

- Information should be transmitted in a private area.
- Students should receive information from somebody they trust and respect.
- Unnecessary details should be avoided.
- The person informing students should be prepared for a variety of reactions.
- The students should not be alone after being informed.
- Some students need expressions of sympathy.
- Silence is perfectly normal, but students should know that it's appropriate to express emotions if they need to.

Depending on the severity of the crisis, some students may need assistance from individuals with counseling expertise. School administrators need to recognize this and must have these individuals on alert should their services be needed. This is why determining how contacts with community service personnel are made is an integral part of the crisis management plan.

# Media Relations in Crisis Situations

Chapter 7 focused on effective methods for dealing with the media. As mentioned there, some special skills are needed for working with the media during crisis situations. A clear-minded, rational communicator is needed if the school wishes to respond appropriately and provide the media with pertinent facts that will assist the community in understanding what has transpired. Although it is of paramount importance that the individual who communicates with the media during crisis situations embodies the above qualities, everything will be made easier if a foundation, based on the skills and techniques from Chapter 7, has first been established. In other words, as part of a crisis readiness system, the wise school leader establishes a mutually respectful relationship with the media from the very beginning.

If a crisis suddenly hits a school, as crises generally do, the media may be on the scene in a matter of minutes. This gives the school leader and the crisis management team precious little time to prepare. By keeping the suggestions from Exhibit 10.5 in mind, the individual from the school community who is charged with working with the media will find the task to be far less daunting.

Some of these suggestions, though certainly worth repeating, have been discussed at length earlier in this text. However, there are a few important suggestions from Exhibit 10.5 that warrant deeper explanation.

## Provide Facts About the School and the Crisis

It is wise for the person charged with media relations to always have on hand a fact sheet about the school. Though nothing overly elaborate, this fact sheet ought to contain important demographic information such as population numbers, male/female ratio, and grade configurations. The fact sheet also may include some recent positive accomplishments enjoyed by the school. Not only do reporters often need this information, but they also need facts about the crisis being experienced. In initially speaking with reporters, it is unwise to speculate. Giving facts about the school and the crisis will ensure the most accurate media coverage.

## Log All Information Released to the Public

In a time of crisis, it is so easy to forget what you have said and to whom you have said it. Therefore, it is wise to always log all of the information released to the public in these situations. This will assist the school in checking on the accuracy of information once it appears in print or after is has been broadcast. It will also prevent the school personnel from being redundant.

## Exhibit 10.5. Dealing with the Media in Crisis Situations

- ◆ Develop working relationships with reporters.
- ◆ Focus on the question and the feedback from reporters.
- ◆ Provide facts about the school and the crisis.
- ◆ Log all information released to the public.
- ◆ Release names of victims only after the next of kin have been notified.
- ◆ Be aware of your nonverbal communication. Be sure not to send the wrong message.
- ◆ Be calm, even when pressed by reporters.
- ◆ Don't be afraid to say, "I don't know."
- ◆ Tell the truth. Honesty is essential.
- ◆ Be aware of photographers on campus. You have every right to control photographers on your property.
- ◆ Be brief.
- ◆ Don't allow yourself to be bullied or intimidated.
- ◆ Control the length of the interview by informing reporters at the beginning how long the interview will last.
- ◆ Repeat key messages as often as possible and stay focused on those messages.

## Release Names of Victims Only After the Next of Kin Have Been Notified

In addition to the obvious public relations nightmare created by having a victim's next of kin find out about their loss through media outlets, such an error is a potential legal nightmare for the entire school system. Schools hold a tremendous amount of sensitive personal material about their students and staff. The sensitivity of information is magnified during a crisis situation. Whoever has the task of communicating with the media during crisis situations must remain cognizant of the importance of notifying a victim's next of kin first. There are no exceptions.

## Be Aware of Photographers on Campus— You Have Every Right to Control Photographers on Your Property

Believing that the media has a right to be on school property because of the public nature of such property is a mistake. As chief executive officers of schools, the administration has the right to limit access to photographers on school property. More than the right, they have an obligation to do so. Most parents would cringe at the thought of photographers lurking around their child's school, snapping photographs, and publishing them in the newspaper without the parents' knowledge. This is even truer during a sensitive time, as when a crisis has taken place. There is no need to be rude. However, the school administrators must make it clear to media photographers that they are to remain off-campus until they have been given permission to do otherwise.

## Repeat Key Messages as Often as Possible and Stay Focused on Those Messages

It is important that those speaking with the media remember that they are not there only to answer questions. Although this may certainly be one of their main purposes, these individuals also have an obligation to inform the media of facts that may not be addressed by the reporters' questions. When this happens, it is crucial that these points be repeated often enough to guarantee that they will be included in the media's coverage.

For example, if your school has enjoyed unparalleled safety and has been free of virtually all disturbances prior to this crisis, you may want to share this information with reporters. A skilled communicator will know how to weave this fact into almost all of their responses to best ensure that the media representatives have heard the message loudly and clearly.

# Dealing with the Aftermath of a Crisis

As mentioned, the way in which schools deal with the aftermath of a crisis situation is a most important aspect of how successful their crisis management plan really is. Even if a school administrator has assembled the best crisis management team, conducted meaningful and lasting staff development around his or her school's plan, and overseen its execution with precision, failure to effectively and sensitively deal with the aftermath of a crisis may be the administrator's lasting legacy. What is meant by the crisis aftermath? How does the school leader sensitively deal with the aftermath while still bringing the crisis to closure? Again, though the specific answers to these questions will vary with individual schools and individual crises, there are some common guidelines that can be generalized to most situations.

## Crisis Aftermath

The crisis aftermath refers to that period of time in which individuals really begin dealing with the effects of the crisis. It refers to that time after the proverbial dust has settled and people can pause to reflect upon the situation they have experienced. Obviously, the aftermath of every crisis is different, and each individual who experiences a crisis also experiences the aftermath in his or her own unique way. Also true is the fact that the time period thought of as the crisis aftermath can vary tremendously. Some crises continue causing individuals grief and despair years after they happened. Others, though still considered crisis situations, are successfully dealt with by everybody within a matter of days.

There is special training required to assist members of the school community with ways of coping in the aftermath of a crisis. School administrators are not expected to necessarily possess all of these skills. They are expected, however, to recognize the needs people have and to provide assistance in identifying individuals who can meet those needs. Exhibits 10.6 and 10.7 (both on the next page) contain brief synopses of crisis situations. Exhibit 10.6 describes a more tragic crisis, whereas Exhibit 10.7 describes a crisis less likely to cause great distress. Though very different from one another, notice that as each crisis ends there is an aftermath that must be dealt with.

These two examples showcase the tremendous diversity in what are termed crisis situations. Both of them have an aftermath that must be dealt with carefully to avoid the creation of another crisis. At the same time, the skills and resources required to deal with the aftermaths could not be more diverse.

The crisis situation described in Exhibit 10.6 is tragic and will unquestionably lead to some grief and emotional turmoil. Even though Dr. Lewis has led the school through a successful resolution of the crisis on day one, the emotional issues that could linger as a result of a teacher's death will present real challenges. Although Dr. Lewis does not single-handedly need the skills and resources to resolve these issues, it is imperative that the school community is provided with people who do have them. For this reason, the formation of an aftercare team remains a vital component of crisis planning. The aftercare team in this particular situation will have a monumental task ahead of itself as it successfully assists all members of the school community in dealing with the issues that will surely arise as a result of their recent tragedy.

## Exhibit 10.6. Tragic Crisis Scenario

Many people wondered why Mrs. Thompson wasn't in school. For as long as she worked at Monroe School she had never missed a day. And for her not to call in and notify anybody, something strange must have happened.

When the police arrived at the school and informed the principal, Dr. Lewis that Mrs. Thompson had been tragically killed in an automobile accident, Dr. Lewis was shocked. Aside from the instant grief and sadness were Dr. Lewis's concerns about how members of the school community would cope with this tragedy. Executing her school's plan very carefully, Dr. Lewis mobilized the staff to notify stakeholders, assist upset students, and respond to media inquiries. Somehow, they all got through the day. What would tomorrow bring, though?

## Exhibit 10.7. Inconvenient Crisis Scenario

As Jermaine Brown entered the boy's restroom, it was apparent that somebody had performed a prank. Jermaine stepped quickly into two inches of standing water. Disgusted, he ran into the hall where he almost bumped into a very upset Lisa Wilkins. "My shoes are ruined," screamed Lisa, as similar cries echoed from many other rooms within Harrison High.

It wasn't long before the school was being evacuated and all of the water had been shut off to Harrison High. The unusual freezing temperatures must have been the culprits of this unexpected pipe-bursting disaster. Thanks to a well-executed plan, all of Harrison's students made it home in as safe and orderly a fashion as possible. The question looming over the heads of the administrators was this: "How would Harrison High School possibly be ready to open at 7:00 AM tomorrow morning?"

The crisis described in Exhibit 10.7, on the other hand, will not require the same type of aftercare response. There will probably not be as many emotional issues surrounding the water damage and subsequent school evacuation as there were in Exhibit 10.6. However, the aftermath of this crisis will need to be handled well, too. Although counseling is likely not a significant need here, the members of the aftercare team still need to utilize sufficient skill to get the school up and running again. Additionally, there will likely be upset students and parents to deal with as a result of both the potential damage of personal property and the difficulty parents had in responding to an unexpected dismissal. Additionally, the aftercare team will need to do whatever possible to assure that future occurrences of this problem are avoided.

The aftermath of any crisis, in short, requires as much skill and planning as the crisis management itself. Although it is not possible to anticipate a crisis aftermath any more than it is possible to anticipate a particular crisis, school leaders must take the initiative to ensure that people are ready to make the necessary response.

## Chapter Summary

+ Crises can occur anyplace and at any time.
+ Though we can never be truly prepared, it is imperative that every school has a plan for dealing with a crisis situation.
+ An essential component of a crisis management plan is that it is highly structured.
+ All involved individuals must know what their role is during a crisis situation.
+ It is up to the administrator to see to it that the school's crisis management plan is an integral part of the school's ongoing staff development plans.
+ In some instances, the aftermath of a crisis can require more care than the actual crisis itself.
+ The school administrator must activate all available resources, from the school and the community, to assist students in the aftermath of a crisis.
+ The school must have some means by which closure is brought to a crisis.

# Case Study Analysis

## 3...2...1...Action!

When she arrived at school and saw the emergency service vehicles all over the parking lot, principal Amy Larkin knew something was terribly wrong. "What's going on here?" she demanded as she bolted from her car. "What are you all doing here, and why haven't I been notified?"

After being told of the tragedy by the chief of police, Dr. Larkin stood in the doorway, a thousand thoughts and emotions streaming forward at once. What could have prompted Frank to take his own life? Why hadn't she noticed any signs before? He was the jolliest, most upbeat custodian she had ever worked with. What would happen to his poor family?

Suddenly she was jolted back into consciousness by one thought—the students! They would be arriving in about 18 minutes. How would she inform them? What if the police were still here? What would the parents think when they dropped the children off for school? Should she call the superintendent?

With that thought, Superintendent Fleischmann arrived in his car. Behind him was a white van with a sign on the side that read *Channel 2 Action News*.

## Questions for Analysis

1. Does this school already have a crisis management plan?
2. What should Amy Larkin do first?
3. What are some key steps that need to be taken within the next 20 minutes?
4. After surviving this day, what are some problems Amy Larkin can anticipate tomorrow?
5. What future steps should be taken to ensure that Amy Larkin does not have a day that's as challenging as today promises to be?

# 11

# Three Opportunities
# to Shine

Building positive, enduring relationships between our schools and our communities is complex and demanding. As has been alluded to many times, the growing list of demands on educational leaders often causes many time-consuming tasks to be temporarily placed on the back burner. Many school administrators find themselves dealing with situations that have quick fixes so they can experience some sense of accomplishment.

The concern raised by such behavior is that it causes relationship building to suffer. The cornerstone of a successful school–community relations plan may well be the capacity that the school administration has for fostering and sustaining positive relationships. If you reflect on many of the concepts and ideas presented in the previous ten chapters, there is a consistent theme of relationship building throughout. The school leaders who influence and shape the culture of their schools through a focus on human relationships find it almost impossible to place these time-consuming tasks on the back burner. They recognize that these relationships are the foundation of their schools' success. Though taking time to build, these relationships form the basis for everything these leaders do.

Principals, in particular, need to gain the support and confluence of values of other members of their school community. In striving to do so, they interact with others and have their values and norms shaped as a result of those interactions. Over time, the norms and values of the leader and the followers move closer together. This means, in essence, that principals who concern themselves with developing strong school–community relations must take the time to understand and appreciate the norms and values of their constituents. Only then will they truly be able to develop relationships with them.

Though strong school–community relations is, therefore, a time-consuming and demanding task, there are a few isolated incidents that, if handled correctly, can be of great assistance in a relatively short time. Although these opportunities will not, in and of themselves, create strong school–community relations in any school, they will assist school leaders in establishing the kinds of relationships that are important to them. As all three of these situations are opportunities that occur in virtually all schools anyway, it stands to reason that we ought to do all we can to make the most of them.

# Open House

The school open house is an opportunity, usually held in the fall, for members of the community to visit the school en masse. Although the majority of attendees are ordinarily parents whose children attend the school, in many cases open houses are held for all members of the community, regardless of their status as parents. There are great variances in the format of a school open house, but they most commonly include an opportunity for attendees to experience a tour of the facility. The next section of this text contains descriptions of some of the more common elements of open house tours.

## Open House Tours

Often, during an open house, parents and community members are given a tour of the school facility. This tour, ordinarily conducted by members of the school's internal publics (i.e., teachers, staff, or students), is a tremendous opportunity to point out to visitors objects and artifacts that define what is important in the school. For example, there are schools that display an array of student artwork for an open house. This display serves to inform the public both of the quality of the artwork students are completing and the importance that the school places on the art program.

Academic awards and athletic trophy displays are another part of the tour that visitors to an open house often receive. As is the case with student artwork, there is a tremendous opportunity here for the school to demonstrate the value placed on student achievement in these areas. The display of such awards is often far more important than is the actual feat the awards represent. From a school–community relations perspective, whether or not the football team won their division is often not nearly as important as the fact that the school takes pride in the team's accomplishments, whatever they happen to be.

Tours of the educational facility conducted during an open house generally also include visits to classrooms or labs that house curricular programs of which the school is particularly proud. Examples include technology labs, band rooms, language labs, and reading rooms. The purpose of including brief visits to these locations as a part of the tour is to ensure that all those in attendance are aware of the curricular offerings that the school provides. For many visitors to an open house, this is the only time in which they are shown these areas.

Because many schools in America are in need of renovations and/or expansions, the issues surrounding the use of tax dollars for such ventures often raise great concern and debate among community members. Tours of the school during an open house also play a significant role in these discussions. If the school has recently undergone some improvements, then the open house tour is an opportunity to show off these improvements to stakeholders. This is particularly effective if students are conducting, or assisting in conducting, the tours. The enthusiasm students can display for improvements to their school can be infectious to community members who are otherwise concerned that their tax dollars are not being spent wisely.

The same logic applies to situations in which the school is in need of improvements for which the local community has failed to approve funds. In these cases, including in the tour those areas that are either outdated, built to specifications not currently warranted, or inappropriately sized, can be a very effective method for convincing community members to reconsider their previous dispositions toward funding the school improvement.

The overall cleanliness of the school facility is another consideration in designing an open house tour. This idea is discussed in greater depth further on in this chapter. Although the school facility and grounds ought to always be meticulously cleaned and maintained, a heightened sense of awareness is necessary at open house time. Because the open house will attract visitors who otherwise are never present in the school, a piece of chalk on a classroom floor may have more impact than it would on an everyday visitor. For the attendee who is a first-time visitor to the school, that single piece of chalk may represent messiness that they feel could exist in the building regularly. You never get a second chance to make a first impression.

In planning to provide tours during an open house, another point to consider and to prepare tour guides for is the way in which individuals greet and respond to one another during the tour. If, for example, two separate tour groups pass one another in the hallways, it is important that the tour guides have a friendly, honest greeting for the leader and members of the other group. If staff members are seen during the tour, they must be aware of the importance of being enthused and greeting the touring group of visitors. These seemingly obvious points are essential. In addition to showcasing the facility, the open house tour provides a rich opportunity to demonstrate relationships and the sense of community that the school professes to enjoy.

## Open House Programs

There are also variations in the types of programs schools offer to attendees of an open house. In fact, there are instances in which there is no program at all. At times such as these, the open house may consist of a simple opportunity for visitors to come to the school and visit locations that are of interest to them. However, as the majority of open house experiences involve adherence to some sort of program planned by school employees, some typical elements are described below.

Oftentimes, an open house begins with a program in the school auditorium, gymnasium, or cafeteria. This program will usually involve an address by the school principal, which will highlight curricular goals and/or accomplishments. If there are issues on the horizon that may benefit from as much public involvement as possible, the principal may choose to introduce or discuss those during this session. This section run by the principal may include a question/answer session, or it may serve as an opportunity for the principal merely to address the public before moving on to the next part of the program.

The open house program, in many cases, also includes a performance(s) by students. This performance may be a song that the children have been rehearsing, it may be a short skit consistent with the open house's theme, or it may be an address by a class president or student council official. Again, the actual content of the performance is often not nearly as important in terms of school–community relations as is the fact that students are included as deliverers of the program. The emphasis is less on showcasing the talents of the children and more on demonstrating the important role they play as stakeholders in the educational process. Additionally, if the student performance incorporates a theme or mission that the school has embraced for the given year, then it becomes even more likely that stakeholders will remember the theme and understand its relevance.

During an open house program, the principal may also choose to introduce staff members to the assembled audience. In a smaller school, it is fairly common for all faculty and staff who are present to be introduced and acknowledged by the crowd. This is of great assistance to families who are new to the community and may be familiar with a very limited number of staff members. In larger schools, the principal often introduces only those faculty and staff members who are new to the school.

In some cases, open house programs are opportunities for guests chosen by the principal to address the audience about relevant topics. The guest may be the district superintendent or his/her designee addressing capital improvements, testing, or curricular advances. Sometimes the guest is a community member, such as a local child psychologist, invited to address such issues as homework completion or parent involvement. Still, in other cases, the guest speaker may be somebody from outside of the community hired because of expertise in an area that parents and community members could benefit from.

Finally, many open house programs also provide an opportunity for an officer of the parent–teacher group (e.g., PTO, PTA) to address those assembled. This address usually includes budgetary information and may include a call for all parents to become involved in the association's activities. This address has added value, in many instances, because it illustrates for attendees that parents are leaders in some important school issues. Again, the issues discussed are often not nearly as important as the mere fact that the individual has been chosen to speak about them. The act of including parent association officials in the program, for example, is often more significant than the content of their speech.

## Classroom Visits

Though open house programs are held for a variety of reasons (i.e., back-to-school night, science fair, student author conference), visits to classrooms are ordinarily a part of the scheduled activities. Sometimes, the classroom visits are designed to give visitors a visual image of the integral parts of the school. There may be student projects displayed for visitors to enjoy, or the classroom may look like it ordinarily does.

At other times, the classroom visit is more formal and includes an address by the classroom teacher. This is particularly common on back-to-school night. The purpose of this address is to inform parents of rules, expectations, and events that will make up the school year for their child. Additionally, there is time allotted for visitors to ask questions of the teacher. The interchange occurring during these times is of paramount importance in setting the tone that the teacher hopes to enjoy throughout the school year. For this reason, teachers should take great care in their personal appearance, their nonverbal and verbal communication, and the appearance of their classroom. The school administration must emphasize these points to assist teachers in understanding their importance. Since many teacher-preparation institutions do not adequately prepare teachers for dealing with parents, it is the responsibility of the principal and other school officials to do so.

It is vitally important to the success of classroom visits that teachers receive some training in how to make a positive impression on the public. Particularly, new teachers must be trained in how to convey positive, welcoming feelings to open house attendees. Although it is important that teachers understand policies and procedures they may be asked about during the event, it is perhaps more important that they understand the importance of the image they portray. This image will be remembered by the parents in attendance far longer than whether or not the teacher knew the answer to a policy question. Conveying a caring disposition toward students and a desire to work cooperatively with parents are two of the most important messages teachers can convey during these events.

The back-to-school event is a tremendous opportunity for each classroom teacher to illustrate a positive disposition and for the school, as a whole, to put its best foot forward with members of the community.

## Timing Is Everything

It has become common practice in many school communities to host open house events during the evening hours. This, in many ways, is a throwback to the days of Ward and June Cleaver of television fame. Ward, being the family breadwinner would arrive home from work, the family would enjoy a nice meal together, and then Ward and June Cleaver would venture off to school to hear of faculty plans for Wally and the Beaver's educations. School administrators must realize that the Cleavers do not live in many communities these days. Single-parent families and other unconventionally configured families have replaced them. The changing of the American workforce has further necessitated that schools reconsider the time of day in which they offer activities such as an open house. A vast number of people work hours quite different from those worked by Ward Cleaver. Many of these workers are the mothers of our schoolchildren, another fact that differentiates the current workforce from its predecessor. Consider that in 1940 fewer than nine percent of all women with children worked outside the home (U.S. Bureau of Labor Statistics, 1987). In 1997, the U.S. Bureau of Labor Statistics reported that 76.5 percent of women with children between the ages of 6 and 13 were in the labor force. As the workforce has changed and alternative family configurations have become more commonplace, one would think that schools also would have changed the times in which they offer programs for these parents to enjoy. Whereas this is true in the best schools, it sadly has not yet become the practice in a vast majority of them.

What are needed are school administrators who structure open house programs to meet the needs of their targeted audience. Knowing the community is again an obvious first step that must be taken. Once the school administrator has some information about the work schedules of most families, then he or she can make more informed decisions regarding the scheduling of activities targeted to these individuals. This does not imply that the principal must memorize every parent's work schedule. However, it does imply that the principal at least ought to know something about the industries that employ many of the school's parents. For example, if the school is located in the vicinity of large manufacturing facilities, knowledge of the number of parents who are employed at these facilities will yield some information about the different shifts that these parents work.

Scheduling important events such as open houses should be done with these work shifts in mind. This will mean, in many instances, that events are held shortly after student dismissal instead of during the evening hours. It may mean that there are two separate events held, one after school and one during the evening. What is important is that the decision regarding the event's scheduling is done with the parents' work schedules in mind.

It can be argued that such an emphasis on parents' schedules shows a lack of understanding for the schedules of faculty and staff members. This is not necessarily so. Although it is true that altering an open house schedule to meet the needs of parents and community members may inadvertently make the event less convenient for faculty and staff, the reverse may also be true. Besides, open house events are designed for the visitors and not for the staff. The relative infrequency of such events, at worst, means that faculty and staff will be inconvenienced a few times each year. If the event produces satisfied visitors, cognizant that every effort has been made to make their attendance plausible, then the inconveniences will be a small price to pay. Remember, the open house is an opportunity for your school to shine. Schedule it at a time when the most people can attend.

## Advertising the Open House— Calling All Parents

A common complaint heard from school principals is that they make efforts to make their open house event convenient for parents to attend, and a very small percentage of parents actually show up. Although there is no way to guarantee the attendance of every parent, there are certainly ways in which school personnel can dramatically increase the number of people in attendance. The simplest one is through advertising.

Because an open house is an important event, it should be advertised in newsletters from the principal's office at the earliest possible date. If you know the date of the fall open house on the first day of school, then begin including it in newsletters and other communications from the office on that very day. People need time to plan, and many people need several reminders before they actually pay close attention to something. The same can be said of classroom communications. All of the teachers who send notices or newsletters home to parents should be encouraged to advertise the open house date and time as soon as they become aware of such things.

In some schools, the students create advertisements for open house events. This can be done in a way that integrates the activity with the curriculum. For example, an art class can utilize techniques that the teacher has introduced in designing special open house invitations for students' parents. At almost any grade level, students can utilize technology to create advertisements of the event. There is an added benefit to parents receiving invitations from their children. If invitations are to be delivered to business or community members, creations by children are almost always more appealing and likely to ellicit positive responses.

Although written invitations and notifications of open house events are important, personal telephone calls are one of the best ways to increase attendance. Again, utilizing students for this task is one way to make it more manageable. Student councils can have an evening in which they attempt to call each and every family inviting them to the open house. In conjunction with faculty assistance, the students can develop a short script that they read to every family they reach. If the students reach an answering machine, they can simply read their prepared speech as the message they leave. The goal of such an evening is that each family receives one personal contact (Whitaker and Fiore, 2001).

The same goal can be accomplished with teacher assistance. If each teacher is given the responsibility of contacting the parents of every student they teach, they will be amazed at the positive response parents are likely to give. In large departments with a vast number of students, parent volunteers or students can be utilized for assistance. This may seem like a lot of work, but the benefits will far outweigh the cost. If care has been taken to create an open house event in which the school will really shine, then the goal ought to be to get as many people to attend as humanly possible.

## The Cleanliness of the School

A further consideration in creating a winning open house event involves the cleanliness and maintenance of the school and its grounds. Although keeping a well-groomed and properly maintained facility is always important to school–community relations, it becomes even more important when planning an event that is likely to draw large numbers of people to the school. Though the school facility may be old, there is no reason why it cannot be cleaned and properly maintained. Leaky or rusted plumbing, for example, can be fixed or updated at a relatively small cost. A fresh coat of paint in a high-traffic area need not be expensive. Clean floors ought to be the expectation of the custodial staff, regardless of the school facility's age. Finally, the exterior of the school ought to be neat, vibrant, and aesthetically pleasing to the community. In maintaining the exterior of the school, the custodial and maintenance staff should be encouraged to use flowers and shrubs that are often seen in the community. The school ought not to appear as something alien from the community, but should instead be an example of the best-groomed facility within the community. Make it look beautiful, but make it look like it belongs in the community also.

Newer facilities should be designed with some of these ideas in mind. Although a new building will obviously stand out as different in many communities, the landscaping affords one opportunity to blend the building in with the community. Newer facilities require the same maintenance as older buildings in terms of keeping floors and hallways clean and attractive, also. Again, open house events provide opportunities for the custodial and maintenance staffs to really make a positive impression. The school administrator must assume the responsibility of ensuring that custodial and maintenance staff members are aware of this.

## Parent–Teacher Conferences

Events involving large groups of people, such as those mentioned in the preceding section are important opportunities for schools to shine. The fact that so many people may attend these events adds credence to their value as a chance to make a positive impression on a significant percentage of constituents all at the very same time. It must be noted, however, that there are other very important opportunities to shine, which do not involve presentations to large groups of people. The most common of these is the face-to-face parent–teacher conference.

The parent–teacher conference provides an unparalleled opportunity for concerned teachers to engage in meaningful, two-way communication with concerned parents. As such, the conference ought to be something that both parties look forward to. It ought to be seen as a chance for the parent to inform the teacher of pertinent information about the child that may assist the teacher's educational planning. Further, it ought to provide the opportunity for the teacher to inform the parent of the child's educational progress and/or potential deficiencies, while utilizing teamwork to design a plan to maximize the child's learning potential. Opportunities for such dialogue cannot be found in large-group open house meetings. This is why the parent–teacher conference is such a valuable time for both the parent and the teacher.

Sadly, many teachers have grown to dread the rich opportunities that parent–teacher conferences can provide. In informal conversations with hundreds of teachers, difficult parents is one of the most commonly cited reason why this is so. The solution to these negative feelings so many teachers have toward parent–teacher conferences rests with the principal's ability to see to it that teachers receive the proper training and support for leading conferences. Effectively handled parent–teacher conferences require skills in communication and organization that too many school principals assume their teachers already possess. While staff development dollars are being used for other types of training, an opportunity is being lost to prepare teachers for this highly important interchange.

The first type of training that teachers need is in dealing with difficult parents. Although most parents in any given school community are supportive and cooperative, one difficult parent can lead to a career of dread and fear at the mere mention of parent–teacher conferences. Principals often have more experience in dealing with difficult parents and can provide some of the necessary training themselves. The problem is exacerbated, however, when the principals do not possess skills to effectively work with difficult parents themselves. In these cases, the principal needs to look outside of the school and find other resources for providing such training.

There are several important considerations in dealing with difficult parents that teachers must become aware of. Some of these are mindsets, as listed in Exhibit 11.1, and may represent a paradigm shift of sorts for the teacher. Others are actual skills and techniques that have been proven time and time again to be successful in dealing with the most difficult parents. Among the mindsets are the following:

---

### Exhibit 11.1. Mindsets About Dealing with Parents

---

- More than 90 percent of parents do an excellent job with their children.
- Virtually 100 percent of parents do the best job they know how to do.
- Part of our job, as educators is to assist the less than 10 percent of parents who really need to improve.
- NEVER argue, yell, use sarcasm, or behave unprofessionally with parents.
- Difficult parents are much better at arguing than you are. The reason is that they have more experience. (Whitaker & Fiore, 2001)

---

School administrators must ensure that teachers understand the mindsets listed above. It is up to the principal to model the belief that the vast majority of parents are good ones. The principal must set the tone for recognizing everybody's responsibility to assist those who are not doing such a good job. Finally, the principal must ensure that all teachers understand that it is never wise to argue with or yell at a difficult parent. These mindsets are not, as some think, automatically understood. They must be taught to teachers in much the same way as good classroom management is taught. I know of very few principals who teach teachers that they ought to yell at students to keep the learning environment well managed. The management of students is seen as important to principals, and so they make sure that teachers understand their values and expectations in this area. The same importance must be assigned to dealings with parents and the management of conferences with them. This is the only way that parent–teacher conferences will begin to become real opportunities for the school to shine.

There are many skills that educators can put into their proverbial bags of tricks that will assist them in dealing with difficult parents. They are outlined in the book *Dealing With Difficult Parents and With Parents in Difficult Situations* (Whitaker & Fiore, 2001) and include such ideas as:

- Making positive contacts with parents before problems occur;
- Acknowledging when you have made a mistake;
- Showing parents that you are on their side and have the same goals as they have;
- Illustrating for difficult parents that the situation could be worse and that you've really given them a good deal; and
- Focusing on the future to prevent further occurrences of whatever has caused them to be upset.

By taking the time to train teachers in these areas, principals will notice a marked decrease in the number of teachers who dread conferences with parents. The focus will cease being on the difficult ones once teachers feel that they have some skills for dealing with these difficult situations. Such training represents time that is well spent so that schools do not lose out on this tremendous opportunity to make parent–teacher conferences the meaningful activities they were designed to be.

In addition to staff development for these human relations issues, principals need to be aware that many teachers need assistance in understanding best how to conduct an effective parent–teacher conference. Here again, the assumption that all teachers possess this understanding is misguided at best. Principals must help teachers focus on the reasons for parent–teacher conferences. They must help teachers get their thoughts focused on such topics as these:

- What do you hope to accomplish?
- What steps can you follow during the conference to ensure that you meet your major objectives?
- Will you allow time for parents to ask questions and make comments?
- What materials should be shared with parents?
- How can you wind up the conference with a plan for action? Will you recommend any specific steps? (NAESP & NSPRA, 2000)

It is, therefore, good practice for principals to provide a training or workshop activity early in the year to prepare teachers for conferences. In addition to informing teachers of the goals of parent–teacher conferences, which essentially are to get information and to give information, the workshop ought to focus on such things as room arrangements and time structuring techniques to ensure that teachers make the most of the opportunities they have for conferring with parents. Part of this training should be devoted to helping teachers understand what the goals of parent–teacher conferences ought to be. Specifically addressed should be the contributions that both parties make to a successful conference.

Exhibits 11.2 and 11.3 outline specific contributions both parents and teachers make to successful conferences.

## Exhibit 11.2. Parents' Contributions to Successful Conferences

+ Their feelings about school from their own childhood
+ Their perceptions of their child's reaction to school
+ A description and understanding of their child's responsibilities at home
+ Information regarding their child's adherence to rules at home
+ An outline of their child's interests or hobbies
+ Health information about their child
+ Sudden changes at home (e.g., divorce or death of a pet or relative)

## Exhibit 11.3. Teachers' Contributions to Successful Conferences

+ An update on the child's academic and social progress at school
+ Perceptions of the child's work habits
+ Opinions about the child's preferred learning style
+ Information about the child's relationships with other children
+ Observations about the child's ability to listen and concentrate
+ An overview of the assessments the child will face during the school year
+ Areas of needed improvement

Acknowledging the achievements possible when these goals are accomplished is helpful to teachers as they prepare to meet with parents. When teachers understand that conferences are give-and-take opportunities replete with the abilities to strengthen an understanding of the child and his or her home life, and the potential for building home and school partnerships, then they are more likely to prepare for them with eager anticipation.

## Helping Teachers Prepare for Conferences

If parent–teacher conferences are going to be opportunities to shine, then the entire school community must be part of the effort in preparing for them and carrying them out. Although teachers are on the front line and, therefore, must be the most prepared for conferences, there are steps that school administrators can take to assist teachers in coordinating smooth, productive conferences.

The first task of the school administrator involves the scheduling and timing of parent–teacher conferences. Just as he or she must do in scheduling open house events, the administrator must try to schedule conferences at a convenient time for parents that is least likely to be in conflict with other community events. Care in scheduling will produce two desirable results. First, attendance is likely to be increased if there are no known scheduling conflicts, and secondly, parents are more likely to arrive at conferences in a cooperative mood if they believe that the school has already made efforts to be cooperative with them.

Another way that the school administrator can provide assistance to teachers is in the advertising of the conferences. Although it is always good practice for individual teachers to include conference reminders in any publications they send home to parents, timely information and reminders from the principal's office can be equally effective and can take some of the burden off the teachers.

In many schools, the scheduling and informing of conferences occurs simultaneously. This is very effective as it not only informs parents that conference days are coming, but it gives them advance notice of scheduling opportunities in case they need to make adjustments to their schedules. Exhibit 11.4 is an example of a letter sent home from a school principal. Note how the letter initially informs parents that conference days are coming, and then gives them an opportunity to indicate their preferred time for scheduling. Although there is no guarantee that parents' preferences can be honored, this letter does serve the purpose of attempting to schedule the conference at a convenient time for both parties. It is believed that parents appreciate this thoughtfulness.

Exhibit 11.4. Parent–Teacher
Conference Notification Letter

## Woodview School

123 Woodview Lane
Anytown, USA

**Ima Goodfellow, Principal**
**Susie Sunshine, Administrative Assistant**

Dear Parents,

It is with excitement that I inform you of our upcoming parent–teacher conferences. These conferences signify a school year that is solidly underway. Allow me to say that I believe we are off to an excellent start here at Woodview. This is due, in large part, to the cooperative relationship between our staff and you, the parents. Parent–teacher conferences will be an outstanding opportunity to enhance these already positive, cooperative relationships we all enjoy.

For your convenience, we are offering both afternoon and evening conferences once again this year. To facilitate this schedule, please be reminded that school will dismiss early on Wednesday, Thursday, and Friday, October 10, 11, and 12. We will follow our early dismissal policy as set forth in our parent handbook. Transportation will be provided as always.

To assist us in scheduling your conference with your child's teacher, please indicate your availability below. So that every effort can be made to ensure that conferences of multiple children in the same family can be accommodated reasonably, please list all of your children's names and grades in the appropriate place below as well. It is important that this form is returned to your child's teacher by September 25. Final confirmation of conference schedules will be sent home on Friday, September 28.

I thank you again for your cooperation, and I assure you that we look forward to the opportunity for strengthening our relationships with you via parent–teacher conferences.

Yours truly,

Ima Goodfellow
Principal

*Please place a "1" by your first choice and a "2" by your second choice. If only one option is plausible, then a "2" is not necessary.*

_____Wednesday, October 10 (5:30 PM–8:30 PM)
_____Thursday, October 11 (1:00 PM–4:00 PM)
_____Thursday, October 11 (5:30 PM–8:30 PM)
_____Friday, October 12 (1:00 PM–4:00 PM)

Child(ren)'s Name(s):

_____ Grade_____
_____ Grade_____
_____ Grade_____
_____ Grade_____

## Conducting the Conference

Methods for actually conducting parent–teacher conferences ought to be explained and periodically reviewed with teachers. Though it is likely not a good idea to develop a single systematic way for conferences to proceed, as such steps run the risk of dehumanizing the entire process, teachers do benefit from some guidance as to how they should best structure and conduct parent–teacher conferences.

The first steps to prepare for conferences involve the arrangement of the conference areas. To begin with, teachers should develop positively worded signs to post outside their classroom doors informing people that conferences are in progress. Posting such signs will lead to a decrease in the number of interruptions and will stress the importance of the conversations taking place inside the classroom. Placed near these signs should be chairs for parents who arrive early to sit in. It is also a good idea to have small puzzles or other toys to occupy the attention of young children who may have needed to accompany the parents to the conference.

Inside the classroom, care should be given to the placement of chairs and tables at which parents and the teacher will confer. These should be placed away from the classroom door to lessen distraction and, above all else, should be comfortable for parents to sit in. It is patently disrespectful for the teacher to sit in his or her desk chair while the parent is squeezed into a student's chair. This is particularly so in early childhood settings. If there are not enough adult-sized chairs available to accommodate all parties, then the teacher must also sit in a student's chair. The comfort of the parents and their feelings of equality should be the primary concerns in creating conference environments.

It is further unwise for teachers to hold conferences with a desk between the parents and themselves. Doing so creates an immediate barrier between parents and teacher that should be avoided. Teachers must be perceived as caring and approachable if conferences are to be successful. This is better accomplished if all parties sit in positions of equality, facing one another.

To maximize the limited time typically allotted for parent–teacher conferences, teachers are well served if they have all relevant data (i.e., test scores, work samples) available before the conference begins. Time is wasted if the teacher is searching for artifacts and examples during the conference, and parents may perceive such searching as disorganization on the part of the teacher.

Once the actual conference has begun, there are other important steps teachers should take to maximize effectiveness. These include:

- Teachers must recognize that they immediately set the tone and climate for the conference by the way in which they greet parents. A friendly smile and an expression of appreciation that the parents were able to attend the conference, go a long way in this regard.

- Begin the conference with a positive comment about the student. For the best students, positive comments will dominate conversations with their parents. Even the students who are experiencing difficulties have positive points, though. The teacher should acknowledge these before discussing areas in need of improvement.
- Allow parents ample opportunities to express their points of view. It can be very frustrating for a parent to listen to a teacher for 15 minutes, only to be told that there is no time left for parent reactions. Therefore, teachers must temper the points that they feel are urgent to discuss with the concerns parents have brought to the conference. It is always possible to schedule a follow-up conference if necessary.
- Sum up any agreements made before the conference ends. The teacher needs to be aware of actions agreed upon and steps to be taken before ending the conference. Just as he or she would do when teaching a lesson to students, the teacher should close the conference by summing these points up for the parents.
- End on the same positive note you began with. Teachers should express appreciation to the parents and make a positive comment about the future. If the conference resulted in a good deal of negative discussion centered on student problems, it is particularly important for the teacher to end with a positive focus on the future.
- The teacher should immediately document any follow-up steps he or she agreed to before beginning a new conference with other parents. Commitments made at a conference but not followed through with can be very damaging to a teacher's reputation.

The principal's role in parent–teacher conferences extends beyond providing training in the areas previously discussed. Although it is important that the principal first take steps to ensure that teachers are prepared for leading parent–teacher conferences, that is only the beginning of the principal's work.

Principals must be highly visible during conference time. Research shows (Fiore, 1999) that teachers and parents feel a sense of comfort knowing that the principal is around. As often as possible, the principal should circulate through the school building. In doing this, the principal will discover opportunities to confer with parents who are waiting for their conference to begin, assist teachers who may have been asked questions that they were unprepared for by parents, and even coordinate conferences that have the expectation of being particularly difficult.

In addition to being visible throughout the building, the principal should be prepared to remain available until the last parent–teacher conference has ended. It is of great comfort to teachers knowing that the principal is still in the building, even if all other teachers have left. Remaining in the building until it is otherwise empty also shows all stakeholders that the principal is willing to work whatever hours are necessary to ensure that parent–teacher conferences are run properly. If they are run properly, then parent–teacher conferences become one more golden opportunity for a school to really shine.

Finally, an evaluation form such as the one depicted in Exhibit 11.5 should be sent to all parents who attended conferences. The form depicted, which was developed by NAESP and NSPRA (2000) can be adapted to include questions specific to a particular school environment.

## Convocations and Celebrations

Throughout the typical academic year many situations occur that warrant a convocation or celebration of some sort. The degree to which the school is perceived as preparing for and assigning importance to these assembly programs and events says a great deal to the public about the pride taken in students and their accomplishments. Therefore, these situations present the third big opportunity that schools have to really shine.

---

### Showcase

My former school is located in an affluent neighborhood in Tampa. There was no shortage of parental involvement because of an active Parent Teacher Association (PTA). One program that the former principal, Mr. Lynn Wade, implemented, was the Achievement of Excellence Breakfast for fifth graders. Students who had earned 20 points or all A's in the fourth grade received a patch with the school emblem. If they received all A's in the fifth grade for the report card grading periods, they received a star-shaped pin for specific points earned. Parents and grandparents were invited to the function, as was a guest speaker from the community or district office. Teachers were able to meet parents in a relaxed atmosphere and share in the celebration.

*Doreen Duncan, former Fifth Grade Teacher and Team Leader,*
*Northwest Elementary School, Tampa, FL*

---

## Exhibit 11.5. Parent Survey

1. All things considered, how would you rate your parent–teacher conference?

     ___ Excellent
     ___ Good
     ___ Average
     ___ Poor

2. What part of the conference was most helpful to you?

3. How could we have improved the conference?

4. What kinds of information about our school would you like to see in our newsletter?

5. Are there any general comments you'd like to make about our schools?

6. Did the conference help you better understand your child's progress?

     ___ Yes
     ___ No; Please explain:

7. Do you feel you had adequate opportunity to contribute to the school's understanding of your child?

     ___ Yes
     ___ No; Please explain:

8. What grade is your child (or children) in?

     ___ Kindergarten, first, second
     ___ Third, fourth
     ___ Fifth, sixth

# Graduation

The most common convocation in all schools is student graduation. Although this is an occurrence in virtually every high school, many elementary and middle schools also honor students who have matriculated through them. The way in which this honor is bestowed on students communicates the importance of students in a school's overall mission to more people than do many of its other methods.

The elements of a high school graduation are essentially similar in most communities. Typically, students are garbed in caps and gowns, there is a processional march, a student leader and an administrator address the graduates, and diplomas are awarded atop a stage. The ceremony oftentimes is one of the most formal convocations students have yet experienced. The fact that its sole purpose is to honor them makes many students very appreciative of having experienced their high school graduation many years after it has occurred.

At other school levels, speaking mainly of middle and elementary schools, student graduations can be opportunities for school leaders to provide acknowledgment of student achievements while also giving closure to the experiences students have enjoyed while at the school. This sense of closure is important to students, and it helps ease the trauma that some students and their families experience during transitional periods. Many parents, for example, feel a sense of unease when their children move from the nurturing environment of elementary school to the often perceived less nurturing environment of middle school. Even though both student and parent typically find the middle school's environment to be wonderful and appropriately nurturing once they get there, if the school can acknowledge trepidations and assist in the transition by implementing a graduation or similar convocation, then the fear of the unknown can be allayed somewhat.

Further, it is a good idea to recognize student achievements at intervals occurring more frequently than every 12 years. A graduation ceremony at each significant transitional period in a child's schooling provides such recognition at appropriately placed intervals.

The particular features of a graduation oftentimes are not as important as the symbolism for which the event stands. Students appreciate being acknowledged and celebrated for their accomplishments. Knowing that school officials have put effort into creating this special occasion just for students delivers a powerful message that otherwise can be taken for granted. Students who feel respected and appreciated can be very good stewards of a school–community relations plan.

## Awards Programs

Awards programs are also opportunities for school administrators, teachers, and staff members to honor students and celebrate their accomplishments. Though these typically involve only family members of the honored students, this arrangement need not be the only way to conduct such convocations. Community members should also be invited, if space allows, so that they can share in the accomplishments of their community's young people. In this way, awards programs become other opportunities for the school to shine. Recall a premise from the first chapter of this book: If we do not tell the public about the great things we are accomplishing in our schools, then nobody will. It is up to educational leaders in all positions to celebrate the successes of their own students.

Another terrific aspect presented by the staging of awards programs and convocations is that the school officials are at liberty to decide which accomplishments to honor. As such, awards programs need not only celebrate those students with sterling academic accomplishments. All students, whether academically gifted or not, have the opportunity to be recognized. Many schools also honor those students who have achieved athletically. Some schools honor students whose achievements are in artistic endeavors.

Other schools, while honoring students for academic achievements, give equal honor to students who have shown academic improvement, even if such improvements do not put students on any honor roll. BUG, an acronym for Bringing Up Grades, is a program at Parkview Elementary School in Valparaiso, Indiana. The goal of BUG is to honor students who have done precisely what the name implies; they have brought up their grades from where they were at the conclusion of the previous grading period. Students who earn a BUG award are honored at the same ceremony as those students who have achieved honor-roll status.

By publicly recognizing and honoring students for their accomplishments, schools deliver the message that students are the purpose of their existence. Furthermore, these convocations show the community that students accomplish a great deal at school. Finally, convocations demonstrate that the school wishes to celebrate successes with the community. The message is that schools do not choose to isolate themselves from the community, allowing the community to learn about what happens inside the school only from media outlets. Instead, through convocations, schools clearly illustrate that they are vibrant, integral parts of the community. Though much of what happens inside may be veiled somewhat from the community, the community has ample opportunity to remove the veil and join in celebrations.

## Showcase

As a local superintendent in two large districts, I always needed to create identity in organizations where shear size and geography were enemies of developing a sense of family. An annual event that focused on this need was the convocation. The goals were simple: (1) Bring everyone together in one place where there is a sense of common purpose; (2) Give colleagues a chance to visualize the size of the organization; (3) Foster an understanding that there are "no secondary citizens" in our family; (4) Recognize teachers and administrators for outstanding achievement and contributions; and (5) Celebrate student achievement in the classroom, on stage, on the field, and in the community. The emphasis was always on qualities that led to an outstanding organization—not on policies, politics, or platform presentations. The desired result was to have colleagues leave (teachers, custodians, secretaries, bus drivers, mechanics, and administrators) saying, "I may not agree with every decision, but this is a great place to work."

*Dr. William C. Bosher, former Superintendent, Chesterfield County Schools, Chesterfield, VA, now Director of the Commonwealth Educational Policy Institute, Richmond, VA*

## Chapter Summary

- An open house creates a rich opportunity to invite members of the community into our schools.

- It is essential that great care go into the design and implementation of an open house so that the school may put its best foot forward.

- Parent–teacher conferences present teachers with an opportunity to give and receive pertinent information that can make a school year more productive.

- Most parents do an excellent job supporting education, so educators should be excited about opportunities to confer with them.

- There are specific skills and techniques that greatly assist educators in dealing with difficult parents.

- The school principal must ensure that teachers are properly trained and prepared for productive parent–teacher conferences.

- Graduations and convocations present opportunities for school officials to demonstrate the pride they have in student accomplishments.
- There are a wide variety of ways in which schools can recognize and honor their students.
- Convocations and open houses should include and involve as many members of the community as is feasible.

# Case Study Analysis

## But They Scare Me

The calendar showed it, and the falling leaves confirmed it; the autumn season had arrived. Whereas that meant many good things to other people, for Jeff Bowman it spelled doom. Early October signified that parent–teacher conferences were on the horizon. Though he had not experienced them before, as this was his first year teaching, Jeff had heard horror stories about angry, uncooperative parents with very unrealistic expectations. Jeff hated conflict. In fact, he entered the teaching profession because he felt there would be far less conflict to deal with than he would have experienced if he entered his family's automobile sales business.

Sitting at home and staring into space one evening, Jeff was startled back into consciousness by his new bride, Gretchen. "Honey," she began. "What's been bothering you so much lately? You look as though you've seen a ghost."

Jeff tried to explain his fear at the prospect of meeting all of the parents he'd have to face in a few weeks. He told his wife that he was really concerned about all of the horrific tales he'd heard about parents in this community. After all, he reasoned, he had one of the lowest achieving literature classes in the school. His ability to motivate people and his excitement for literature prompted the principal to schedule many students who needed a boost of some sort in Jeff's class. He was positive, he explained, that these students' parents would expect great things from Jeff. The fact was eight students were barely passing.

"Well honey," Gretchen retorted, "can't you just talk to the principal about this? Surely he's planning to help you prepare for these conferences anyway." "After all," Gretchen concluded, "if you had joined the family business, your father would have trained you before putting you in front of a customer, wouldn't he have?"

Jeff could only smirk. "You know, honey, I never thought of it that way before."

## Questions for Analysis

1. What are the real bases for Jeff's fear of parent–teacher conferences? Why do you believe as you do?

2. Other than Jeff himself, is anybody else responsible for his feelings that he is not adequately prepared for parent–teacher conferences?

3. If you were Jeff, would you speak with the principal about your trepidation? If so, what would you say?

4. Explain the principal's role in parent–teacher conferences. Which aspects do you think are the most important? Has Jeff's principal been remiss in any of his duties?

# 12

# Evaluating Effectiveness and Building Confidence— The Future

The previous eleven chapters have been designed to influence and assist every educational leader in developing and sustaining the aptitude required to build bridges between schools and communities. Whereas some chapters have focused on specific communication techniques that will make this mission easier, there have also been numerous citations of research to convince all readers that strong, purposeful communication between the school and the community is, in fact, beneficial. Examples have been provided to further assist in this process.

As the previous chapters have been read and studied, there undoubtedly have been parts of the text that have sparked readers to realize that the concept or communication element being illustrated is already being practiced to an adequate or, perhaps superior, extent in their schools. Wherever this is the case, the accompanying text may have served as a reinforcement of the school's great efforts. At other times, parts of the text may have caused readers to realize that improvements are needed to maximize relationships between the school and the community. Hopefully, the examples and explanations from the text will allow these readers to begin developing and utilizing techniques that are parts of a superior school–community relations plan.

Regardless of the feelings evoked, whether they are of satisfaction at the adequacy of efforts or concern about the improvements needed, the task before all readers is now to begin focusing on the future. If a school's plan for communicating with the communities it serves is adequate or superior, then the focus must be on how to make it even better. If a school's plan and efforts appear inadequate at present, then the present must be pushed aside and replaced with a focus on the future and the improvements that future will bring.

# Determing the Effectivess of Your
# School–Community Relations Efforts

In the field of education, determining effectiveness in any area is fraught with difficulty. Unlike some of the sciences, there are often untold variables or intangibles in educational settings that are difficult to control and/or measure. So while readers may feel that their school is performing school–community relations' tasks with a certain degree of success, this determination is often based on feelings or observations that are challenging to quantify.

As our nation becomes further entrenched in discussions of school choice, the call for school administrators to prove their successes will become increasingly loud. School administrators at both the building and school district levels will be asked to verify that the programs they implement do produce measurable results. Additionally, the task of demonstrating that communications programs contribute to better student learning will fall squarely on the administrators' shoulders.

How can the results of efforts in school–community relations be verified? Furthermore, because these efforts contain many intangibles, can these intangibles in some way be measured? Finally, does the concept of school choice create additional concerns for school administrators? These questions will be answered throughout the remainder of this chapter.

## Verifying Results in School–Community Relations

Evaluating the results of school–community relations efforts, whether they are individual steps or an entire comprehensive plan, encompasses three separate examinations or steps, as outlined here:

1. Examining the present components of the school–community relations plan. Here, the focus is on the actual components that are present. The purpose is to verify whether or not anything is actually being done. For example, if written communication with external groups is what a school leader wishes to verify, then the first step is to simply examine evidence that such communication actually exists.

2. Examining the extent to which these efforts are producing intended results. Here, the focus is on the results of the components examined in the first step. Using the example of written communication with external groups, the school leader would now examine whether or not the written examples already evidenced did, in fact, improve communication with external groups. The purpose would be to discover if the writ-

ten examples were circulated to, read by, understood by, and appreciated by the intended audiences.

3.  Examining whether or not the results of the effort justified the resources required to achieve them. Here, the focus is on the time and/or cost of implementing the components examined in steps one and two. Continuing with the written communication example, the leader must now weigh the time and/or cost expended in creating and circulating these written examples with the benefit that they appear to have given the school.

The above three steps are essential in verifying the results of any school–community relations' efforts. School administrators must regularly examine whether or not any evidence exists that indicates there actually are efforts being made in school–community relations. They then must examine the results of these efforts. Moreover, they must ascertain whether or not these results warrant the resources being expended to attain the results. Each step, or separate examination, can be verified through a variety of evaluation methods. School administrators ought to understand the benefits of each method, and then choose the method that will best deliver the results they intend to measure in the first place. Methods of evaluation include:

+ *Questionnaires*—Questionnaires are widely used in schools for surveying the opinions of select internal or external groups. Their relative design ease and the different ways for distributing them make questionnaires an attractive choice for discovering public opinion on a wide range of topics. Questionnaires can be personally handed out to individuals at the conclusion of a meeting. If attendees are urged to respond to the questionnaire before leaving the meeting, then quick, immediate results can be obtained. Questionnaires can also be mailed to parents or community members or inserted into publications that are then sent home with students to avoid postage costs. If a large sample size is desired, then the school administrator can include prepaid postage with questionnaires sent to external public groups so that respondents are not burdened with postage costs.

+ *Rating Scales*—Rating scales, with the most widely used model having been developed by Rensis Likert, ask respondents to choose from between two and five degrees of feeling or opinion on a series of questions. For example, respondents may be asked, "How well does your child's teacher communicate with you regarding your child's academic progress—extremely well, fairly well, barely adequately, not well at all?" The purpose of a rating scale is to attempt to quantify human expression. Receiving a majority of responses that state "not well at all," gives the administrator a quantitative representation of respondents' attitudes that would be more difficult to verify with open-ended responses.

- *Telephone Surveys*—As people increasingly are becoming frustrated with unsolicited telemarketing contacts, telephone surveys may not be the most accepted method for discovering public opinion. However, their low cost and the fact that they can be conducted quickly make them popular in some schools. Essentially, telephone surveys are conducted by calling parents or community members at random and asking their opinions or reactions to a few brief items. Comments are recorded and then school administrators look for patterns in the results. Telephone surveys are primarily used to get reactions to previously printed news stories or school events.

Although there are other methods that can be employed to evaluate school–community relations efforts and gather public opinion data, these three are among the most widely used. It is up to school administrators to know how best to survey the community they are targeting. For example, if a school administrator needs to know what teachers are doing, if anything, in terms of communicating with parents about their students standardized test performances, then a telephone survey of parents likely is not the most efficient or effective method to employ. Likewise, it would be unwise to send questionnaires home with students designed to show parents' perceptions of school wide effectiveness in school–community relations on the last day of school. Exhibit 12.1 shows a sample questionnaire regarding a school's communication with parents. A questionnaire like this can be included in a newsletter that is sent home with student, or it can be mailed home to parents.

A final, less formal means for assessing program effectiveness is through observation. Although this method may be widely criticized because of the lack of quantifiable evidence it produces, it is also the method most often employed in schools. Effective administrators practice MBWA (Management By Wandering Around). As Frase & Melton explain, "MBWA leaders are seldom in their offices during school hours. MBWA principals are on their feet, wandering with a purpose. They spend their time in classrooms and hallways, with teachers and students." (1992, p. 19) As principals and other administrators practice MBWA, they cannot help but make observations. Knowing what they intend to observe accomplishes the task of program evaluation in the context of an already planned part of the administrator's day. For example, if an administrator desires information about the effectiveness of parent–teacher conferences,

## Exhibit 12.1. Communication Questionnaire

Please take a few minutes to answer these important questions. They are designed to assist us in evaluating our efforts at communicating with you, the parents. By returning this completed questionnaire to your child's teacher by *February 26, 2002*, you will be assisting us greatly. Thank you in advance!

1. Do you read the principal's weekly newsletter? Is the information it contains helpful to you?

2. Does your child's teacher send home regularly scheduled newsletter? If so, are they helpful to you?

3. Please comment on school staff members' efforts at communicating with you if your child is having a problem.

4. Please comment on school staff members' efforts at communicating good news to you.

5. Do you feel that the principal is accessible to you if you need to speak with her?

6. Do you feel that your child's teacher is accessible to you?

7. Do you feel welcome at Sunnyvale School? Why/Why Not?

---

evidence can be targeted for observation while the principal is moving around the school building, as he or she already would have planned to be doing.

Other opportunities school administrators have to conduct informal observations designed to inform them of public opinion or program effectiveness occur when the administrators are appearing in public settings. People's reactions at civic organizations, outside of school board meetings, or at sporting and artistic events give administrators a great deal of information regarding public opinions. Again, though this information is difficult to quantify, it should be noted by the administrator and used as part of the assessment process.

---

## Showcase

Being recognized as an effective leader requires more than the sign on the door or the title on you desk. Influencing others is a critical skill in today's workplace where you must interact with many school critics and supporters. Looking ahead into the twenty-first century, principals will continue to need public support to endorse school initiatives. One of the many ways to win support from others is to systematically promote school achievements and programs through brochures, flyers, and other marketing tools.

*Dr. India Podsen, former Assistant Principal, Lindle Middle School, Smyrna, GA, now Associate Professor, North Georgia College and State University, and author of Written Expression: The Principal's Survival Guide*

---

## Making Intangibles More Tangible

As mentioned earlier, there are many intangible elements at work in our schools that interfere with our ability to get quantifiable, indisputable results to our measurement attempts. The classic example of this paradox occurs each year as schools administer standardized tests to students. Because these tests measure student achievement in clearly defined areas, the inherent nature of being large-scale, norm-referenced tests, prevents them from measuring other areas that may be important in certain schools. Similarly, these standardized tests obviously ignore social–emotional factors affecting student performance. This is not a criticism of any particular tests. It is, instead, a fundamental limitation of norm-referenced, standardized tests designed for national distribution.

Interpreting and utilizing results from these tests presents further challenges. As standardized tests, often referred to as "high-stakes" tests, become litmus tests for gauging teacher and school success, other less tangible issues become larger and more significant. One such issue is the number of transient students taking these tests. Many teachers have commented that they have students entering their classrooms days before these tests are to be administered. The results these students achieve are somehow included in an overall composite that is then used to judge particular teacher performance. With as much as 50 percent of the student body moving in and out of a particular classroom during an academic year, judging teachers based on test results seems unfair, at best. Many of the students are not in the classrooms long enough to receive much of an impact from the teacher. This point is not included to generate discussions about standardized tests. It is included, however, to illustrate that the social dynamics of schools make quantifiable measurements and judgments a challenge to obtain and utilize.

This is particularly so in the realm of school–community relations. Truly uncovering public opinion, for example, is a challenge. Knowledge of sampling techniques and margins of error reduces some of the ambiguity, but the fact still remains that quantifying people's feelings and attitudes is a challenge facing school administrators. The challenge is compounded when a public that demands answers in quantifiable terminology confronts school administrators.

This challenge is why multiple measures of a school–community relations plan's effectiveness must be obtained. Let us say, for example, that a questionnaire is sent to parents asking them for their opinions regarding school personnel and their aptitudes at external communication. Let us assume that this questionnaire enjoys a 30 percent return rate, meaning that of those questionnaires sent out, 30 percent are completed and returned to school. Further assuming that the questionnaire was sent to all parents, a feat that may or may not have been possible, there are still 70 percent of parents whose opinions are not accounted for. To make the results more tangible and easier to give credence to, the school administrator must do more to gather a greater number of opinions regarding the issue in question. Telephone polls, as an example, may be conducted next. Through these polls, a greater number of respondents should be reached. However, the administrator's efforts need not end at this step. Informal conversations with parents who visit the school can be easily conducted. Questions about external communication can be asked of parents who are in attendance for conferences with the teacher or who attend meetings of the school's parent–teacher organization.

The result of this combination of efforts may be a portfolio of responses that can be used to verify the success or limitation of a school's efforts at communicating with external publics. Depending on the specific questions that were asked, this portfolio can point out specific areas within the category of external communication that the school does well, or it can illustrate specific areas that need to be strengthened.

It is important that school administrators recognize the ever-increasing importance of verifying their efforts in communicating with all of the publics they serve. It is further important that school administrators understand the challenges of gathering information that can, in fact, be verified. By understanding some simple techniques and by utilizing them appropriately and in combination, a portfolio can be developed that will offer information that is more tangible and easier to quantify.

# School Choice in
# the Twenty-First Century

Upon mentioning the idea of school choice to teachers and administrators, one is often greeted with anger, fear, hostility, or any combination of these emotions. The concept of choice has become synonymous with an unfair conspiracy against public education. It need not be viewed in this way, though. Educators can learn to embrace the concept of choice and to use school choice to their advantage. All educators need to face one simple fact. The public's right to choose schools for their children to attend is an idea that is here to stay, at least for the foreseeable future.

What is less certain is what school choice will look like on a national basis 10 or 20 years from now. As this textbook goes to press, the administration of President George W. Bush continues pressing for wider school choice options for American families. Politicians on both sides of the issue continue to grapple with issues of funding and equity in such choice. The political landscape of this enormous issue can overshadow what school choice actually means to educators across the country. Educators, though also concerned with funding and equity issues, must also be aware of what choice programs may mean to their schools' enrollment. These individuals must learn, at least for the time being, how to lead the public to choose their school as the place to educate their children.

One of the first questions that school administrators and teachers consider when faced with the school choice issue is similar to this one: "If parents in this community could send their children to any school they choose, how many of them would choose to stay right here?" Although all of the complexities of the school choice issue are not within the control of individual educators, the answer to the above question certainly is. Each and every school staff member has a role to play in ensuring that parents in their community would choose their school, if they were given the choice.

If you think of the best schools you know of—the real superstar schools—how many people in those schools' communities do you think would choose to stay in their school if given the choice to go anyplace they want to go? The answer is probably close to 100 percent of the people. It is within every reader's grasp to turn the school that they are employed at into a superstar school. Utilizing many of the techniques already discussed in this book will lead all readers in that direction.

The essential feeling educators ought to begin experiencing when confronted with the school choice questions that previously angered, threatened, and concerned them is a feeling of hope. School choice ought not be a threat, assuming educational leaders keep in mind a few suggestions that will lead people, if given the choice, to choose their schools. These suggestions are listed and explained below:

- *Focus energies on the overall climate of your school.* Pay particular attention to the entryway that greets all visitors to your school facility. Keeping this area especially clean, warm, and inviting will go a long way toward improving visitors' perceptions of the overall climate as soon as they enter the building.

- *Pay similar attention to the exterior of your school facility.* Because this is the only part of the school that most community members see, it ought to be well groomed and free of debris. When the exterior of a school looks as though it has been taken care of, there is a positive impact on people's perceptions of the pride employees have in the school.

- *Remind all staff members that they are the best spokespersons for the school.* Comments that staff members make about the school while out in the community are taken as the truth. Community members assume that employees ought to know what the school is really like because they work there every day. Staff members must exercise great care in what they say about the school to members of the community.

- *The above item is less of an issue when employees are glad they work at the school.* School administrators, therefore, must pay close attention to employee needs. Recognizing good work, judiciously giving staff members responsibility and authority, and rewarding all good deeds noted are practices that every school administrator ought to follow.

- *Recruit and retain the best teachers you can find.* There is no substitute for excellent teaching. In fact, great teachers are the cornerstones of every great school. Principals who are open, honest, and fair and who understand what excellent teaching is have the easiest time attracting the best teachers. Remaining mindful of how best to acknowledge and reward great teachers is of great assistance in retaining them.

- *Communicate with external groups as effectively as you possibly can.* School administrators must regularly reach out to the community, asking for their guidance and assistance, and thanking them for any input they give. The administration cannot do it alone, though. In the best schools, teachers communicate regularly with all parents. Many teachers in these schools are also active in organizations within the community, and they use this involvement to get business and community support for educational ventures.

- *Inform the press of **every** good thing that happens in your school.* By respecting the wishes of local media in terms of how and when you inform them of news, you can avoid getting on their bad side. Give the news to them in the format they want, but give all positive news, without exception, to media outlets.

♦ *Focus on the students.* The schools that never fail to remember that everything they do is done for students and their education are the schools that tend to be seen as the most successful. Moreover, when students understand how important they are to the adults in the school building, then they feel better about school. Happy, respected students are the best publicity a school could ever ask for.

These suggestions will not, by themselves, transform a school into a place that all community members support and consider to be great. Obviously, there are a multitude of factors that affect what people think of the schools in their communities. In some communities, for example, schools that perform poorly on standardized tests are considered by many not to be good schools. Legislatures in many of our states, unfortunately, have fed this misconception. However, as the administrators of these schools can attest, even their personal best efforts will not, by themselves, have a dramatic impact on test scores.

This is not to say that improved test scores ought to be a secondary goal of schools. However, if administrators know that they have the best teachers, if they reach out to the community to keep them involved in their school, and if students feel good about being in school, then there is a greater likelihood that students will be achieving at their potential. School administrators who devote their attention toward the people in their schools, this author believes, will find that achievement will follow.

Not every school can perform at an above-average level on standardized test measures. However, every school can perform at, or even above, the expected level of performance for the students it serves. Schools that consistently turn out students performing at or above expected levels given their individual abilities will be schools of choice, regardless of the dynamics of the school choice program.

It is time for educational leaders to become proactive and to stop operating in a fear mentality. School administration is not a career characterized by people as victims of an unfair public. It is not a field that people ought to enter with an expectation of being unfairly judged and scrutinized. It is not a field that requires people who can formulate quick responses in the face of irrational demands and expectations.

School administration is a field for educational leaders. It is a field for those individuals who have vision and a passion for turning this vision into a reality. It is a profession for that special person who can take the collective beliefs of a variety of individuals and form a cohesive mission around them. School administration is a field for leaders who wish to help correct and inform an often-misunderstanding public.

Whether the issue is school choice or a curricular one of deeper meaning to education, it is up to educational leaders to educate the entire community. This is done, as the previous eleven chapters have illustrated, through a paradigm of communication. This paradigm has listening, understanding, openness, honesty, and respect as its core elements. If school administrators will adopt this paradigm and begin focusing on the needs and beliefs of the many publics they have been hired to serve, then they will gain a richer understanding of education's role in their community. If school administrators will passionately communicate what they know to be sound educational practices to all concerned stakeholders, then they will create more informed publics than those already existing. This two-way communication will, the author is convinced, restore confidence to American public education.

School–community relations is essential to the success of all school administrators. Hopefully, this book has helped you, the reader, to realize that and to better understand your own personal role in developing and enhancing the relationships that characterize it.

## Chapter Summary

+ The many publics served by a school are increasingly expecting schools to verify their results and to be accountable.

+ The effects of a school–community relations plan are often difficult to assess and verify.

+ A combination of methods is the best way to illustrate that efforts in school–community relations are paying desired dividends.

+ Questionnaires, rating scales, and telephone surveys are three common ways school administrators attempt to ascertain public opinion.

+ Combining these methods with personal observations helps the school administrator develop an even clearer picture.

+ School choice is a concept that has many forms, but is here to stay for the foreseeable future.

+ School leaders must stop fearing choice and must, instead, see this as an opportunity to illustrate why their schools ought to be among those "chosen."

+ There is no substitute for excellent teaching. It is the cornerstone of a school, and when it is present, there is an increased likelihood that the public will look favorably on the school.

- Focusing on students and the overall climate of a school will go a long way toward demonstrating school quality to the public.
- The most successful administrators are those who are the most adept at developing strong school–community relations.

# Case Study Analysis

## The Proof is in the Pudding

As Linda Perry sat outside of Bud McCaffrey's office waiting for her annual review conference, she couldn't help but smile. This had been a great year at Lake Vista Elementary School, and she knew that Bud was happy with the work she had done. And really, she thought, why shouldn't he be. The Lake Vista parents, a traditionally apathetic group, were volunteering hundreds of hours, their attendance at parent–teacher conferences had steadily increased in the three years Linda had been principal, and complaints to Bud's office were virtually nonexistent. As Assistant Superintendent for Elementary Education, a reduction in parental complaints pleased Bud greatly.

Linda also reflected on the improvements in student achievement and student attendance noted at Lake Vista. Increased attendance meant increased funding for the district, and improved test scores kept the media from printing negative stories. This conference with Bud, she was sure, would be a great one!

Thirty minutes later, Linda still had that same smile on her face. Bud McCaffrey was praising her for all of Lake Vista's many accomplishments. Linda was actually a bit embarrassed, because she knew she wasn't responsible for all of the good things happening at the school. Nevertheless, it felt great to have Bud giving her so much credit. Then Bud raised an issue that Linda really didn't know how to respond to. It wasn't a negative issue, but it certainly was a perplexing one, and it addressed something that Linda Perry had never before considered.

"Linda," Bud began, "the board is impressed with your efforts at improving parental and community involvement in your school. In fact, several board members have acknowledged that you gave impressive presentations to Rotary and Kiwanis about programs at your school. Because one board member is a Lake Vista parent, I have even heard how impressed parents are with the three-column, color newsletter you send home each week. However, in closed session last month, one board member raised concern about money being spent at Lake Vista for all of these "good" things. He specifically cited the color laser printer and toner cartridges purchased from your supply account. There was even mention of the extravagant afternoon teas you provide on a monthly basis for members of the local community." Bud chuckled, "I was specifically told that I must find out where you purchase those sponge cakes with the flavored pudding inside."

"I don't understand," Linda mustered. "All good things come at a cost."

"I know," came Bud's reply. "The thing is, the board wants proof that all of this effort is doing more than just making people happy. If you just give me some data, some numbers to verify that more members of the community are involved and that this involvement makes Lake Vista a better school, I know the board will be happy. Look Linda, some test data indicates improvement and I don't get nearly as many complaints from Lake Vista parents as I used to, but that's not enough evidence. Do Lake Vista parents believe that the three-column color newsletters are so good looking that they justify the costs? Is it worth having you out of the building making presentations to civic organizations? Does the food you provide for these afternoon teas improve attendance and benefit kids in any way? These are questions that you need to answer, Linda."

## Questions for Analysis

1. How can Linda gather the information requested by the Assistant Superintendent for Elementary Education?
2. Why should she choose one method for data collection over another?
3. Could there be any underlying reasons why the school board wants this information? If so, what are they?
4. What can you learn from Linda's situation that will help you if you are in similar shoes?

# References

*Achieving the goals: Goal 8—Parental involvement & participation* (1997). Retrieved from http://www.ed.gov/pubs/AchGoals/pidds.htm

American Association of Retired Persons (2001). *AARP facts.* Retrieved from http://www.aarp.org/whatis.html

Beach, R.H., & Trent, J. (2000). In T. Kowalski. *Public relations in schools* (2nd Ed.). Columbus, OH: Merrill.

Benson, C., Buckley, S., & Elliott, A. (1980). Families as educators: Time use contributions to school achievement. In J. Gutherie (Ed.), *School finance policy in the 1980's.* Cambridge, MA: Ballinger.

Berliner, D.C. (1993). Education's present misleading myths undermine confidence in one of america's most cherished institutions. *Journal of Educational Public Relations, 15*(2), 4–11.

Brum v. Town of Dartmouth, 690 N.E.2d 844 (Mass. App. 1998).

Buell, N. (1992). Building a shared vision—The principal's leadership challenge. *NASSP Bulletin, 76*(542), 88–92.

Burgoon, J.K., Buller, D.B., & Woodall, W.G. (1989). *Nonverbal communication: The unspoken dialogue.* New York: Harper & Row.

Cattagni, A. & Farris, E. (2001). Internet access in US public schools and classrooms: 1994-2000. National Center for Educational Statistics. Retrieved from http://nces.ed.gov/pubsearch/pubsinfo.asp?pubid= 2001071

Covey, S. R. (1997). *The 7 habits of highly effective families.* New York: Golden Books.

Dietz, M.J. (1997). *School, family, and community: Techniques and models for successful collaboration.* Gaithersburg, MD: Aspen Publishers.

Educational Excellence for all Learners Act of 2001, S.7, 107th Cong., 1st Sess. (2001).

Epstein, J. (1992). Schools reaching out increase family–community involvement. Report: Current research and development (No.1, p. 15). Baltimore, MD: Center on Families, Communities, Schools, and Children Learning, Johns Hopkins University.

Fiore, D.J. (2001). *Creating connections for better schools: How leaders enhance school culture.* Larchmont, NY: Eye On Education.

Fiore, D.J. (1999). The relationship between principal effectiveness and school culture in elementary schools. (Doctoral dissertation, Indiana State University, 1999).

Frase, L.E., & Melton, R.G. (1992). Manager or participatory leader? What does it take? *NASSP Bulletin, 76*(540), 17–24.

Generations United Goals (2000). Retrieved from http://www.gu.org/about.htm

Ginott, H.G. (1972). *Teacher and child: A book for parents and teachers.* New York: Macmillan.

Greenleaf, R. (1977). *Servant leadership: A journey into the nature of legitimate power and greatness.* New York: Paulist Press.

Goals 2000 (1995). The National Education Goals Report 1995. Washington, DC: U.S. Government Printing Office.

Hall, E.T. (1969). *The hidden dimension.* Garden City, NY: Anchor.

Heckman, P.E. (1993). School restructuring in practice: Reckoning with the culture of school. *International Journal of Educational Reform, 2*(3), 263–271.

Herzberg, F. (1975). "One more time: How do you motivate employees?" *Business classics: Fifteen key concepts for managerial success.* President And Fellows of Harvard College.

Human Development Report (6th ed.) (1995). Cary, NC: Oxford University Press.

Immigration and Naturalization Service Statistics Division (2001). Retrieved from http://www.ins.usdoj.gov/graphics/aboutins/ statisics/index.htm

Maeroff, G.I., (1998). Good neighbors. *The American School Board Journal, 185*(3), 26–29.

McCormack, M. (1989). *What they still don't teach you at Harvard business school.* New York: Bantam Books.

McEwan, Elaine K. (1998). *How to deal with parents who are angry, troubled, afraid or just plain crazy.* Thousand Oaks, CA: Corwin Press.

National Association of Broadcasters (1984). *If you want air time.* Washington DC: Author.

National Association of Elementary School Principals(2001). *Conventions and exhibits.* Retrieved from http://www.naesp.org/conventions.html

National Association of Elementary School Principals & National School Public Relations Association (2000). *Principals in the public*

National Association of Secondary School Principals (2001). *86th Annual convention and exposition.* Retrieved from http://www. nasspconvention.org

National Data Book (2000). *Statistical abstract of the United States,* (120th ed.). Baton Rouge, LA: Claitors.

National PTA (1997). *National standards for parent/family involvement.* Retrieved from http://www.pta.org/issues/invstand.htm

National School Safety Center. (2000). Available at http://www.nsscl.org

No Child Left Behind Act of 2001, H.R. 1, 107th Cong., 1ˢᵗ Sess. § 4 (2001).

NUA Surveys (1999). *How many on line?*, 4(16). Retrieved from http://www.nua.ie/surveys/how_many_online/index.html

O'Hair, M.J., & Ropo, E. (1994). Unspoken messages: Understanding diversity in education requires emphasis on nonverbal communication. *Teacher Education Quarterly, 21*(3), 91–112.

Ordovensky, P. & Marx, G. (1993). *Working with the news media.* Arlington, VA: American Association of School Administration.

Pawlas, G.E. (1995). *The administrator's guide to school–community relations.* Princeton Junction, NJ: Eye On Education.

Podsen, I., Allen, C., Pethel, G., & Waide, J. (1997). *Written expression: The principal's survival guide.* Larchmont, NY: Eye On Education.

Rich, D. (1998). What parents want from teachers. *Educational Leadership, 55*(8), 37–39.

Rioux, J.W., & Berla, N. (1993). *Innovations in parent & family involvement.* Larchmont, NY: Eye On Education.

Rodham-Clinton, H. (1996). *It takes a village and other lessons children teach us.* Carmichael, CA: Touchstone.

Rogers, E. M., & Shoemaker, F. F. (1971). *Communication of innovations: A cross-cultural approach,* (2nd ed.). New York: Macmillan.

Rose, L.C., & Gallup, A.M. (2001). *The 33rd annual Phi Delta Kappa/Gallup Poll of the public's attitudes toward the public schools.* Retrieved from http://www.pdkintl.org/kappan/ko109gal.htm

Rose, L.C., Gallup, A.M., & Elam, (1998). *The 30th annual Phi Delta Kappa/Gallup Poll of the public's attitudes toward the public schools.* Retrieved from http://www.pdkintl.org/kappan/kp9809-a.htm

Scarnati, J. (1994). Beyond technical competence: Nine rules for administrators. *NASSP Bulletin, 78*(561), 76–83.

Schlechty, P. (1997). *Inventing better schools: An action plan for educational reform.* San Francisco: Jossey-Bass.

Schlechty, P. (1990). *Schools for the 21st century: Leadership imperatives for educational reform.* San Francisco: Jossey-Bass.

Schueckler, LP., & West, P.T. (1991). Principals and PR directors mostly agree on the ideal PR role for senior high school principals, but substantially disagree on their PR performance. *Journal of Educational Public Relations, 13*(4), 24–26.

Shell Oil Company (1998). The Shell Poll: Schools and Careers: 1(1)

Standards for school leaders (1996). Washington, DC: Council of Chief State School Officers.

Stolp, S. (1996). Leadership for school culture. *Emergency Librarian, 23*(3), 30–31.

Teixeira, R.A. (2000). The tax cut nobody wants. *The American Prospect, 11*(14).

Toastmasters International (2001). *10 Tips for successful public speaking.* Retrieved from http://www.toastmasters.org/tips.htm

United States Bureau of the Census (1990). *Language use and English availability.* Retrieved from http://www. census.gov/population/ socdemo/language/table1.txt.

United States Bureau of Labor Statistics (1987). Retrieved from http:// stats.bls.gov

United States Department of Education (1997). *Achieving the goals, goal 8: Parental involvement and participation.* Washington DC: U.S. Department of Education

University of Chicago's National Opinion Research Center (2001). Available at http://www.norc.uchicago.edu/about/homepage.htm

West, P. T. (1993). The elementary school principal's role in school–community relations. *Georgia's Elementary Principal, 1*(2), 9–10.

Whitaker, M.E. (1997). Principal leadership behaviors in school operations and change implementations in elementary schools in relation to climate (Doctoral Dissertation, Indiana State University, 1997).

Whitaker, T., & Fiore, D. J. (2001). *Dealing with difficult parents: And with parents in difficult situations.* Larchmont, NY: Eye On Education.

Whitaker, T., Whitaker, B., & Lumpa, D. (2000). *Motivating & inspiring educators: The ultimate guide for building staff morale.* Larchmont, NY: Eye On Education.

Whitaker, T. (1999). *Dealing with difficult teachers.* Larchmont, NY: Eye On Education.

Wirthlin Report (1999). *Current trends in public opinion, 9*(2). Retrieved from http://209.204.197.52/publicns/report/wr9902.htm

# Index

Academic Competitions 114–115
Achieving the Goals 102
Administrators
    And student discipline 90–91
    And non instructional staff 93–95
    As role models 84–87
    Communication during a campaign
        172–178
    Importance of involving students
        87–89
    Importance of visibility 85–86
Advisory Committees 106, 150, 175–177
American Association of Retired Persons (AARP) 111
American Association of School Administrators 64
American Education Week 130, 149
American Federation of Teachers 64
Announcements 77, 87, 130–132, 185
Appearance of School 208–209
Artistic Endeavors 114
Assembly Programs 217
Athletics 113
Audit of School Community Relations Plan 14
Awards Programs 220
Background Checks 104
Beach, R.H. 12
Benson, C. 101
Berla, N. 101
Berliner, D 9
Board of Education (also see school board) 88
Bomb Threats 183
Brum v. Town of Dartmouth 192
Buckley, S. 101
Budgetary Information 2, 204
Buell, N. 85
Building- level School Community Relations
    Roles of office staff 49–51
    Roles of principal 45–48
    Roles of teacher 48–49
Buller, D. 76
Burgoon, J. 76

Bus Drivers 51
Bush, G. W. 57, 58, 133, 232
Business and Community Leaders 21
Campaigns
    Communication during 172–175
    Conclusion of 177–178
Cattagni, A. 159
Census 75
Centers for Disease Control and Prevention 65
Centralized Plan of School Community Relations 16, 18
Checklists 14, 150–151
Choice 232–235
Citizen Advisory Committee 175–177
Civic and Cultural Organizations 22–23
Climate 12, 35, 42, 46, 167, 215
Closing Schools 149, 187
Coalition for Community Schools 64
Columbine High School 183, 185
Communication
    Barriers 75–77
    Channel 32, 35, 69–70, 187
    During a campaign 172–175
    Face to face 168–170
    In a time of crisis 192–193
    In the office 97–98
    Internal 91–93
    Large group 170–172
    Letters 28, 152–153, 179, 214
    Non-verbal 72–74
    Negative and Positive Expressions 155
    Newsletter 144–150
    Open Houses 203–205
    Perception checking 77–78
    Process 68–72
    Purposeful 79–80
    Regular 78–79
    Through local radio 127, 130–132
    Through television 132–135
    Through print media 120–125
    Through the student report card 150–151
    Through technology 159–162

Through writing 141–159
    Words to avoid 154
    Zones 75–76
Communication Barriers 75–78
    Cultural 75–76
    Language 75
    Overcoming 77–80
    Related to time 77
Communication Plan 80, 150
Community
    Leaders 21–22, 25
    Members with grown children 111
    Pockets 22
    Traditions 50, 146
Community Groups 57, 144
Complaints 15, 42
Conferences, Parent-Teacher 209–217
    Conducting 215–217
    Helping teachers prepare 213
    Parents' contributions 212
    Teachers' contributions 212
Coordinated Plan of School Community
    Relations 15–16, 18
Council of Chief State School Officers
    60, 62
Covey, S. 136
Crisis Situations
    Activating community support 186–
        187
    Aftercare teams 185
    Aftermath 196–199
    Assessing crisis management plan
        188
    Bringing closure to 189
    Communicating during 192–193
    Controlling rumors 187–188
    Designing a plan 184–189
    Developing communication channel
        187
    Establishing a headquarters 185–186
    Importance of planning 183–192
    Informing staff of 193
    Informing students of 193
    Media relations in 194–196
    Official spokesperson 186
    Opportunity for staff development
        190–192
    Selecting individuals to serve on
        crisis teams 185
Cultural Diversity 34–36, 71

Culture, School 12, 35–36, 46
Curriculum Planning 106
Custodians 94
Deadlines 121–122
Decentralized Plan of School Commu-
    nity Relations 16–18
Decision-Making 12, 106, 174
    Involving students in the process 88
    Deitz, M. 106
Desktop Publishing 148
Director of School Community Rela-
    tions
    Duties of 45
    Position titles 44
Discipline 90–91
Dollar Bill Test 146
Dramatic Productions 114
E-mail 77, 163
Editorial Staff 126
Elliott, A. 101
Epstein, J. 101
Evaluating School-Community Rela-
    tions plan
    Questionnaires 227, 229, 231
    Rating scales 227
    Telephone surveys 228
External Communication 9, 41, 84, 92,
    160, 231
External Publics
    Communication with 84, 101, 115
    Community members with grown
        children 111
    Key communicators 110–111
    Opinions 9
    Parents as 102–107
Family Educational Rights and Privacy
    Act (FERPA) 103
Farris, E. 160
Field Trips 31, 159
Food Service 51, 150
Frase, L. 13, 228
Friday Focus 92–93
Gallup, A. 4, 7
Ginott, H. 48 Goals 2000 52–57, 102
Grades 220
Graduation 219
Greenleaf, R. 166
Hall, E.T 76
Heckman, P. 36
Herzberg, F. 86, 94, 99

Higher Education 21, 60, 109
Homework Assignments 106–107, 150
House Visits 25–27
Human Development Report 10
Hygiene Motivation Theory 86, 94
ISLLC Standards 60–63
Idea Encoding 69
Idea Formation 68–69
Immigration and Naturalization 34
Information Age 1–2
In-service Training 45, 92, 148
Instructional Methodology 13
Instructional Program 147
Intergenerational Programs 112
Internal Publics
    Non-instructional staff 93–95
    Opening up to 83–84
    School secretary 97–98
    Student teachers 97
    Students 87–90
    Substitute teachers 95–96
Teachers 91–93
Internet 107, 159–162
Interviews, Television 132–135
Invitations 29, 110, 207–208
Jargon, Use of 143
Job Dissatisfiers 86
Key Communicators 109–111
Letters 28, 152–153, 179, 214
Local Radio 127–132
Maeroff, G. 25
Maintenance Staff 208–209
Management by Walking Around 13, 228
Marx, G. 138
McCormack, M. 85
McEwan, E. 102
Media Relations
    During inconvenient times 120–122
    Improving 119
    In crisis situations 194–196
    Involving staff members 123–125
    News release 126–129
    Proactivity with 135–136
    School leader initiated 122–123
    Tips in dealing with 138–139
Melton, R. 13, 228
Multiculturalism 34–36
Musical Productions 114
NUA Surveys 161

National Association of Broadcasters 134
National Association of Elementary School Principals 64, 211
National Association of Secondary School Principals 64
National Association of State Boards of Education 64
National Center for Educational Statistics 159
National Coalition for Parent Involvement in Education 64
National Committee for Citizens in Education 106
National Community Education Association 64
National Council on Aging 112
National Education Association 64, 112
National School Boards Association 64
National School Public Relations Association 211
National School Safety Center 191
National Opinion Research Center 4
National PTA 51, 63, 102
National Standards for Parent/Family Involvement
Programs 63–64
National School to Work Office 64
Negative and Positive Expressions in Writing 155
Neighborhood
    Schools 25–30
Tea 29–30
Newsletter 157–158
    As a public relations tool 144–145
    Layout 146–147
    Reasons for 145
    Topics to include in 147–149
News Media 119, 125
Newspapers 120, 123–124, 126–129
News Release 126–129
No Child Left Behind 57–58
Non-Instructional Staff 93–94
Non-Verbal Communication
    Examples 74
    Misunderstanding 72–73
    Office staff 50–51
    Typical interpretation 74
Off the record comments 138
Office of Adolescent Health 65

Office of Assistant Secretary for Planning and Evaluation 65
Office of Education, Research, and Improvement 64
Office of Elementary and Secondary Education 65
Office of Juvenile Justice and Delinquency Prevention 65
Office of Special Education Programs 65
Office of the Secretary, U.S. Dept. of Education 65
Office of University Partnerships 65
O'Hair, M. 76
Older Adults in the Community 111–112, 116
Open House
    Advertising 207–208
    Classroom visits 205
    Cleanliness of school during 208–209
    Communication during 31
    Programs 203–205
    Timing of 206–207
    Tours during 202–203
Ordovensky, P. 138
Organizational Strategies
    Goals 2000 52–57
    National standards for parent/family involvement
    programs 63
    Senate Bill S.7: Subtitle C—Parental involvement 58–60
    Title IV (No child left behind) 57–58
Organizations, Civic and Cultural 22–24
Overcoming Communication Barriers
    Perception checking 77–78
    Purposeful communication 79–80
    Regular communication 78–79
Parent Teacher Conferences 31, 209–213, 215–217
Parents
    Appropriate involvement 101–107
    Complaints 15
    Contributions to successful conferences 212
    Dealing with angry 168–170
    Difficult 33, 145, 209–211
    Involvement at home 105–107
    Involvement at school 102–104

Mindsets about dealing with 210–211
    Reasons for parent teacher conferences 211–212
Parent Partnership Program 107
Pawlas, G. 109
Perception Checking 77–78
Personality 132, 147
Persuasion 173
Phi Delta Kappa 4–8
Planning 11–15, 29, 65, 70, 92, 106, 148, 174, 183–189
Plans, School-Community Relations
    Coordinated 15–16, 18
    Centralized 16, 18
    Decentralized 16–18
Plays 114
Polls
    NBC/Wall Street journal 7
    PDK/Gallup 4–8
    Shell Oil company 4
Positive Expressions 155
Principal
    As role model 84–85
    Face to face communication 168–170, 192
    Letters from 151–155
    Speaking to large groups 170–172
    Tasks of 45–48
    Telephone calls from 167–168
    Visibility 85–86
Print Media
    News release 126–127
    Reporter initiated contact 120–122
    School initiated contact 122–123
    Staff members and 123–125
Promoting Parental Options and Innovative Programs 57–58
Public Opinion
    Misconceptions of 9–10
    Polls of 4–9
Public Service Announcements 130–132
Publications 47, 113, 148, 213, 227
Publicity 234
Punishment 90–91
Purposeful Communication 79–80
Questionnaires 9, 227, 229, 231
Radio and School Community Relations 127, 130–132

Readers, Types of
    20–second 141–142
    Newspaper 142
    Novel 142–143
Receiver Decoding 71–72
Regular Communication 78–79, 107
Report Cards 150–151, 162
Reporters 120–125, 137–138, 194–196
Retired Persons 111
Rich, D. 33
Riley, R. 52
Rioux, J. 101
Rogers, E. 173
Ropo, E. 76
Rose, L. 4, 7
Rumors 99, 184, 187–188, 193
Safe and Drug-free Schools Program 65
Sampling 9, 231
Scarnati, J. 84–85
Schlecty, P. 9–10, 40
School Board 1, 41, 44, 45, 49, 64, 187,
    229
School Cafeteria 35, 124, 186, 204
School Calendar 161
School Choice 232–235
School-Community Relations
    At building level 45–51
    At district level 39–45
    Checklist 14
    Communication and 67–72
    Determining effectiveness of 226
    Planning yardstick 14–15
    Verifying results in 226–230
School Facility 9, 90, 176, 177–178, 202–
    203, 208, 233
School Newsletter
    Format 146–147
    Reasons for 144–145
    Topics to include 147–148
School Office 49–51
School Secretary
    Role in school-community relations
        plan 49–50
    As an internal public 97–98
Schueckler, L. 47
Senate bill S.7: subtitle C—Parental
    Involvement 59–60
September 11, 2001 190
Shoemaker, F. 173

Staff Development 35, 45, 92, 147, 148,
    190–191
Staff Morale 12, 35, 48, 86
Staff Working Conditions 94–95
Standardized Test 2, 122, 168, 228, 230–
    231, 234
Standards for School Leaders 60–63
Stolp, S. 46, 72
Strategic Planning 14
Student Advisory Council 88
Student Teachers 97
Students
    As internal publics 87–90
    Discipline and 90–91
    Presenting to the community 113–
        115
    Report cards 150–151
    Welcoming new 89–90
Substitute Teachers 95–96
Superintendent
    As leader 40–42
    Information shared by 33–34
    Mistakes made by 42–43
    Tasks carried out by 41
Surveys 4, 7–8, 44, 218, 227–228
Teachers
    As internal publics 90–92
    Contacting media 123–125
    Information shared by 30–31
    Parent-teacher conferences 209–217
    Written communication from 156–
        159
Technology
    Information age 1–2
    Use of 148, 150, 159–162
Telephone Use 78, 97, 110, 121, 138, 162,
    165–168, 187–188, 208, 228
Television Appearances 132–135
Test Scores 122, 215, 234
Title IV (No child left behind) 57–58
Toastmasters International 171–172
Trent, J. 12
U.S. Bureau of Labor Statistics 206
U.S. Department of Education 64
U.S. Department of Health and Human
    Services 65
U.S. Department of Housing and Urban
    Development 65
U.S. Department of Justice 65
Violence in Schools 191–192

Visibility 12–13, 85–86
Volunteers 102–104
Welcoming
    Letters 27–29
    Signs 104–105
West, P.T. 47

Whitaker, M. 12, 31, 46, 72, 165, 171
Whitaker, T. 2, 33, 92, 101, 102, 106, 107,
    208, 210, 211
World Wide Web 159–162
Written Communication 27–29, 70, 78–
    80, 92, 141–159, 207–208, 214